BERNARD OF *Hollywood*

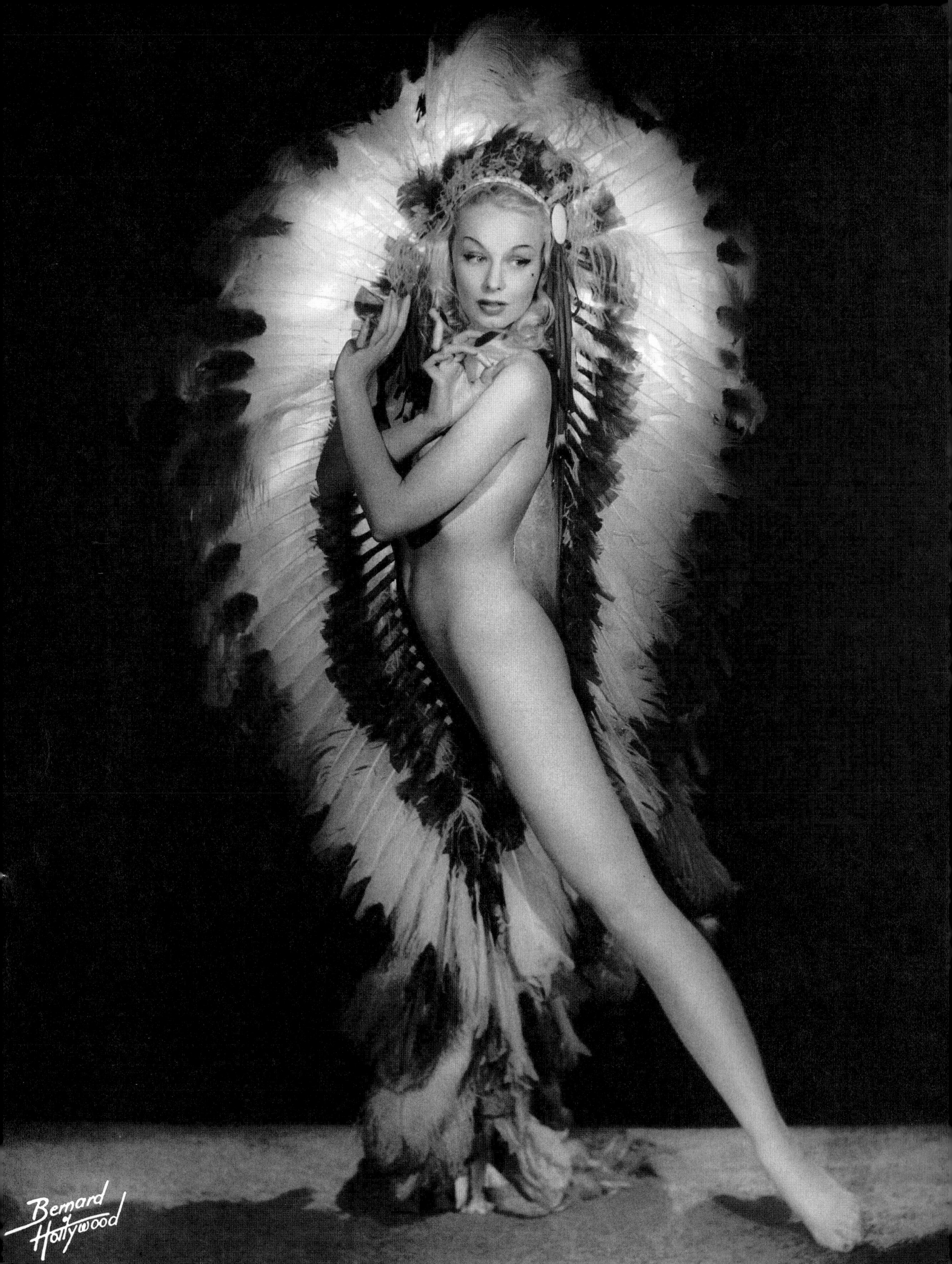
Bernard
Hollywood

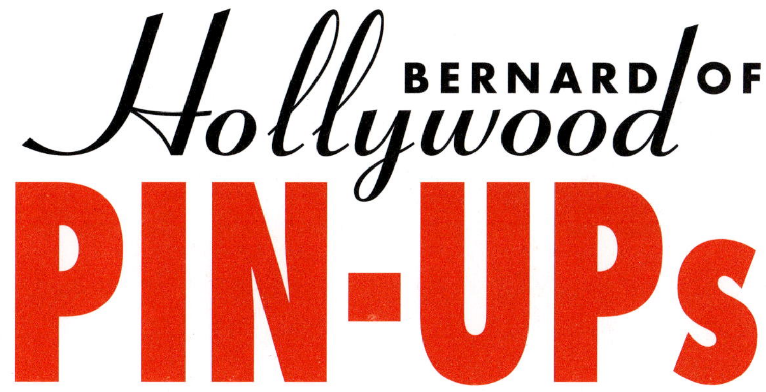

GUIDE TO PIN-UP PHOTOGRAPHY

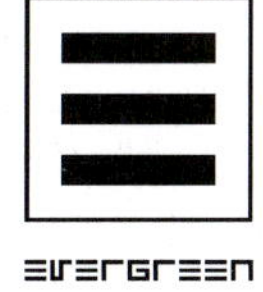

Front Cover:
"A Step Beyond"
Ann Melton

Back Cover:
Robert Mitchum reading "A Step Beyond"

Page 2:
"Early American"
Lili St. Cyr

EVERGREEN is an imprint of
Benedikt Taschen Verlag GmbH

First published in 1950 by Bernard of Hollywood Publishing Co.
Foreword: Harald Hellmann, Cologne
French translation: Philippe Safavi, Paris
German translation: Harald Hellmann, Cologne
English translation of pp. 6–7: Michael Hulse, Cologne
French translation of pp. 10–11: Thérèse Chatelain-Südkamp, Lohmar

Printed in Germany
ISBN 3-8228-7172-9

Contents Inhalt Sommaire

Foreword

In 1953 the magazine "Art Photography" asked Bruno Bernard which were his favorite photographs. With disarming confidence he replied that he had not yet taken his two best pictures: the one would be that perfect photo that every photographer aspires his whole life long to take, and the other would show the document awarding him U. S. citizenship. At that date, Bernard had already become an institution in Hollywood. Those whose outsize portraits were displayed in the windows of Bernard's studio on Sunset Boulevard had definitely made it in the dream factory.

For one who had emigrated to the New World with little more than nebulous plans and hopes, Bernard already had an impressive career behind him. He had left Germany sixteen years before, a young man who had studied psychology in Heidelberg, Berlin and elsewhere, putting the racist hysteria of that country behind him. He had booked a passage to Brazil, but a few days before he was due to sail he saw the Clark Gable movie "San Francisco" and was so taken with the spirit of camaraderie and optimism it displayed that he promptly changed his plans. When Bernard arrived at Ellis Island in 1937 he had five dollars, a knowledge of seven languages, and a camera which his mother had given him when he was eleven.

Bernard had originally intended to read for a doctorate in criminal psychology. But in the event that never worked out, any more than his wish, born of an enthusiasm for Hollywood and the movies, to be a film director. He did find a way of working in a movie-related area, though. A passionate photographer, he began in a modest way by taking pictures of the children of stars and movie moguls. His photos met with such acclaim that he became one of Hollywood's most sought-after portrait photographers. Most of the Golden Age greats – among them Tyrone Power, John Wayne, Elizabeth Taylor, Jane Russell, Gregory Peck, Joseph Cotten, Robert Mitchum, Alan Ladd and many more – put their trust in Bernard's psychological insight. The photographer himself told "Art Photography" that in his view portrait shooting was ninety-nine per cent psychology: it simply wasn't possible to produce a valuable portrait if you were not emotionally and mentally affected by your subject.

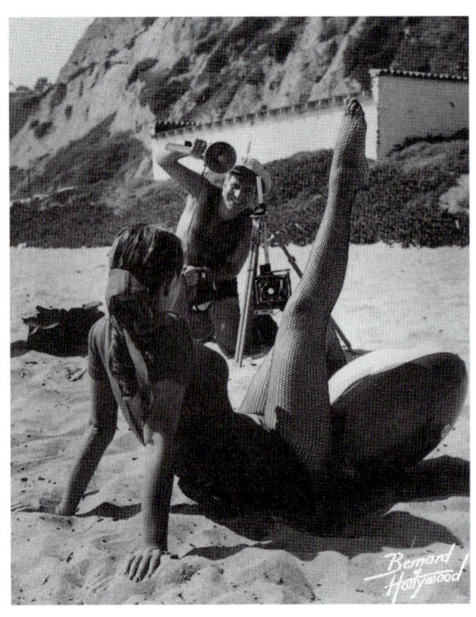

BERNARD & JUNE McCALL

By his own account, Bernard turned increasingly to pin-up and glamor photography because he needed a change from the technical monotony of classic portrait photography. Glamor photography, as one contemporary periodical put it, is a curious medium that emphasizes illusions and heightens the inexplicable aura that surrounds beautiful women. Bernard was so proficient at transforming beauties into supernatural beings that his friend and mentor Alberto Vargas dubbed him the "King of Glamor". And Vargas was not alone in his admiration.

In his guide to the art of pin-up photography, "Pin-Ups. A Step Beyond" (1950), Bernard was less concerned with glamor than with the girl-next-door look of the classic pin-up. The best-known of the models from our present-day point of view is of course Marilyn Monroe, whom Bernard met one day in the street outside his dentist's. Marilyn was still just Norma Jean in those days. Bernard was one of the first to take professional photographs of her, and they remained friends till she died.

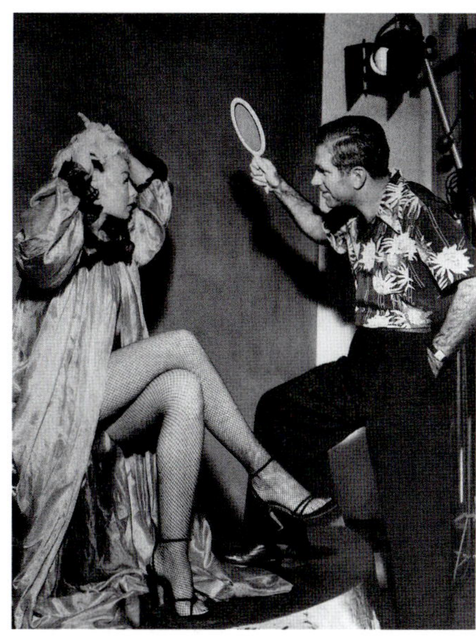

BERNARD & LILI ST. CYR

Bernard had great expectations of "Pin-Ups. A Step Beyond". The book was intended as the first title in a regular series. In fact the series never materialized, thanks to Lili St. Cyr, a woman who had men firing on every cylinder if she so much as strolled by a parking lot. Politely known as a variety girl, Lili – whose real name was Naarie van Scheck – was one of the most celebrated strippers of her day, and her legendary foam bath routine attracted the likes of Humphrey Bogart to Ciro's Night Club on Sunset Strip. Lili was Bernard's muse, and he photographed her as a bathing belle, as an ancient goddess, or as the classically seductive vamp. In "Pin-Ups. A Step Beyond" she also appears as a native American chieftain, clad only in a resplendent headdress. Though all her intimate parts were decently covered in the photograph, the moral watchdogs of the Fifties put their imagination to work on what they couldn't see, and the upshot was that they took Bernard to court. Following the scandal that ensued, no distributor would touch his publications.

Apart from Marilyn Monroe and Lili St. Cyr (who now enjoys the kind of cult status accorded to a Betty Page), the other models in this book are now largely forgotten, though some had their fifteen minutes of fame in their day. Maila Nurmi, seen here as the Lorelei in fishnet stockings (p. 99), became a TV legend as "Vampira" and notched up various film credits, among them Ed Wood's notorious sci-fi movie "Plan Nine from Outer Space". And Jane Greer, shown passing the time on a surfboard on p. 49, featured alongside Kirk Douglas and Robert Mitchum in the *film noir* classic "Out of the Past". But whether they ever really made it on the big or small screen, or not, the dancers and B-movie starlets and provincial beauty queens in this book were all stars for a moment when Bernard of Hollywood put them center-stage.

HARALD HELLMANN

Vorwort

Als die Zeitschrift „Art Photography" Bruno Bernard 1953 nach seinen Lieblingsfotografien fragte, erklärte er mit lässigem Selbstbewußtsein, seine zwei besten Aufnahmen habe er noch gar nicht gemacht: die eine wäre jenes perfekte Foto, nach dem jeder Fotograf zeitlebens streben müsse, die andere müßte seine Einbürgerungsurkunde zeigen. Zu diesem Zeitpunkt war Bernard bereits eine feste Institution in Hollywood. Jeder, der das eigene Porträt überlebensgroß im Schaukasten vor Bernards Studio auf dem Sunset Boulevard entdeckte, konnte sicher sein, es in der Traumfabrik geschafft zu haben.

Für einen Emigranten, der mit wenig mehr als vagen Plänen und Hoffnungen in die Neue Welt gekommen war, konnte Bernard auf eine beeindruckende Karriere zurückblicken. Um dem Rassenwahn Deutschlands zu entkommen, hatte der junge Bernard Sommers, der u. a. in Heidelberg und Berlin Psychologie studiert hatte, 16 Jahre zuvor eine Passage nach Brasilien gebucht. Ein paar Tage vor seiner Abreise sah er jedoch den Clark-Gable-Film „San Francisco" und war vom Geist der Kameraderie und dem Optimismus des Films so beeindruckt, daß er seine Pläne kurzentschlossen änderte. Als Bernard 1937 auf Ellis Island eintraf, besaß er fünf Dollar, Kenntnisse in sieben Sprachen und einen Fotoapparat, den er als Elfjähriger von seiner Mutter geschenkt bekommen hatte.

Bernard wurde nicht, wie er es ursprünglich beabsichtigt hatte, promovierter Kriminalpsychologe. Er wurde auch nicht Regisseur, wie er es – von Film und Hollywood begeistert – nun gerne geworden wäre. Zugang zur Welt des Films fand er dennoch. Er besann sich auf seine Leidenschaft für die Fotografie und begann im kleinen: er fotografierte die Kinder der Hollywoodstars und Filmbosse. Seine Fotos waren so erfolgreich, daß er zu einem der beliebtesten Porträtfotografen Hollywoods aufstieg. Nahezu alle großen Stars der goldenen Jahre Hollywoods standen vor seiner Kamera. Tyrone Power, John Wayne, Elizabeth Taylor, Jane Russell, Gregory Peck, Joseph Cotten, Robert Mitchum, Alan Ladd – sie alle und zahlreiche mehr vertrauten Bernards psychologischem Einfühlungsvermögen. „Ich bin der Meinung", so Bernard, „daß neunundneunzig Prozent der Porträtfotografie Psychologie ist. Es scheint mir einfach unmöglich, irgend etwas Wertvolles mit der Bezeichnung ‚Porträt' zu erhalten, wenn man von der emotionellen und geistigen Art des Objekts unberührt bleibt." (Art Photography)

Daß Bernard sich schließlich der Pin-Up- und Glamour-Fotografie zuwandte, ist – nach seinem Bekunden – dem Verdruß über die beschränkten Entfaltungsmöglichkeiten auf dem Gebiet der klassischen Porträtfotografie zu verdanken. „Die Glamour-Fotografie", so fabuliert ein zeitgenössisches Fotomagazin, „ist ein eigenartiges Medium, das Illusionen verstärkt und gleichsam beseelt ist vom unerklärlichen Fluidum schöner Frauen." Und Bernard verstand sich so gut darauf, Frauen in überirdische Wesen zu verwandeln, die eine Fee mit ihrem glitzernden Sternenstaub verzaubert zu haben schien, daß ihn nicht nur sein Freund und Mentor Alberto Vargas zum „King of Glamour" kürte. In seinem 1950 erschienen Leitfaden zur Pin-Up-Fotografie „A Step Beyond ..." setzt Bernard weniger auf Glamour denn auf den „Mädchen von nebenan"-Look des klassischen Pin-Ups. Das bekannteste Modell aus dieser Sammlung ist natürlich Marilyn Monroe, der Bernard eines Tages vor der Tür seines Zahnarztes auf der Straße begegnet war. Marilyn hieß damals noch Norma Jean, und Bernard, einer der ersten, der professionelle Aufnahmen von ihr machte, sollte ihr bis zu ihrem Tod freundschaftlich verbunden bleiben.

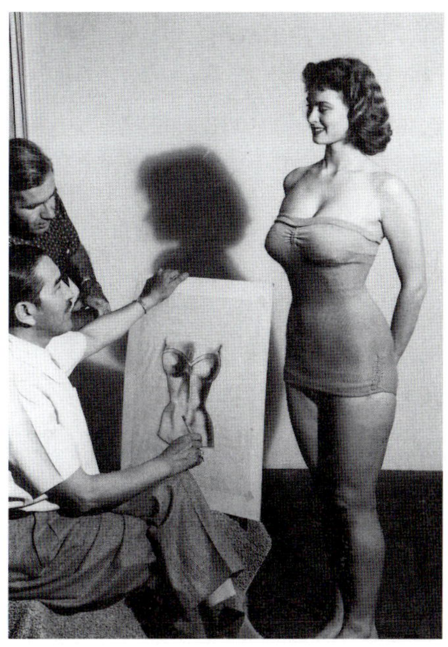
BERNARD, ALBERTO VARGAS (SEATED) & IRISH McCULLA

In die Veröffentlichung von „A Step Beyond ..." hatte Bernard große Hoffnungen gesetzt. Ursprünglich sollte dies nur der Auftaktband einer regelmäßig erscheinenden Reihe werden. Daß es dazu nicht kam, lag an Lili St. Cyr, einer Frau, die alle Motoren anspringen ließ, wenn sie an einem Parkplatz vorbeiging. Euphemistisch als „Varieté-Tänzerin" tituliert, war Lili (mit bürgerlichem Namen Naarie van Scheck) eine der berühmtesten Stripperinnen ihrer Zeit, und ihre legendäre Schaumbadnummer lockte nicht nur Humphrey Bogart in Ciro's Nachtclub auf den Sunset Strip. Lili war Bernards Muse, und er inszenierte sie mal als Badenixe, mal als antike Göttin oder als verführerischen Vamp. In „A Step Beyond ..." sehen wir Lili als Indianerin, mit nichts bekleidet als einem langen Federkopfschmuck. Obschon alle intimen Körperteile schamhaft bedeckt sind, waren die Tugendwächter der 50er Jahre doch phantasiebegabt genug, Bernard für diese Aufnahme vor den Kadi zu zerren. Nach diesem Skandal ließ sich kein Vertrieb mehr für weitere Ausgaben finden.

Neben Marilyn Monroe und der heute, ähnlich wie Betty Page, wieder zu Kultstatus gelangten Lili St. Cyr finden sich in diesem Buch zahlreiche nun vergessene Modelle, aber auch einige, denen zumindest begrenzter Ruhm beschert war. Maila Nurmi etwa, die uns hier als Lorelei in Netzstrümpfen begegnet, wurde als „Vampira" zur TV-Legende und spielte u. a. in Ed Woods berüchtigtem „Plan Nine from Outer Space" mit, und Jane Greer, die Müßiggängerin auf dem Surfboard (S. 49), konnte man u. a. an der Seite von Kirk Douglas und Robert Mitchum in dem Film Noir-Klassiker „Out of the Past" sehen. Doch auch jene, die es nicht auf die Leinwand oder den Bildschirm schafften, die kleinen Tänzerinnen, B-Film-Starlets und Schönheitsköniginnen aus der Provinz, wurden für den Moment, in dem Bernard of Hollywood sie in Szene setzte, zu Stars.

HARALD HELLMANN

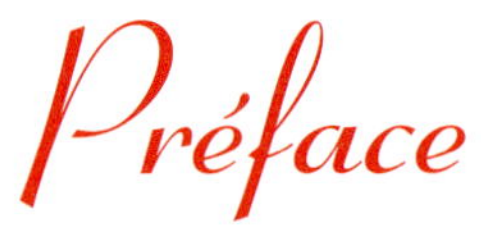

Lorsque le magazine « Art Photography » demanda en 1953 à Bruno Bernard quelles étaient ses photos préférées, il répondit d'un ton désinvolte qu'il n'avait pas encore réalisé ses deux meilleurs clichés : le premier serait la photo parfaite après laquelle chaque photographe devait courir toute sa vie, le second devrait montrer sa carte de naturalisation. A cette époque, Bernard était devenu une véritable institution à Hollywood. Celui qui découvrait son portrait plus grand que nature dans la vitrine de son studio sur le Sunset Boulevard pouvait être sûr de sa réussite dans ce haut lieu du 7ème art.

Pour un émigrant arrivé dans le Nouveau Monde la tête remplie de projets et de rêves, Bernard pouvait être fier de sa carrière impressionnante. C'est pour fuir la folie raciste de son pays que Bernard Sommers qui avait étudié entre autres la psychologie à Heidelberg et à Berlin avait voulu embarquer pour le Brésil seize ans auparavant. Toutefois, quelques jours avant son départ, il alla voir le film de Clark Gable « San Francisco ». Il fut si impressionné par l'esprit de camaraderie et l'optimisme du film qu'il modifia ses projets sans hésiter. Lorsque Bernard arriva à Ellis Island en 1937, il avait cinq dollars en poche, « baragouinait » sept langues et possédait un appareil photo que sa mère lui avait offert à l'âge de onze ans.

Bernard ne devint pas, comme il en avait l'intention au départ, diplômé en psychologie criminelle. Il ne devint pas non plus metteur en scène comme il aurait tant voulu l'être, vu son enthousiasme pour le cinéma et Hollywood. Néanmoins, il trouva le moyen d'entrer dans cet univers. Se souvenant de sa passion pour la photographie, il commença petit et photographia les rejetons des vedettes d'Hollywood et des grands producteurs. Ses photos eurent tant de succès qu'il devint l'un des photographes de portraits les plus prisés d'Hollywood. Presque toutes les grandes stars de la grande époque d'Hollywood posèrent devant son objectif. Tyrone Power, John Wayne, Elizabeth Taylor, Jane Russell, Gregory Peck, Joseph Cotten, Robert Mitchum, Alan Ladd et bien d'autres encore firent confiance à son intuition. « Je pense », affirma Bernard un jour, « que quatre-vingt-dix pour cent de la photographie de portrait relève de la psychologie. Il me semble impossible de désigner quelque chose de précieux sous le nom de ‹ portrait › si je reste insensible au côté émotionnel et spirituel de l'objet. » (Art Photography).

Bernard se consacra finalement de plus en plus à la photographie glamour et des pin-up afin de changer un peu, comme il le dit lui-même, de la monotonie technique du portrait classique. « La photographie glamour », raconte un magazine contemporain, « est un support étrange qui glorifie les illusions et rend palpable le fluide inexplicable qui entoure les jolies femmes. » Bernard s'y entendait si bien à métamorphoser les jolies femmes en êtres supraterrestres que son ami et mentor Alberto Vargas ne fut pas le seul à le baptiser « King of Glamour ». Dans « A Step Beyond … », guide de la photographie de pin-up paru en 1950, Bernard s'intéressa moins au glamour qu'au look de la pin-up classique, la « fille bien de chez nous ». Le modèle le plus connu de cette collection est naturellement Marilyn Monroe que Bernard rencontra un jour dans la rue, devant la porte de son dentiste. Marilyn s'appelait encore Norma Jean et Bernard, qui fut l'un des premiers à prendre d'elle des clichés professionnels, devait rester son ami jusqu'à sa mort.

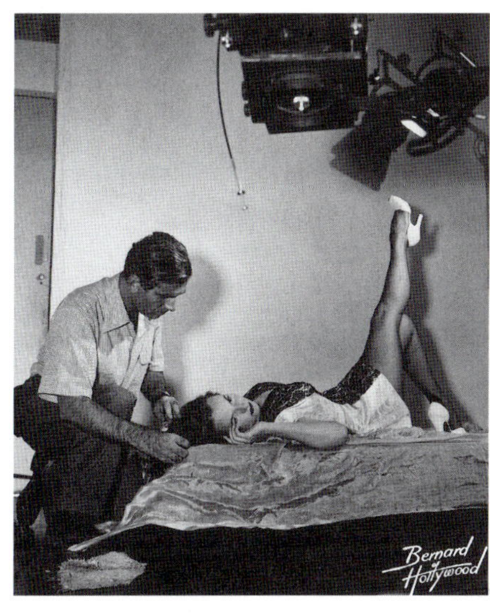

BERNARD & JUNE McCALL

Bernard espérait beaucoup de la publication de « A Step Beyond … ». A l'origine, cet ouvrage devait être le premier de toute une série de publications périodiques. S'il n'en fut pas ainsi, c'est la faute à Lili St. Cyr, une femme qui faisait s'emballer tous les moteurs de voitures rien qu'en traversant un parking. Qualifiée avec euphémisme de « danseuse de variétés », Lili qui s'appelait plus prosaïquement Naarie van Scheck, était l'une des strip-teaseuses les plus célèbres de son temps et son numéro légendaire du bain moussant n'attira pas seulement Humphrey Bogart au night-club Ciro's. Lili était la muse de Bernard qui la changea en naïade, en déesse antique ou en vamp dévastatrice. Dans « A Step Beyond … » on peut voir Lili en squaw portant uniquement une immense coiffe d'Indien. Bien que ses « parties honteuses » aient été pudiquement recouvertes, les gardiens de la vertu des années 1950 étaient doués d'assez d'imagination pour traîner Bernard devant le juge. Après ce scandale, Bernard dut renoncer aux autres publications.

A côté de Marilyn Monroe et de Lili St. Cyr qui, comme Betty Page, fait de nouveau l'objet d'un culte, ce livre présente de nombreux modèles tombés dans l'oubli, mais aussi quelques-uns qui connurent la gloire, même si celle-ci fut éphémère. Maila Nurmi par exemple, que nous rencontrons ici en Lorelei et bas résilles devint légendaire dans « Vampira » au petit écran et joua entres autres dans « Plan Nine from Outer Space ». Quant à Jane Greer, qui se prélasse sur la planche à voile (p. 49), on a pu la voir aux côtés de Kirk Douglas et de Robert Mitchum dans le classique du film noir « Out of the Past ». Mais même celles qui n'arrivèrent jamais à percer au petit ou au grand écran, les petites danseuses, les starlettes de films de série B et les Miss de province devenaient des stars l'espace d'un instant quand Bernard of Hollywood leur faisait prendre la pose.

HARALD HELLMANN

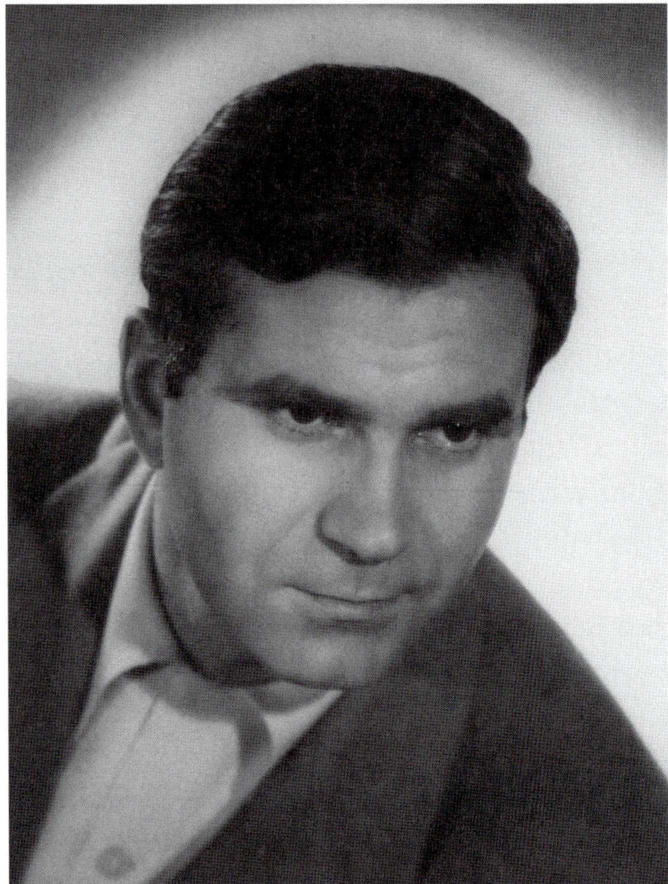

BERNARD OF HOLLYWOOD

A Step Beyond . . .

Just a short time ago, a well-known publicity man phoned Bernard of Hollywood. One of his clients, a nationally prominent hosiery manufacturer, needed an eye-catching shot to spark the photographic illustrations for his new fall advertising campaign. Would Bernard handle the assignment?

To Bernard, one of the top glamor photographers in the country, it was just a routine request, and the following day he and the publicity man were going through the files, looking for a model with well-nigh perfect legs. After the first few hundred beautiful pictures, the publicity man exclaimed:

"These are terrific, Bernard! You've really gone a step beyond all the run of the mill leg-art. These look more like paintings or illustrations than just the usual type of pin-ups. You've got enough here for a whole book."

This was a thought that had already occurred to Bernard, but as with practically every artist, it had been one of those personal projects which always seem to get stuck way back in the bottom drawer. Still, this particular incident resulted in this collection of "Bernard's Best."

Since he moved to the motion picture capital in 1937, Bernard has snapped the shutter on most of the big-name stars in Hollywood. Born in Switzerland and now a U. S. citizien, he came to America, oddly enough, to do graduate work at the University of California in psychology, which he had studied abroad at the universities of Heidelberg, Kiel, Berlin and Paris. Photography was his hobby; dramatics and the theater secret yearnings.

The latter drew him to Hollywood, where he turned his hobby into a successful career by applying his knowledge of psychology to the kind of people he likes best – the famous personalities of stage and screen.

A former member of the Little Theater Group at the University of California, Bernard is also a student of the late Max Reinhardt, and of the motion picture director, William Dieterle. Through a series of developments, Bernard has introduced the directorial approach to still photography, in which the actor is not "posed," but directed in a series of theatrical situations which are recorded in split-second synchronization.

His unique, so-called "posed candids" of Hollywood stars have been reproduced in practically all of the leading publications, both here and abroad. The photographs in this collection are from his private files, and, most of them, now being published for the first time.

They have not only been selected to cover the gamut of model types – from the demure and "cute" to the ultra sultry – but they have also been chosen as study material for the amateur photographer and artist. Bernard hopes that his book will contribute to make *shooting* pin-ups as widespread and enjoyable a pastime as *collecting* them.

To those interested in pin-ups for their own sake, the text gives some idea of the vast amount of work that goes into the making of a pretty picture. The pictures themselves show why Bernard is acclaimed one of the top personality photographers in America.

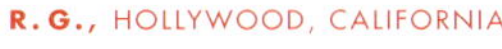

R. G., HOLLYWOOD, CALIFORNIA

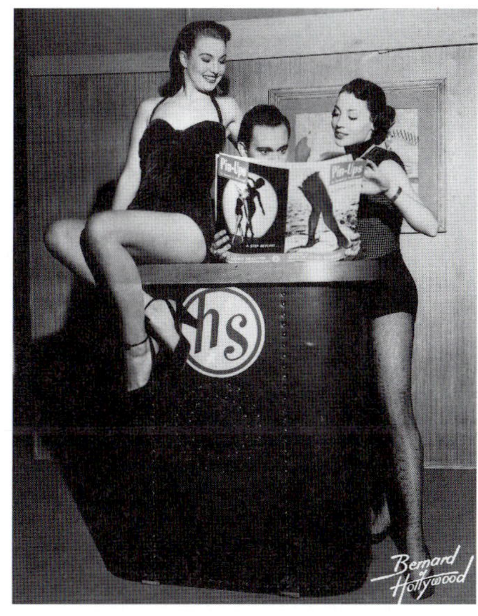

JUNE McCALL & ANN MELTON

Einen Schritt weiter . . .

Vor nicht allzu langer Zeit erreichte Bernard of Hollywood der Anruf eines renommierten Werbefachmanns, der für die neue Anzeigenkampagne eines landesweit bekannten Strumpfmodenherstellers ein aussagestarkes Foto benötigte. Ob Bernard diesen Auftrag übernehmen könnte?

Für Bernard, einen der berühmtesten Glamour-Fotografen im Lande, war eine solche Anfrage Routine, und am nächsten Tag durchsuchte er gemeinsam mit dem Werbefachmann sein Archiv nach einem Modell mit dem perfekten Bein. Nachdem hunderte von hervorragenden Aufnahmen durchgesehen waren, rief Bernards Klient begeistert: „Die sind ja umwerfend, Bernard! Du bist wirklich einen Schritt über die ganzen 08/15-Aufnahmen hinausgegangen. Diese Bilder sehen eher wie Gemälde oder Illustrationen denn wie herkömmliche Pin-Ups aus. Dein Material reicht ja für ein ganzes Buch."

Der Gedanke war Bernard auch schon gekommen, doch wie bei den meisten Künstlern war es auch bei ihm einer dieser Pläne geblieben, die immer wieder auf die lange Bank geschoben werden. Diese zufällige Bemerkung führte schließlich zur Veröffentlichung von „Bernard's Best".

Seit er 1937 in die Filmmetropole gekommen war, hatte Bernard die meisten Hollywoodstars vor die Linse bekommen. Eigentlich war der gebürtige Schweizer und heutige US-Bürger in die Vereinigten Staaten gekommen, um an der University of California sein Psychologiestudium fortzuführen, das er in Heidelberg, Kiel, Berlin und Paris begonnen hatte. Die Fotografie war sein Hobby, die Schauspielerei und das Theater seine heimliche Leidenschaft.

Sie führten ihn nach Hollywood, und hier machte er sein Hobby erfolgreich zum Beruf: seine Kenntnisse in der Psychologie nutzte er für die Arbeit mit den Menschen, die er am meisten schätzte, den Berühmtheiten von Bühne und Film.

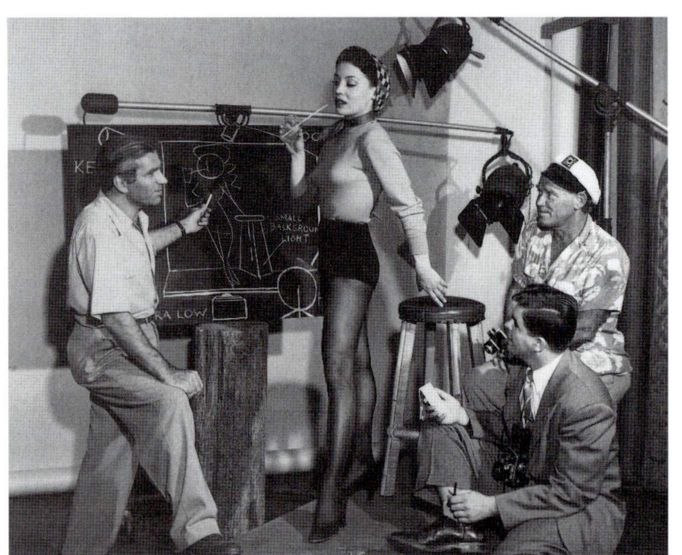

BERNARD, ANN MELTON & FRIENDS

Als ehemaliges Mitglied der Little Theater Group der University of California hatte Bernard auch bei Max Reinhardt und dem Filmregisseur William Dieterle studiert. Die Arbeitsweise eines Regisseurs übertrug Bernard Schritt für Schritt auf die Porträtfotografie: der Darsteller wird nicht in eine Pose gezwängt, sondern durch eine Abfolge dramatischer Szenen geführt, die in ihrem charakteristischsten Moment „eingefroren" werden.

Seine einzigartigen sogenannten „posed candids", inszenierte Schnappschüsse, von

Hollywoodstars sind in nahezu jeder wichtigen Zeitschrift im In- und Ausland veröffentlicht worden. Die Aufnahmen in diesem Buch stammen aus seinem Privatarchiv und werden hier zum größten Teil erstmals gezeigt.

Sie wurden nicht nur deshalb ausgewählt, weil sie die ganze Palette von Modelltypen wiedergeben – vom spröden und „süßen“ bis zum ultra-verruchten Typ – sondern auch, um dem Fotoamateur und Künstler als Anschauungsmaterial zu dienen. Bernard möchte mit dieser Veröffentlichung dazu beitragen, daß das „Ablichten“ von Pin-Ups ein ebenso populärer und vergnüglicher Zeitvertreib wird wie das Sammeln von Pin-Ups.

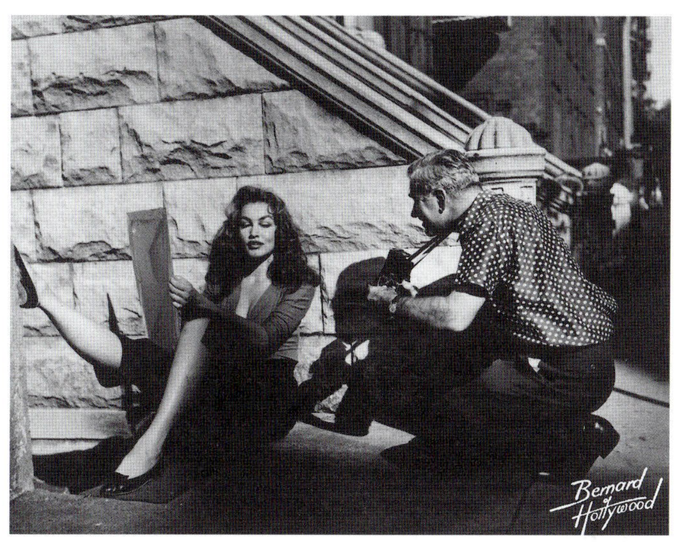

BERNARD & JULIE NEWMER

Jedem ernsthaft an der Pin-Up-Fotografie Interessierten vermittelt der Text, wieviel Arbeit in einem gelungenen Bild steckt. Die Fotos selbst illustrieren, warum Bernard zu den besten Porträtfotografen Amerikas zählt.

R. G., HOLLYWOOD, CALIFORNIA

Une longueur d'avance...

Récemment, Bernard of Hollywood fut contacté par un célèbre agent de publicité. Un client de ce dernier, grand fabriquant américain de bonneterie, avait besoin d'une image séduisante et forte pour égayer les photographies du catalogue de sa prochaine campagne publicitaire. Bernard acceptait-il de s'en charger?

Pour le photographe, un des meilleurs spécialistes du style glamour, il s'agissait d'une commande de routine. Le lendemain, il rencontra le publiciste et parcourut avec lui ses archives, cherchant un modèle aux jambes parfaites. Après avoir examiné plusieurs centaines de photographies toutes plus belles les unes que les autres, l'agent s'exclama:

« Bernard! C'est tout simplement magnifique! Tu as une longueur d'avance sur tous les experts en ‹ Leg Art ›. Ces images tiennent davantage de la peinture ou de l'illustration que de la photographie habituelle de pin-up. Tu as là de quoi faire tout un livre!»

Bernard y avait déjà songé mais, comme il arrive souvent avec les artistes, le projet était resté au fond d'un tiroir. Néanmoins, cet incident le convainquit de le ressortir et de publier ce florilège.

Depuis son arrivée dans la capitale du cinéma en 1937, Bernard a capturé dans son objectif la plupart des grandes stars d'Hollywood. Aujourd'hui citoyen américain, il est né en Suisse. Etrangement, il est venu aux Etats-Unis pour poursuivre ses études de troisième cycle en psychologie à l'University of California, après avoir étudié à Heidelberg, Kiel, Berlin et Paris. La photographie était son violon d'Ingres, l'art dramatique et le théâtre ses passions secrètes.

Ce furent ces dernières qui l'attirèrent à Hollywood, où son passe-temps se transforma bientôt en une carrière fructueuse. Là, il put appliquer ses connaissances en matière de psychologie au genre de personnes qu'il aimait le plus: les célébrités des planches et du grand écran.

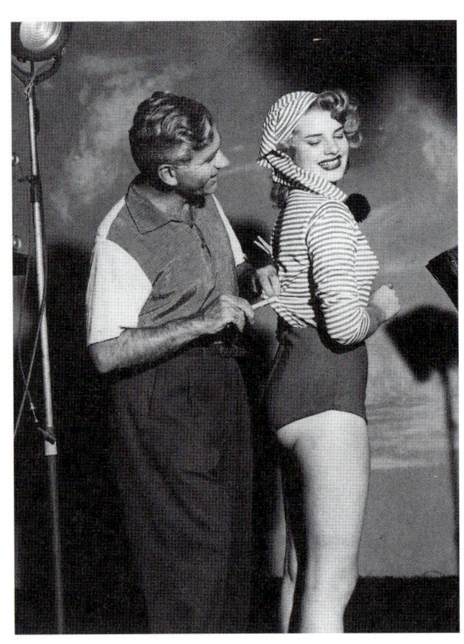

BERNARD & MODEL

Ancien membre de la compagnie du Little Theater à l'University of California, Bernard a également étudié auprès du grand Max Reinhardt, aujourd'hui disparu, et du réalisateur de cinéma William Dieterle. Cela explique sans doute qu'il ait adopté une démarche de metteur de scène dans sa manière de photographier: au lieu d'imposer une attitude figée à son sujet, il le dirige dans une série de situations théâtrales qu'il capture ensuite dans son objectif à la fraction de seconde près.

Ses « instantanés posés » de stars d'Hollywood ont été publiés dans pratiquement toutes les grandes revues américaines et étrangères. Les photos de cet album proviennent de ses archives personnelles et sont, pour la plupart, présentées pour la première fois.

Elles ont été choisies pour refléter toute la gamme de ses modèles, de la plus ingénue à la plus sulfureuse, mais également pour servir de matériel d'étude aux photographes et artistes amateurs. Bernard espère que, grâce à ce livre, « capturer » des pin-up deviendra un passe-temps aussi répandu et agréable que celui qui consiste à les collectionner.

Pour ceux qui s'intéressent à la photographie en tant que telle, le texte donne une petite idée de l'énorme travail nécessaire pour obtenir une bonne photographie. Quant aux images, elles démontrent, si besoin était, pourquoi Bernard est considéré aujourd'hui comme l'un des plus grands photographes de célébrités en Amérique.

R. G., HOLLYWOOD, CALIFORNIA

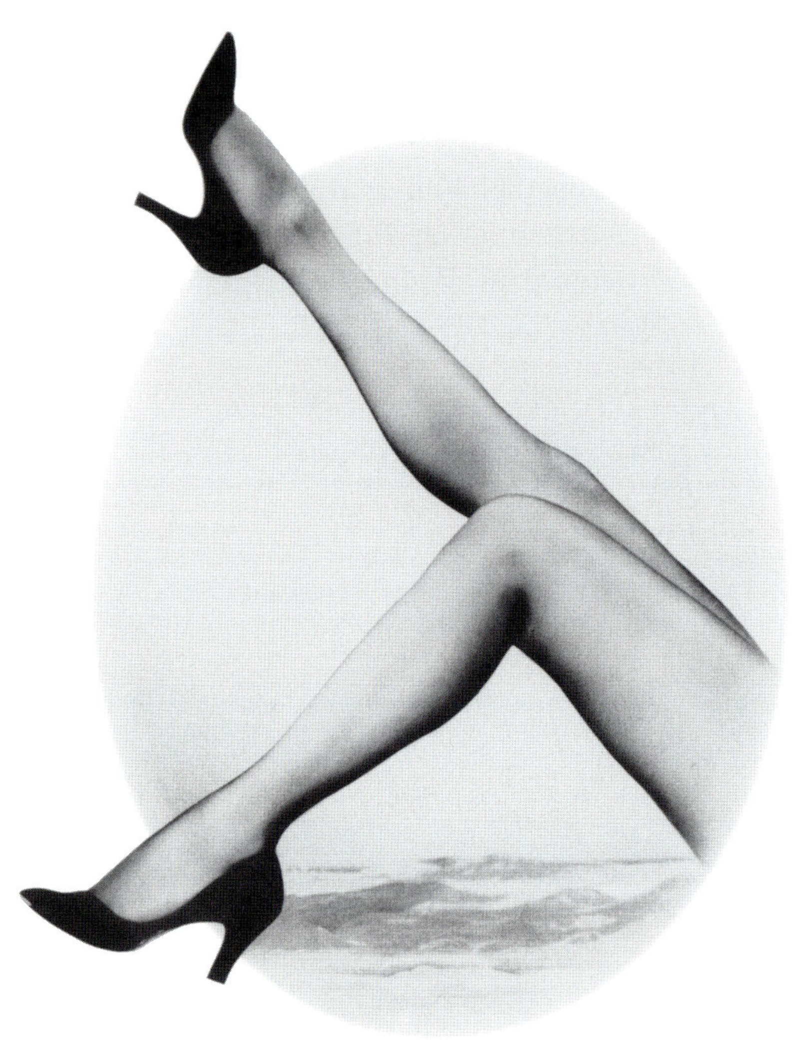

A Couple of Good Reasons

This is how it all started. A Hollywood publicity man needed an advertising shot for a nationally known hosiery manufacturer. Hundreds of pictures of beautiful models were examined before the one with the most beautiful legs was selected. The by-products are collected in this book.
5x7 Ansco studio camera, 1/5 second at f/16.

Zwei gute Gründe

So fing alles an. Ein PR-Mann aus Hollywood suchte ein Reklamefoto für einen landesweit bekannten Strumpffabrikanten. Einige hundert Fotografien bildhübscher Modelle wurden durchgesehen, bis schließlich das mit den schönsten Beinen gefunden war. Die anderen „Schätze", die bei dieser Suche entdeckt wurden, finden sich in diesem Buch. 5x7 Ansco studio camera, 1/5 Sekunde bei f/16.

Quelques bonnes raisons

Voici comment tout a commencé. Un publiciste d'Hollywood avait besoin d'une image publicitaire pour un grand fabriquant de bas. Des centaines de photos de superbes modèles ont été passées en revue avant de choisir celle aux plus belles jambes. Un grand nombre des images non retenues ont été rassemblées dans ce livre. 5x7 Ansco studio camera, 1/5ème de seconde à f/16.

Fresh and invigorating as an ocean breeze is this medium shot of a bathing beauty. Since the white sand on the beach acted as a reflector no flash fill-in was necessary. Super D Graflex, 1/200 second at f/22.

Die Halbtotale dieser Strandschönheit ist erfrischend und belebend wie eine Meeresbrise. Da der weiße Sand des Strandes wie ein Reflektor wirkte, wurde kein zusätzlicher Aufhellblitz benötigt. Super D Graflex, 1/200 Sekunde bei f/22.

Ce plan moyen d'une belle baigneuse est aussi frais et revigorant qu'une brise marine. Le sable blanc reflétant la lumière du soleil, je n'ai pas eu besoin de flash. Super D Graflex, 1/200ème de seconde à f/22.

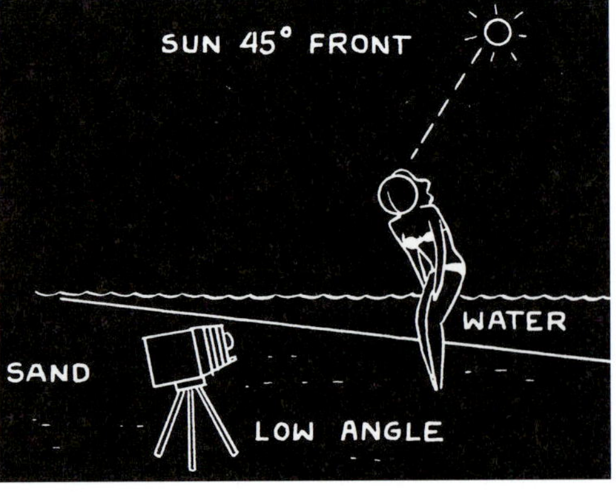

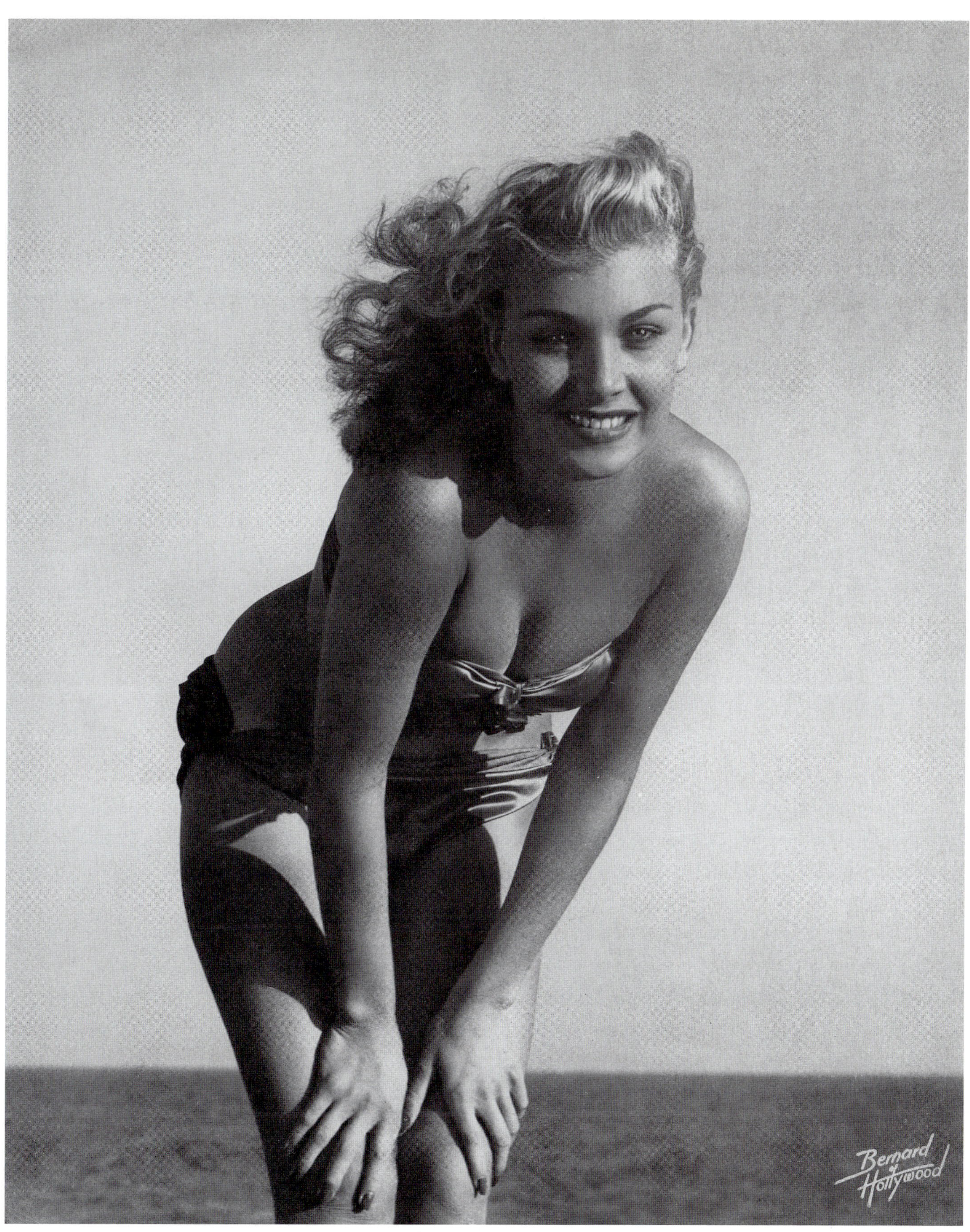

Hi There!

NA, DU? · COUCOU, C'EST MOI !

Pin-Ups as an Art

Pin-ups, the pictorial reproduction of the Female Form Divine, are nothing new. The cave drawings of the early stone age might very well be considered the forerunners of the modern pin-up girls who "bewitch, bother and bewilder" us on calendars, magazines and billboards.

The evolvement of pin-ups as an art form, however, is of recent date, and is due mainly to their liberal use in American advertising. All advertising boils down to the stimulation of certain wants, and, once they are established, channeling them in one direction – the house of the advertiser.

Small wonder, then, that the smart American huckster has recruited the services of the ravishing pin-up creature, who calls upon our basic hunger for love which is best stimulated by beauty.

Feminine allure has been ingeniously used to make us buy anything from socks to racing cars, from food to girdles. Our dream girl won't kiss us unless we shave off our whiskers with some particular shaving cream, and once she's kissed us, we risk losing her instantly unless we happen to be using the right kind of mouthwash.

The foremost exploiters of the pin-up have been the Hollywood motion picture publicity men. The imagination of the heads of the art departments and studio galleries works overtime when it comes to getting a pair of gorgeous gams and a come-hither look in ever new variations on an advertising poster. No matter how little bearing it has on the story content – the provocative display of the perfect feminine figure has always been used as a sure-fire bait to lure the public to the box office.

Motion picture exploitation has made "Cheesecake" (Hollywood lingo for glamorized leg art) as typically American as apple pie. Pressed into the services of a multi-billion-dollar industry, our innocent little pin-up cutie has now the double function of turning not only our heads but also the big wheels of our economy. "Noblesse Oblige," as the Frenchman says, and with its new importance, the pin-up is subjected to certain requirements of the graphic arts.

Let it be emphasized at the outset that in this book we are concerned with the photographically artistic rendition of the pin-up. The borderline between a mere vulgar display of the feminine body and a legitimate work of commercial art cannot be found in the margin of what is revealed to the eye and what is left to the imagination. No one in his right mind will dispute the artistry of the master painters and sculptors in depicting nudes. It is up to the artistic integrity and ability of the artist whether his work merely arouses the animal instincts, or transmits aesthetic values.

The author hopefully submits that his collection of pin-ups falls into the latter category. Each picture has been the result of careful study in composition and lighting, costuming and background as well as purposeful direction. While the different art elements are discussed with each individual picture, let us attempt here to summarize what gives the pin-up universal appeal.

Obviously, every one of us has a different idea of what constitutes beauty. However, motion pictures, magazines, and the different advertising media have crystallized certain standards of modern beauty. With the proverbial grain of salt contained in all generalizations, it is safe to say that the classic shape of Venus and the buxom ideal of Rubens have given way to the lissom, curvaceous, long-stemmed American beauty as the almost-universally accepted beauty ideal of the Western World.

If an enterprising archeologist, several thousand years from now, should find no other trace of our civilization than a capsule containing pin-ups, he could not only deduce from them the beauty ideal of the mid-century Jones and Smith, but could easily reconstruct from them a large sector of our present-day life.

Pin-Ups als Kunstform

Pin-Ups, die bildliche Darstellung des „ewig Weiblichen", sind nichts Neues. Schon die Höhlenzeichnungen aus der Steinzeit könnte man durchaus als Vorläufer des modernen Pin-Ups betrachten, das uns heute auf Kalenderblättern, Titelbildern und Reklametafeln begegnet und „bezaubert, fesselt und verwirrt".

Die Entwicklung des Pin-Ups zur Kunstform ist allerdings jüngeren Datums und verdankt seine Popularität vornehmlich der amerikanischen Werbung. Alle Werbung zielt auf die Erwekkung bestimmter Bedürfnisse und lenkt diese, sind sie erst einmal da, in eine einzige Richtung: auf das Produkt.

Wen wundert es da, daß sich der gewiefte amerikanische Werbefachmann der Dienste des atemberaubenden Pin-Ups versichert hat, das durch seine Schönheit unsere ewige Sehnsucht nach Liebe anspricht.

Seit jeher werden weibliche Reize geschickt dazu eingesetzt, uns alles mögliche zu verkaufen, von Socken über Sportwagen und Lebensmittel bis hin zu Hüfthaltern. Unser Traumgirl wird uns erst küssen, wenn wir unsere Bartstoppeln mit einer ganz bestimmten Rasiercreme abrasieren, und hat es uns dann geküßt, könnten wir es umgehend wieder verlieren, wenn wir nicht das richtige Mundwasser benutzen.

Die Männer aus den Werbeabteilungen Hollywoods setzen am schamlosesten auf das Pin-Up. Wenn es darum geht, ein Paar umwerfender Beine oder einen aufreizenden Blick in allen erdenklichen Spielarten auf ein Filmplakat zu bekommen, arbeiten die kreativen Köpfe in den Werbeabteilungen auf Hochtouren. Egal, wie wenig Bezug es zum jeweiligen Film auch haben mag, die provokative Zurschaustellung weiblicher Schönheit galt schon immer als todsicherer Köder, die Menschen an die Kinokassen zu locken.

Die Filmindustrie hat dafür gesorgt, daß „Cheesecake" (im Hollywood-Jargon der Begriff für verführerisch in Szene gesetzte langbeinige Schönheiten) zu etwas genauso typisch Amerikanischem geworden ist wie ein Doughnut. Im Dienste einer Millionen-Dollar-Industrie erfüllt unsere unschuldige kleine Pin-Up-Schönheit nun eine doppelte Funktion: Sie hält nicht nur unsere Phantasie, sondern auch unsere Wirtschaft in Schwung. „Noblesse oblige", wie der Franzose sagt, und mit seinem neugewonnenen Stellenwert muß das Pin-Up auch bestimmten künstlerischen Anforderungen genügen.

Wir wollen gleich zu Beginn unseres Buches klarstellen, daß wir uns für die künstlerische Pin-Up-Fotografie interessieren. Der feine Unterschied zwischen der vulgären, bloßen Zurschaustellung des weiblichen Körpers und legitimer Werbekunst besteht sicherlich nicht darin, ob etwas dem Blick enthüllt wird oder der Phantasie überlassen bleibt. Wer würde ernsthaft die künstlerische

Leistung der großen Maler oder Bildhauer bei der Darstellung eines Aktes in Frage stellen? Es hängt von der künstlerischen Integrität und Begabung des Künstlers ab, ob sein Werk lediglich animalische Instinkte weckt oder ästhetische Qualitäten vermittelt.

Der Verfasser hofft, sagen zu können, daß seine Sammlung von Pin-Ups zur letztgenannten Kategorie zählt. Jede Aufnahme ist das Ergebnis einer sorgfältigen Studie von Komposition und Ausleuchtung, Kleidung und Hintergrundgestaltung und ganz genauer Regieanweisungen. Die verschiedenen künstlerischen Aspekte werden anhand konkreter Bildbeispiele erläutert, doch hier wollen wir versuchen zusammenzufassen, was den universellen Appeal des Pin-Ups ausmacht.

Selbstverständlich hat jeder von uns andere Vorstellungen von Schönheit. Dennoch haben Film, Zeitschriften und die verschiedenen Werbeträger gewisse Schönheitsideale für unsere Zeit formuliert. Bei allen Vorbehalten gegenüber Verallgemeinerungen darf man wohl dennoch feststellen, daß die klassische Gestalt der Venus und das üppige Schönheitsideal eines Rubens von der geschmeidigen, kurvenreichen und langbeinigen amerikanischen Schönheit abgelöst wurden, die heute das fast überall in der westlichen Welt akzeptierte Schönheitsideal ist.

Sollte ein Archäologe in ferner Zukunft nicht mehr von unserer Zivilisation finden als eine Zeitkapsel mit Pin-Ups, er könnte daraus nicht nur das allgemeine Schönheitsideal der Mitte des 20. Jahrhunderts ablesen, sondern auch mit Leichtigkeit einen großen Ausschnitt unserer Alltagskultur rekonstruieren.

L'art de la pin-up

La pin-up, soit la représentation des formes divines de la femme, ne date pas d'hier. Les peintures rupestres de l'âge de pierre peuvent sans doute être considérées comme les ancêtres des pin-up modernes qui nous « ensorcellent, nous troublent et nous fascinent » sur les calendriers, dans les magazines et sur les affiches.

Cependant, l'élévation de la pin-up au rang de forme artistique est plus récente. On la doit surtout à son utilisation massive dans les publicités américaines. Ces dernières répondent toutes au même principe : stimuler certains désirs et, une fois ceux-ci établis, les canaliser dans une direction déterminée : la marque ou les produits de l'annonceur.

Il n'y a donc rien d'étonnant à ce que le bonimenteur américain ait engagé les services de l'irrésistible pin-up, faisant appel à notre soif primordiale d'amour, celle-ci n'étant jamais autant stimulée que par la beauté.

Les formes féminines sont ingénieusement exploitées pour nous faire acheter pratiquement n'importe quoi. Notre créature de rêve n'acceptera de nous embrasser que si nous rasons notre moustache avec telle marque de crème à raser et, si on parvient à mériter le baiser tant convoité, nous risquons de la perdre aussitôt à moins d'avoir utilisé la marque adéquate de dentifrice.

Les départements de publicité des studios de cinéma d'Hollywood sont sans doute les plus grands producteurs de pin-up. L'imagination de leurs directeurs artistiques ne connaît plus de bornes quand il s'agit de mettre une paire de jolies jambes et un regard aguicheur sur toutes sortes de supports publicitaires. Peu importe qu'elle ait un rapport ou non avec le contenu du message, la représentation provocante de la silhouette féminine idéale a toujours servi d'appât pour attirer le public dans les salles.

Le cinéma a fait du « Cheesecake » (dans le jargon hollywoodien : de jolies filles montrant leurs jambes) un produit typiquement américain. Enrôlée de force dans une industrie qui brasse des milliards de dollars, notre ravissante et innocente pin-up a aujourd'hui la double fonction de faire tourner non seulement nos têtes mais également les rouages de notre économie. Investie de cette nouvelle responsabilité, la pin-up doit désormais se soumettre à certaines exigences graphiques, « Noblesse oblige » comme disent les Français.

Soulignons d'emblée que, dans ce livre, nous ne nous intéresserons qu'à la représentation artistique de la pin-up. La frontière entre l'étalage vulgaire du corps féminin et un véritable travail artistique n'a rien à voir avec celle qui sépare ce que l'on montre et ce qui est laissé à l'imagination. Personne n'oserait remettre en question l'art des grands peintres et des sculpteurs de nus. Il incombe à l'intégrité et au talent de chaque artiste d'établir si son œuvre ne fait que titiller de simples instincts bestiaux ou si elle transmet des valeurs esthétiques.

L'auteur espère que cette collection de pin-up appartient à la seconde catégorie. Toutes ses photographies sont le résultat d'une étude soignée de la composition, de l'éclairage, du costume, du décor et de la mise en scène. Chaque image étant accompagnée d'un commentaire sur ses différents aspects artistiques, nous nous contenterons ici de résumer ce qui fait l'attrait universel de la pin-up.

Naturellement, chacun de nous possède son propre concept de la beauté. Toutefois, les films, les revues et les différents médias publicitaires ont cristallisé certains canons de l'esthétique actuelle. Sans vouloir trop généraliser, on peut avancer sans prendre trop de risques que la Vénus classique et l'idéal plantureux de Rubens ont cédé la place dans l'inconscient collectif occidental à un genre de femme typiquement américain : jeune, svelte, tout en courbes et avec de longues jambes.

Si, d'ici quelques milliers d'années, un archéologue ne découvrait comme seule trace de notre civilisation qu'une capsule contenant des pin-up, il pourra non seulement en déduire quels étaient les canons de la beauté féminine au milieu du vingtième siècle, mais également reconstituer une grande partie de notre vie quotidienne actuelle.

The siren-like lure of the model instantly captures the attention, and is enhanced by the natural setting which is treated in the manner of an old master. The golden sarong, blending perfectly with the gold dust of the sand dunes, turns the model into a child of nature, completely at home in the desert. 4x5 Speed Graphic, Kodak Anastigmat, 1/200 second at f/20.

Der sirenenhafte Reiz dieses Modells nimmt sofort gefangen. Die im Stil eines Alten Meisters gehaltene Szenerie verstärkt diese Wirkung noch. Der goldfarbene Sarong harmoniert perfekt mit dem Sand der Dünen und verwandelt das Modell in ein echtes Naturkind, ein Kind der Wüste. 4x5 Speed Graphic, Kodak Anastigmat, 1/200 Sekunde bei f/20.

L'allure de sirène de ce modèle attire immédiatement le regard, ce qui est encore accentué par le décor naturel traité à la manière d'un maître ancien. Le sarong doré, se fondant parfaitement dans le sable des dunes, lui donne des airs d'enfant sauvage, parfaitement à son aise dans le désert. 4 x 5 Speed Graphic, Kodak Anastigmat, 1/200ème de seconde à f/20.

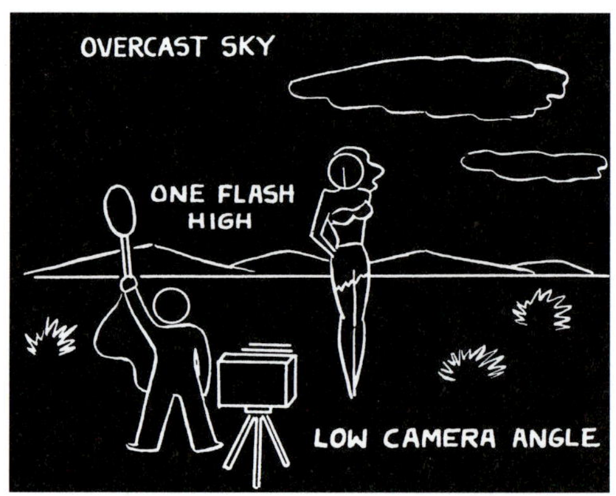

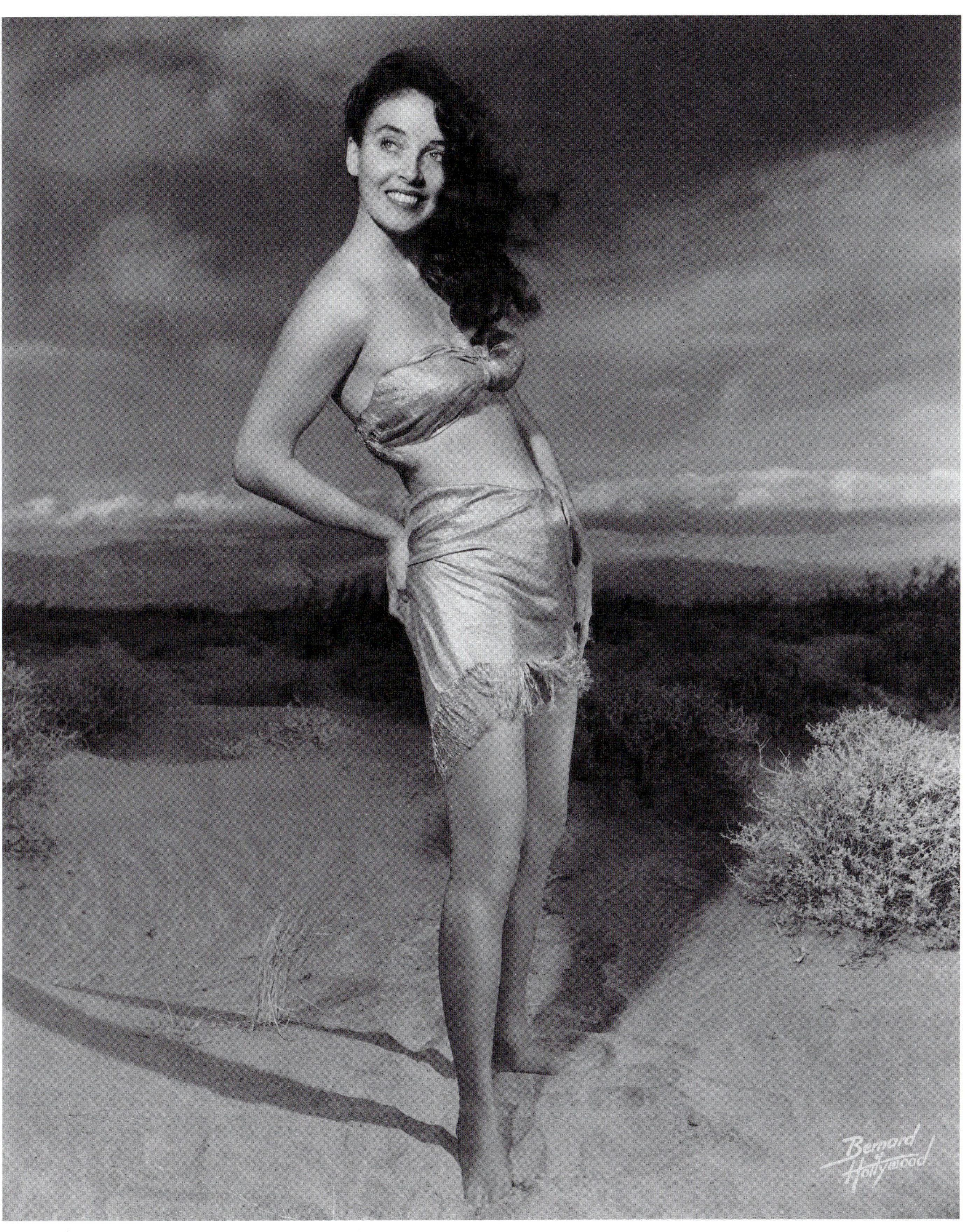

Desert Storm

WÜSTENSTURM · TEMPÊTE DU DÉSERT

A bit of humor has been injected into this carefree, breezy pose on the ocean front. In this case a Bikini suit fits in perfectly with the vivacious personality of the model. The strong feeling of depth is obtained by careful posing of the darker part of the face against the white foam of the wave with an aluminum reflector for added side lighting. Super D Graflex, $5^1/_2$ inch, 1/200 second at f/22. Superpan Press film.

Augenzwinkernder Humor spricht aus dieser sorglos-heiteren Strandszene. Hier paßt der Bikini perfekt zum lebhaften Wesen des Modells. Dadurch daß die im Schatten liegende Gesichtshälfte sorgfältig gegen die weiße Gischt des Meeres abgesetzt wurde und ein Aluminiumreflektor zusätzliches Seitenlicht spendete, wurde eine ausgeprägte räumliche Wirkung erzielt. Super D Graflex, $5^1/_2$ Zoll, 1/200 Sekunde bei f/22. Superpan Press-Film.

Cette pose insouciante devant l'océan a été pimentée avec un peu d'humour. Dans ce cas-ci, le bikini convient parfaitement à la personnalité espiègle du modèle. L'impression de grande profondeur de champ a été obtenue grâce à un réflecteur en aluminium projetant une lumière latérale, faisant contraster la partie ombragée du visage avec l'écume blanche des vagues. Super D Graflex, 13,75cm, 1/200ème de seconde à f/22, pellicule Superpan Press.

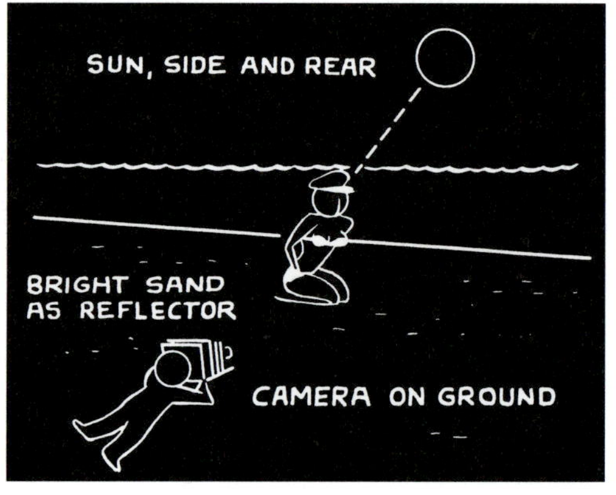

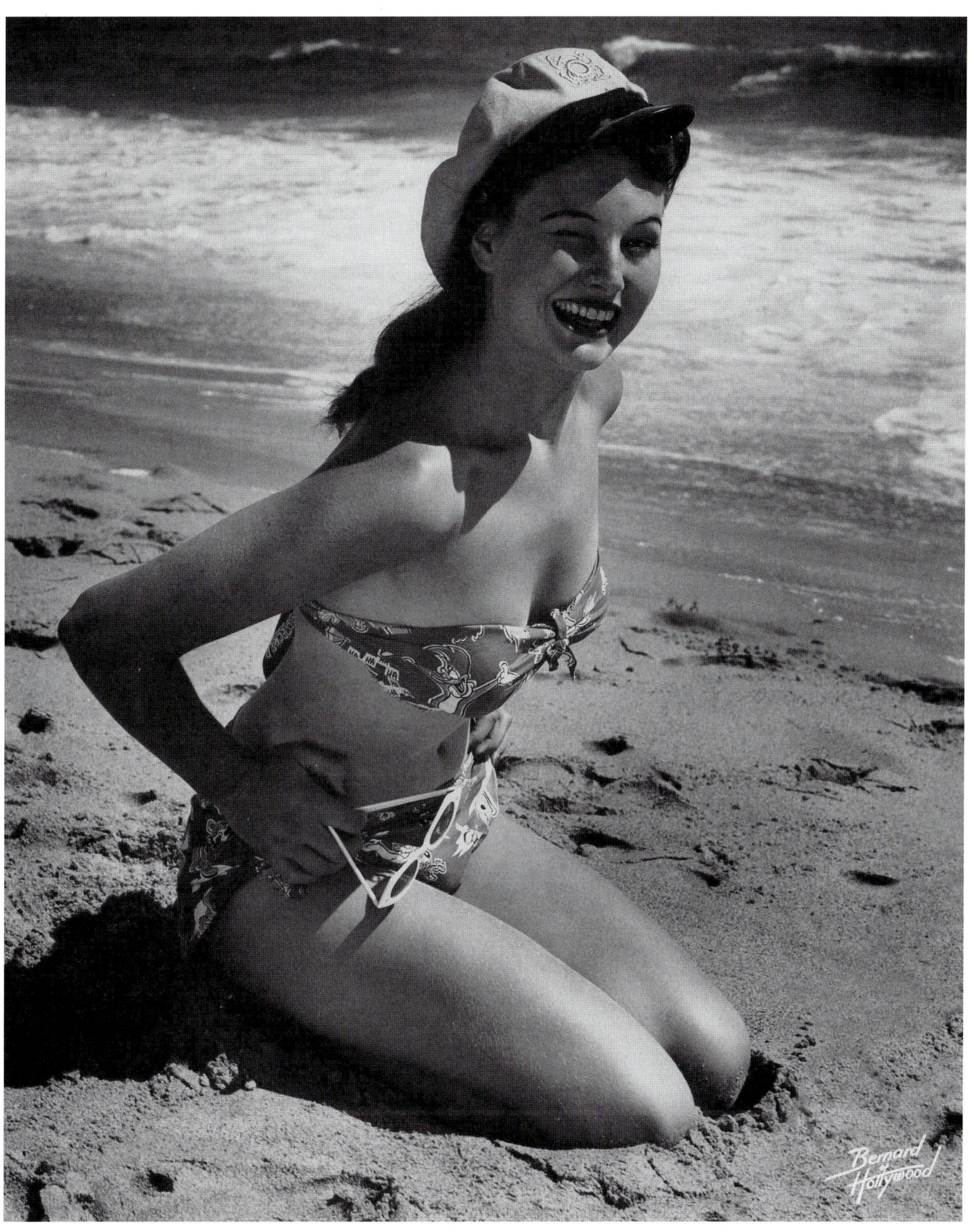

Sailor Beware

SCHIFF AHOI! · OHÉ, DU BATEAU !

An air of casual sophistication is achieved in this "posed-candid," where split-second timing has caught the saucy expression of the model with the wind-tossed spontaneity of her pose. Interest is heightened by the sequin-studded bathing suit, a French original. 1/100 second at f/32.

Dieser „inszenierte Schnappschuß" vermittelt die Atmosphäre lässigen Raffinements. Die kurze Belichtungszeit hat den kessen Ausdruck des Modells und die windzerzauste Spontaneität ihrer Pose eingefangen. Die Aufmerksamkeit wird durch den pailletten-besetzten Badeanzug, eine französische Kreation, noch zusätzlich gefesselt. 1/100 Sekunde bei f/32.

Cet « instantané posé » dégage un air à la fois sophistiqué et naturel grâce à l'expression espiègle du modèle, la spontanéité de sa pose, le mouvement du vent dans ses cheveux et son bikini français brodé de paillettes. 1/100ème de seconde à f/32.

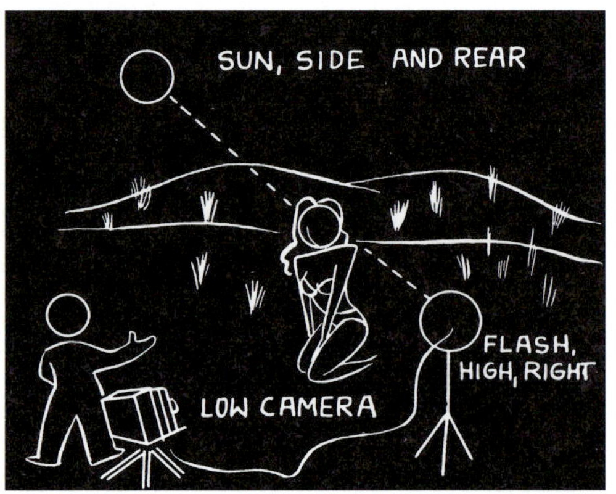

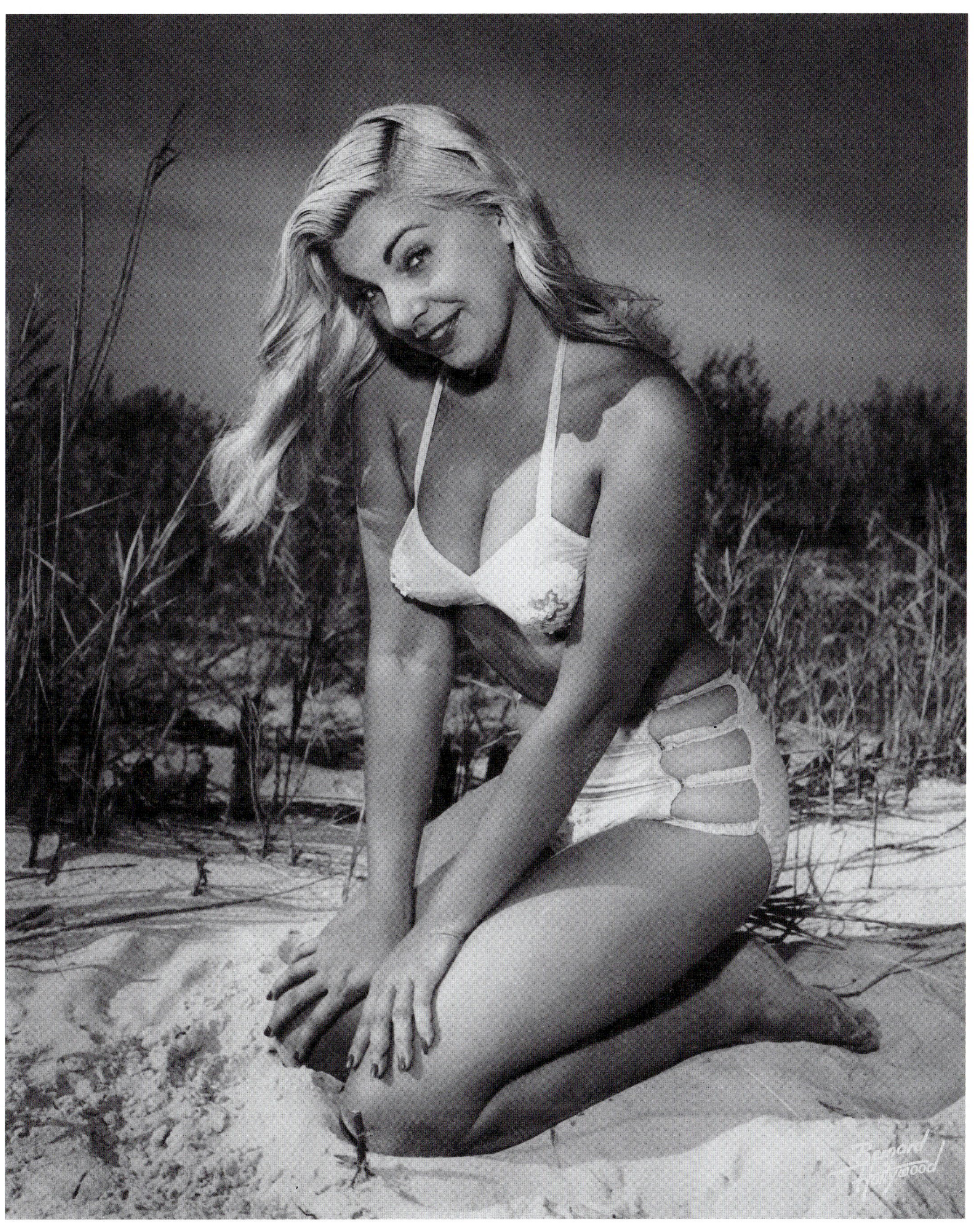

Beauty and the Beach

DIE SCHÖNE UND DER STRAND · BELLE DE PLAGE

With the stark background conjuring up a feeling of an impenetrable jungle, the tiger skin design of the costume helps to create the impression of a lithe, untamed animal. Back side-lighting and boom light on the hair create a three-dimensional effect, separating the figure from the background. 5x7 Ansco view camera, 1/5 second at f/16, Super Panchro-B.

Der neutrale Hintergrund beschwört einen undurchdringlichen Dschungel herauf, und der Tigerfellstoff läßt das Modell wie ein geschmeidiges, wildes Tier erscheinen. Streiflicht und Akzentlicht auf dem Haar erzeugen eine räumliche Wirkung und heben die Gestalt vom Hintergrund ab. 5x7 Ansco view camera, 1/5 Sekunde bei f/16, Super Panchro-B-Film.

Le fond noir qui évoque une jungle impénétrable et le maillot de bain en faux tigre contribuent à donner l'impression d'un animal souple et sauvage. L'éclairage latéral par l'arrière grâce à une lumière de perche orientée sur la chevelure crée un effet tridimensionnel, isolant le personnage de l'arrière-plan. 5 x7 Ansco view camera, 1/5ème de seconde à f/16, pellicule Super Panchro-B.

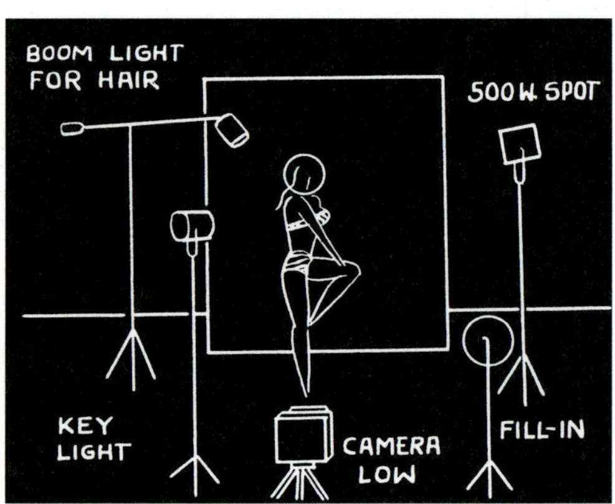

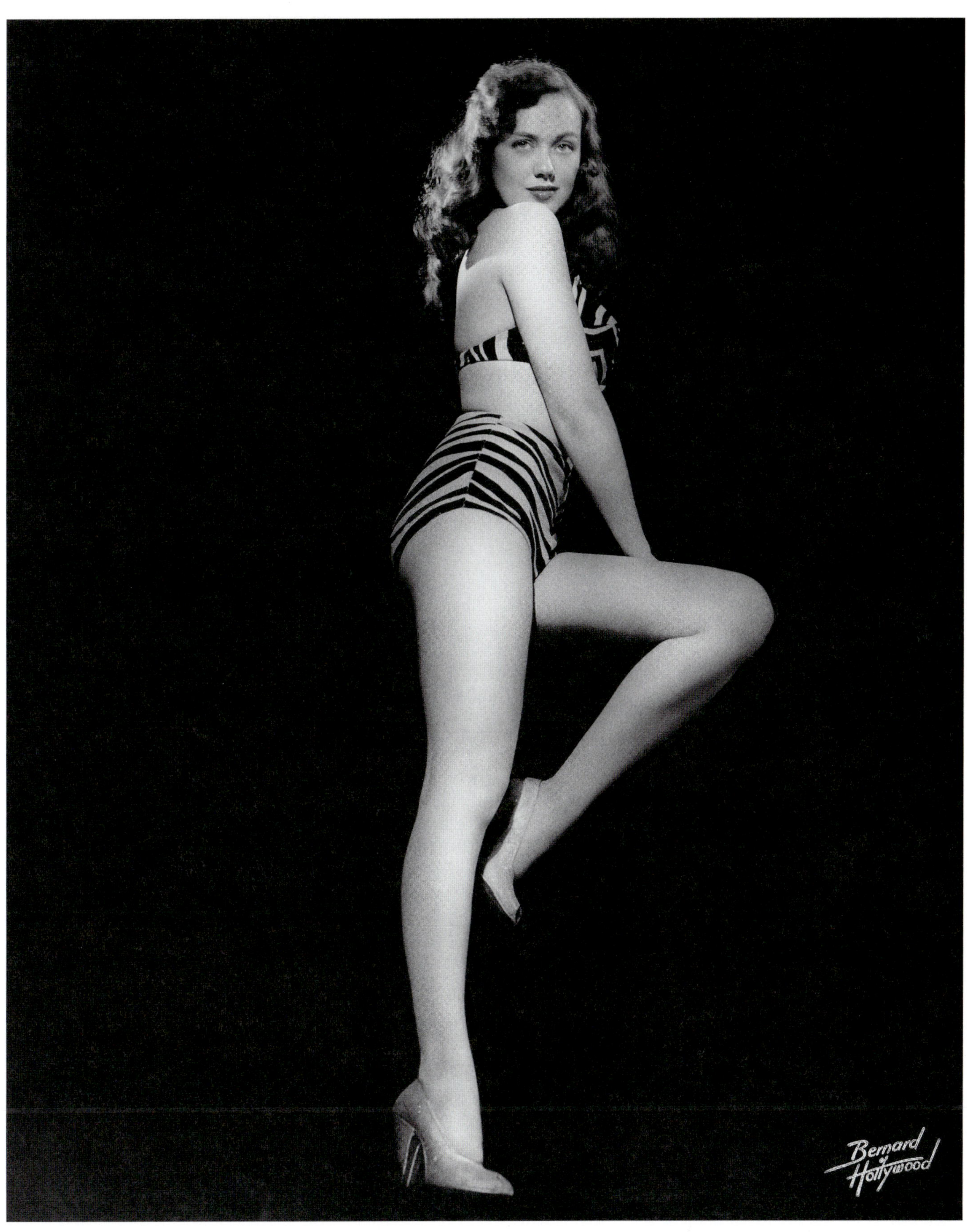

Jungle Juno

DSCHUNGELKÖNIGIN · LA REINE DE LA JUNGLE

The silken texture of the subject's blonde tresses is in perfect harmony with the softness and richness of the furs, and adds warmth to this drawing-like composition. Harsh shadows are avoided by the use of soft, plastic front and side lighting, which at the same time achieves careful balancing of the overall lighting effect. 1/10 second at f/11.

Die seidige Lockenpracht der Blondine harmoniert perfekt mit der luxuriösen Flauschigkeit der Pelzstola und verleiht dieser wie gemalt wirkenden Komposition Wärme. Harte Schatten werden durch weiches Seiten- und Vorderlicht vermieden, das gleichzeitig die Gesamtausleuchtung sorgfältig ausbalanciert.
1/10 Sekunde bei f/11.

La texture soyeuse des cheveux blonds du modèle s'harmonise à merveille avec ses fourrures épaisses et douces et ajoute de la chaleur à cette composition très graphique. J'ai évité les ombres trop dures avec des spots doux orientés de face et de côté, ce qui donne une belle lumière équilibrée à l'ensemble.
1/10ème de seconde à f/11.

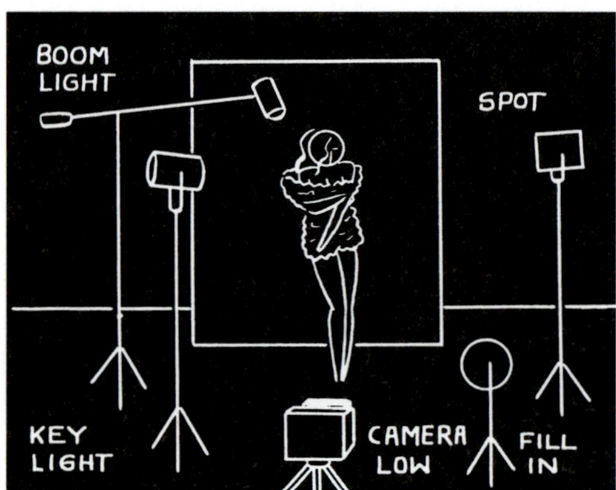

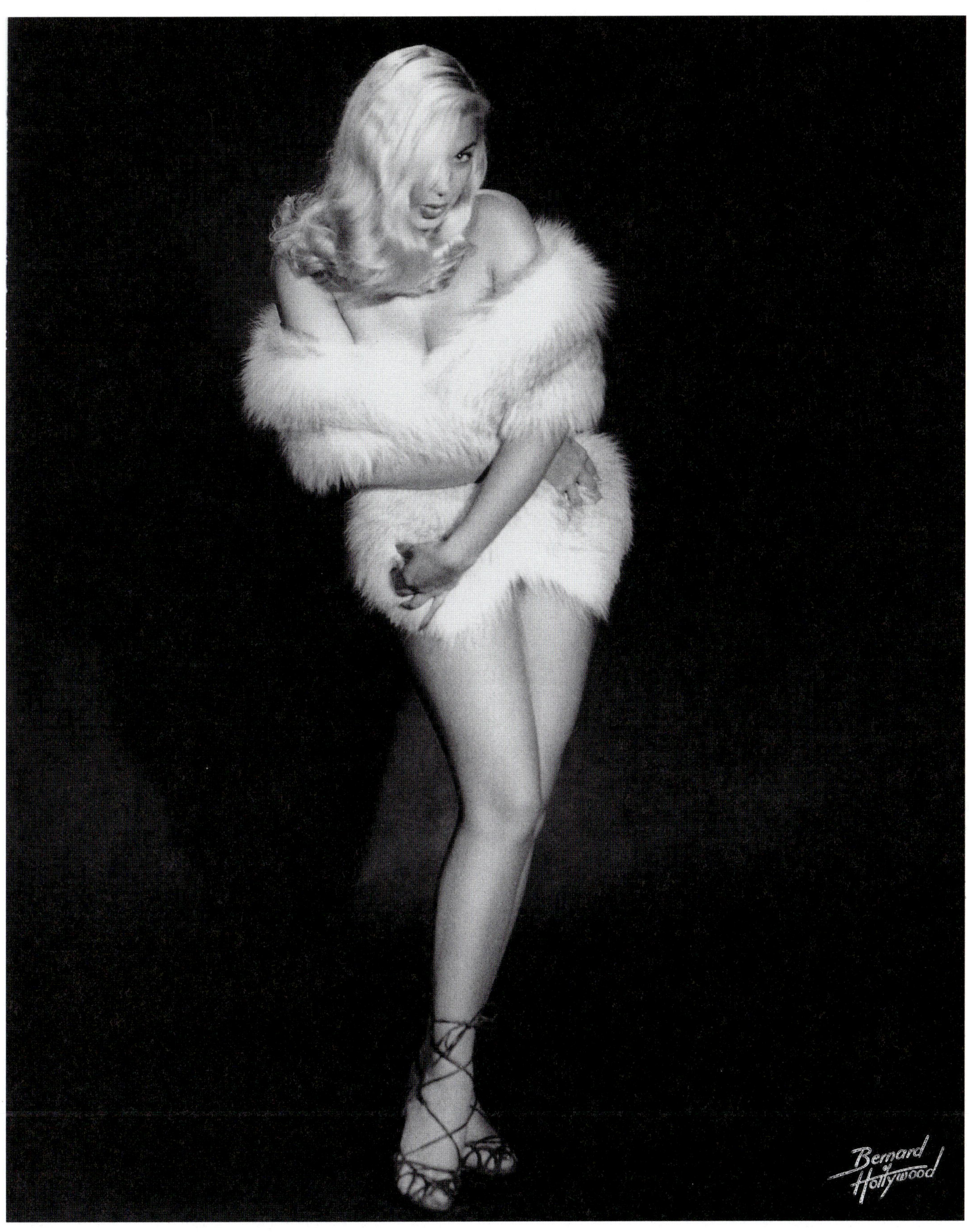

Cold Outside

VENUS IM PELZ · UNE VÉNUS EN FOURRURE

In a static pose such as this, rather in the vein of a Hollywood leg-art poster, the punch has to come from the facial expression. Pictorial intrigue is brought about by atmosphere lighting which accentuates the shape of the legs, and rim-lighting of the head, back and upraised arm.

Bei einer statischen Pose wie dieser, die stark an ein frivoles Filmposter erinnert, macht der Gesichtsausdruck das „gewisse Etwas" aus. Die faszinierende Bildwirkung wird durch die stimmungsvolle Gesamtausleuchtung erzeugt, die die Konturen der Beine betont, und durch das Streiflicht auf Kopf, Schulterpartie und den erhobenen Arm.

Dans une pose statique telle que celle-ci, dans la veine des affiches de pin-up hollywoodiennes, c'est l'expression du modèle qui fait la différence. L'atmosphère d'intrigue est due à un éclairage qui accentue la forme des jambes, alors que la tête, le dos et le bras levé sont illuminés par l'arrière pour créer un halo.

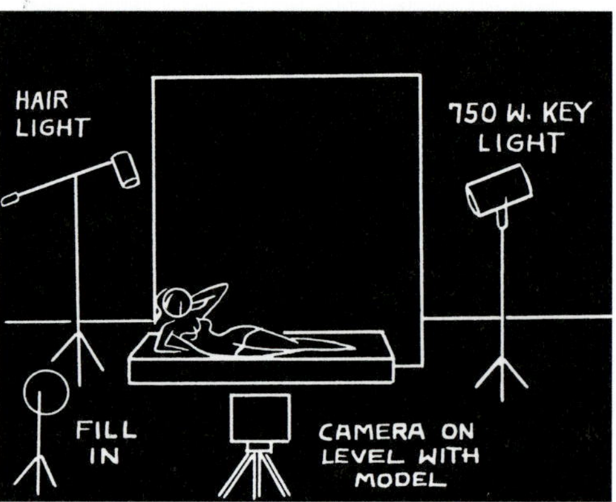

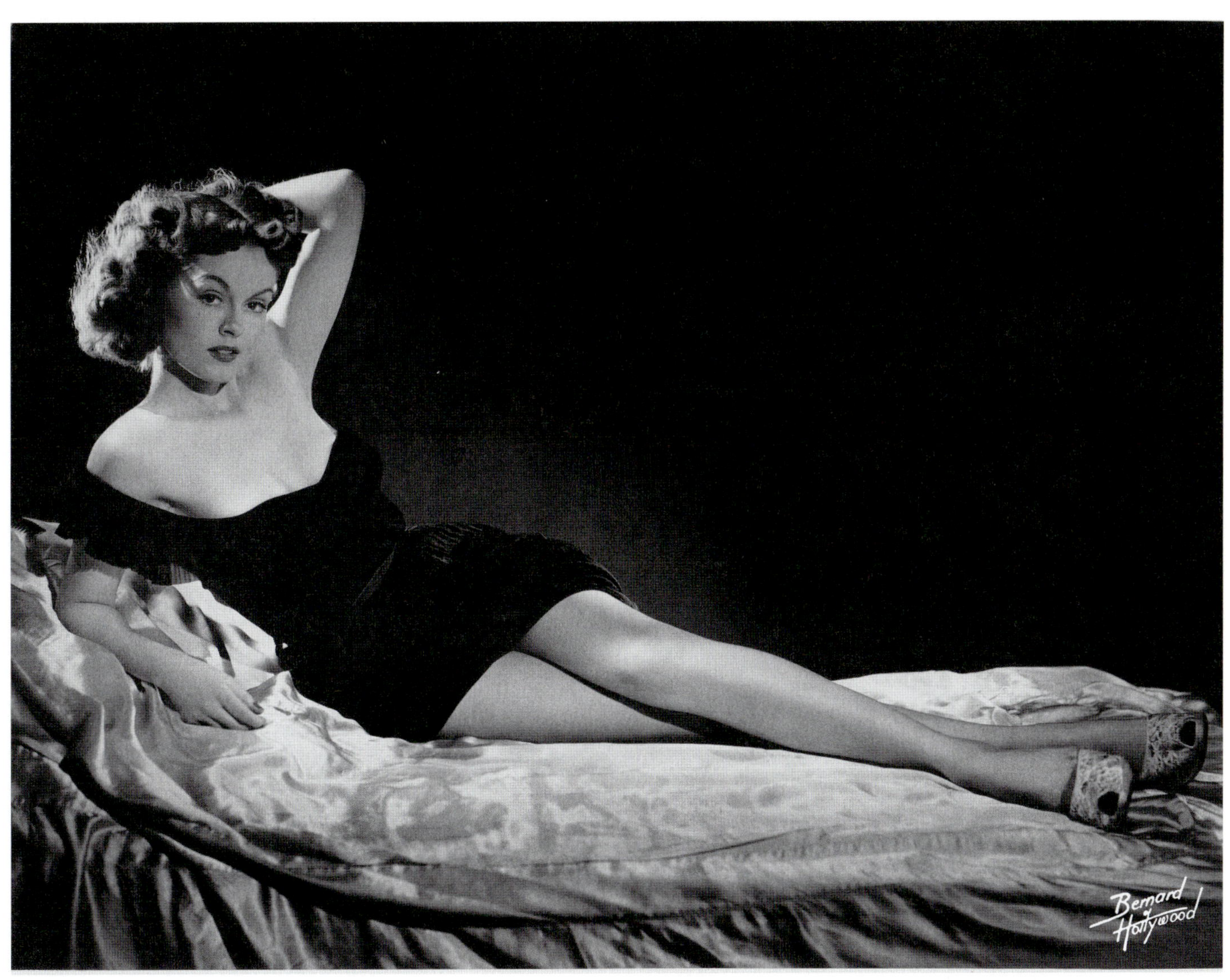

Beauty Rest

SCHÖNHEITSSCHLAF · LE REPOS DE LA BELLE

This mermaid, to all appearances tossed on the shore and left like a piece of driftwood, simulates the form and movement of the receding waves, blending into an eye-appealing compositional pattern. California coastline locale on an overcast day. Soft highlights were achieved by double flash, held eight feet from the model. 1/200 second at f/11.

Diese Meerjungfrau, allem Anschein nach als Treibgut an den Strand gespült, nimmt Linie und Bewegung der zurückweichenden Brandung auf und fügt sich harmonisch in die Komposition ein. Eine weiche Aufhellung wurde mit zwei Blitzlichtern aus drei Metern Entfernung erzielt. 1/200 Sekunde bei f/11.

Cette sirène, qui semble avoir été rejetée sur le rivage et abandonnée sur la plage comme un fragment d'épave, s'harmonise avec le mouvement des vagues mourantes, se fondant dans le paysage. Côte de Californie par un jour nuageux. Un double flash, placé à trois mètres du modèle, permet d'obtenir des reliefs lumineux. 1/200ème de seconde à f/11.

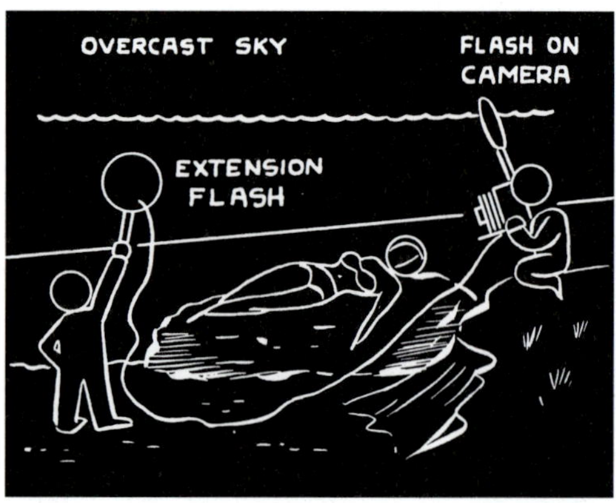

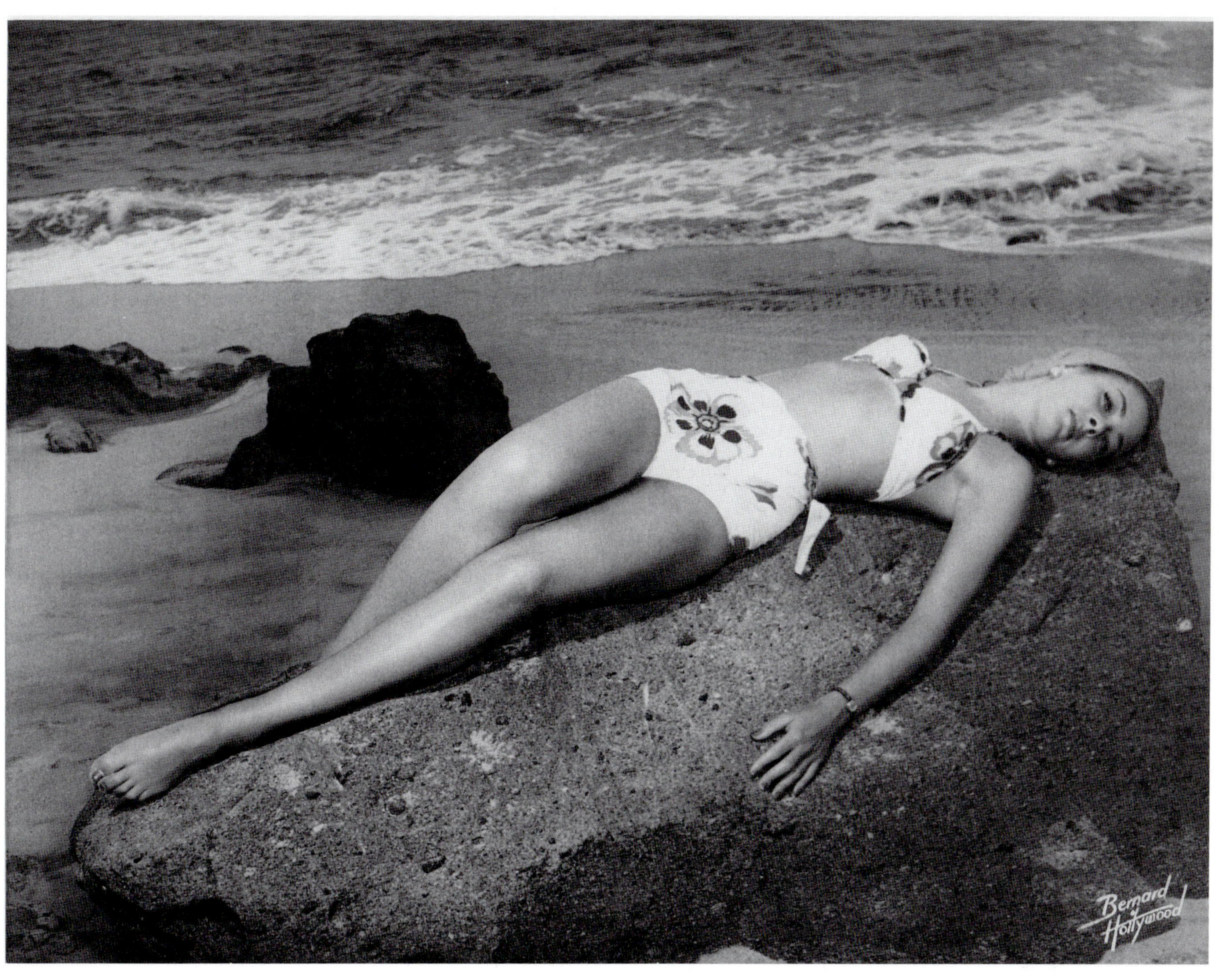

Flotsam

STRANDGUT · LA NAUFRAGÉE

The outstanding feature of this photograph in a simple studio setting is the realism and feeling of immediacy achieved by the forward projection of the model toward the camera – an effect which is currently used to good advantage on television. This is an excellent example of our contention that the photographer has it all over the illustrator when it comes to making models literally "jump out of the picture." 1/10 second at f/11.

Die hervorstechenden Merkmale dieser Fotografie sind die Sachlichkeit und der Ausdruck von Direktheit, der durch den in Richtung Kamera vorgebeugten Oberkörper des Modells vor neutraler Studiokulisse erzeugt wird. Dieser Trick wird in jüngster Zeit erfolgreich im Fernsehen eingesetzt. Das Foto ist ein exzellentes Beispiel für unsere Überzeugung, daß der Fotograf im Vorteil ist gegenüber dem Illustrator, wenn es darum geht, Modelle buchstäblich „aus dem Bild springen zu lassen". 1/10 Sekunde bei f/11.

L'effet saisissant de cette photo prise dans un simple décor de studio provient du réalisme et de l'impression d'instantané fournis par la pose du modèle penché en avant, un stratagème efficace couramment utilisé de nos jours à la télévision. C'est là un excellent exemple de l'avantage que possède le photographe sur l'illustrateur : pouvoir faire littéralement « jaillir » le modèle de l'image. 1/10ème de seconde à f/11.

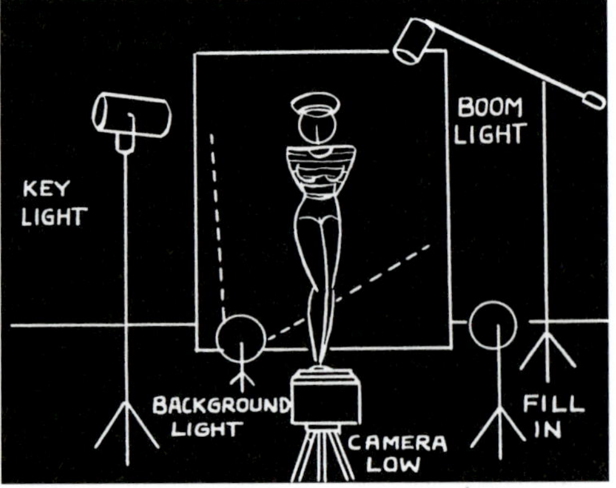

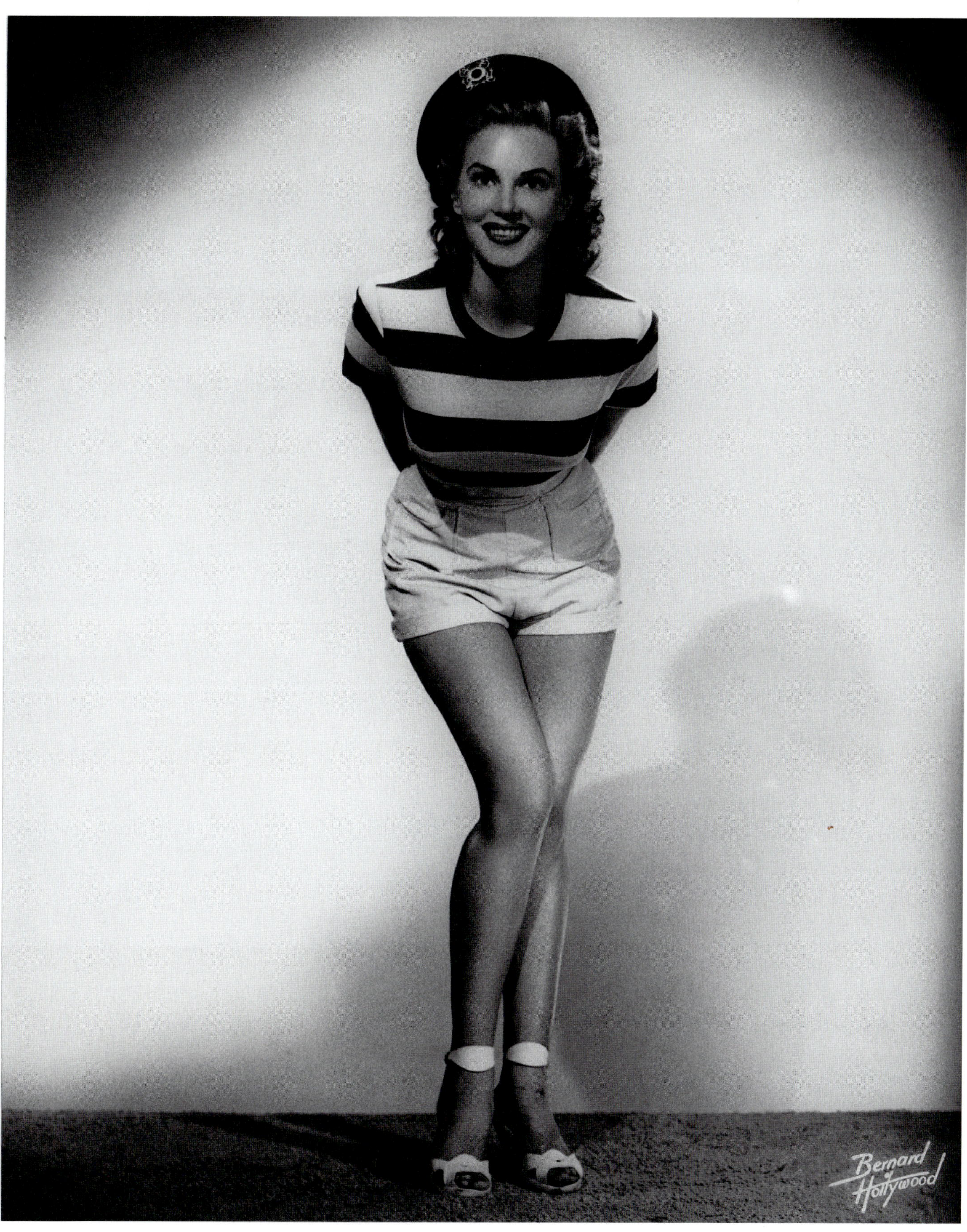

Star and Stripes

STAR UND STREIFEN · LE MATELOT

An elusive, elfin quality keynotes this sensitive study of a fragile, golden-haired beauty. The almost furtive position of the body and the frightened expression of the face make this picture doubly appealing.

Von dieser einfühlsamen Studie einer zarten Schönheit mit goldfarbenem Haar geht eine irritierende Wirkung aus. Die beinah fluchtbereite Körperhaltung und der verängstigte Gesichtsausdruck steigern den Reiz dieser Aufnahme zusätzlich.

Cette étude d'une beauté blonde et fragile possède une qualité de légèreté et de délicatesse. La position presque fuyante du corps et l'expression effarouchée du modèle rendent cette photo doublement attirante.

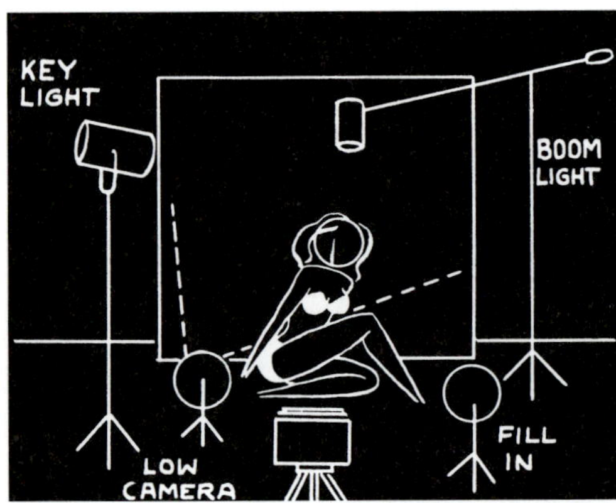

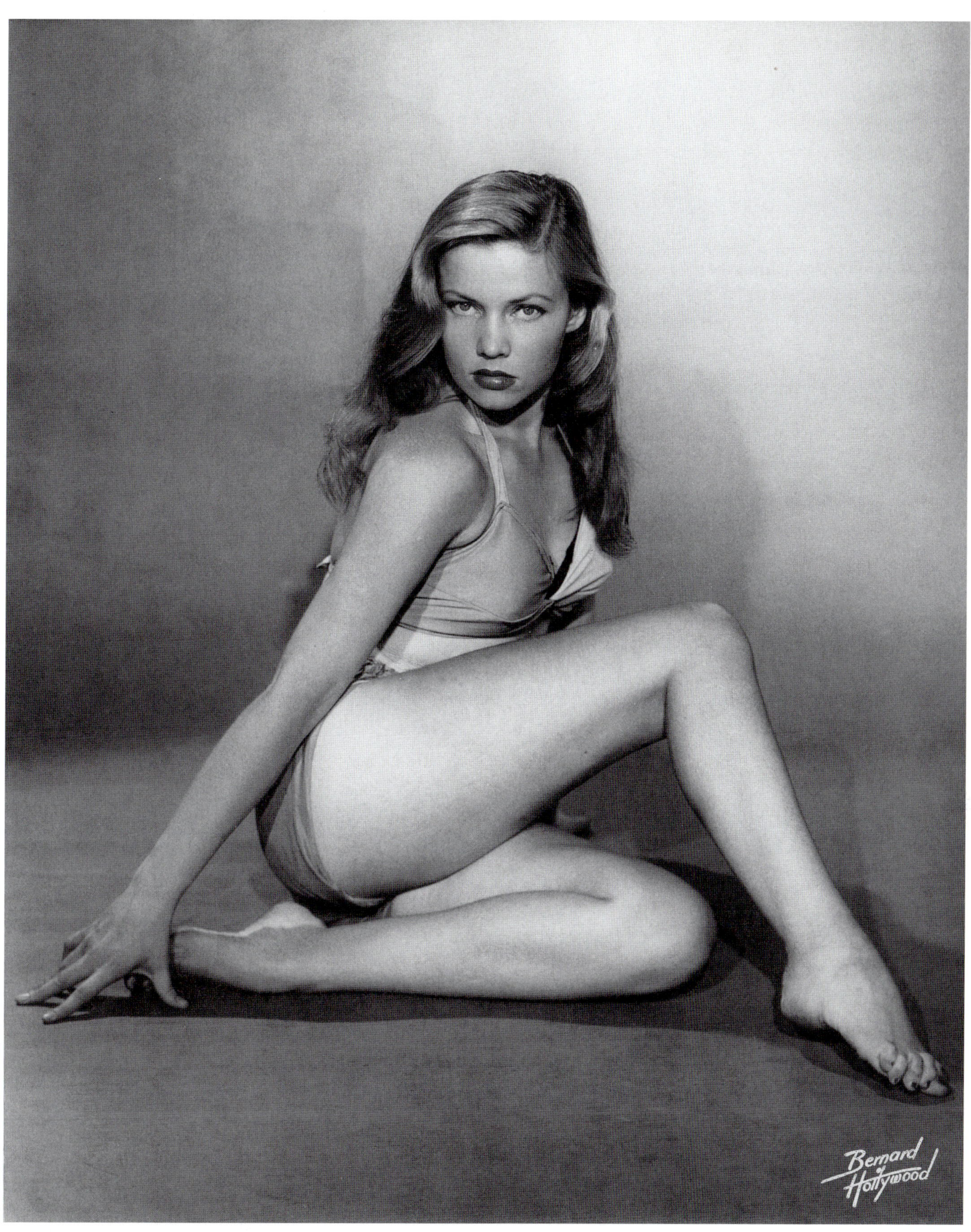

Gamin

WILDFANG · GAMINE

Like the sirens of ancient Greek mythology who lured seamen to destruction with their enthralling voices, this twentieth-century counterpart manages to achieve the same effect with no more than an enticing posture and an inviting expression. Low camera angle accentuates the model's flowing, vertical body lines. 4x5 Speed Graphic, 1/100 second at f/22.

Lockten die Sirenen der griechischen Mythologie die Seeleute noch mit ihren verführerischen Stimmen ins Verderben, so genügt ihrer Schwester aus dem zwanzigsten Jahrhundert bereits eine verführerische Pose und ein einladender Blick. Eine niedrige Kameraposition betont die fließenden, vertikalen Konturen des Modells. 4x5 Speed Graphic, 1/100 Sekunde bei f/22.

Contrairement aux créatures de la Grèce antique qui attiraient les marins par le fond avec leurs voix enchanteresses, cette sirène des temps modernes se contente d'une pose attirante et d'une expression engageante. L'objectif placé bas accentue les lignes fluides et verticales du corps. 4 x 5 Speed Graphic, 1/100ème de seconde à f/22.

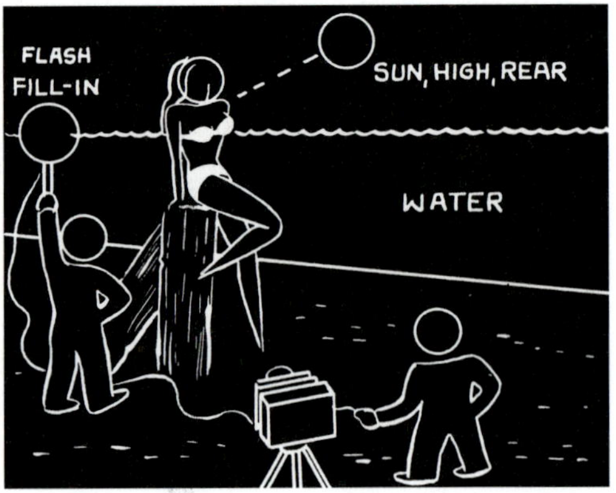

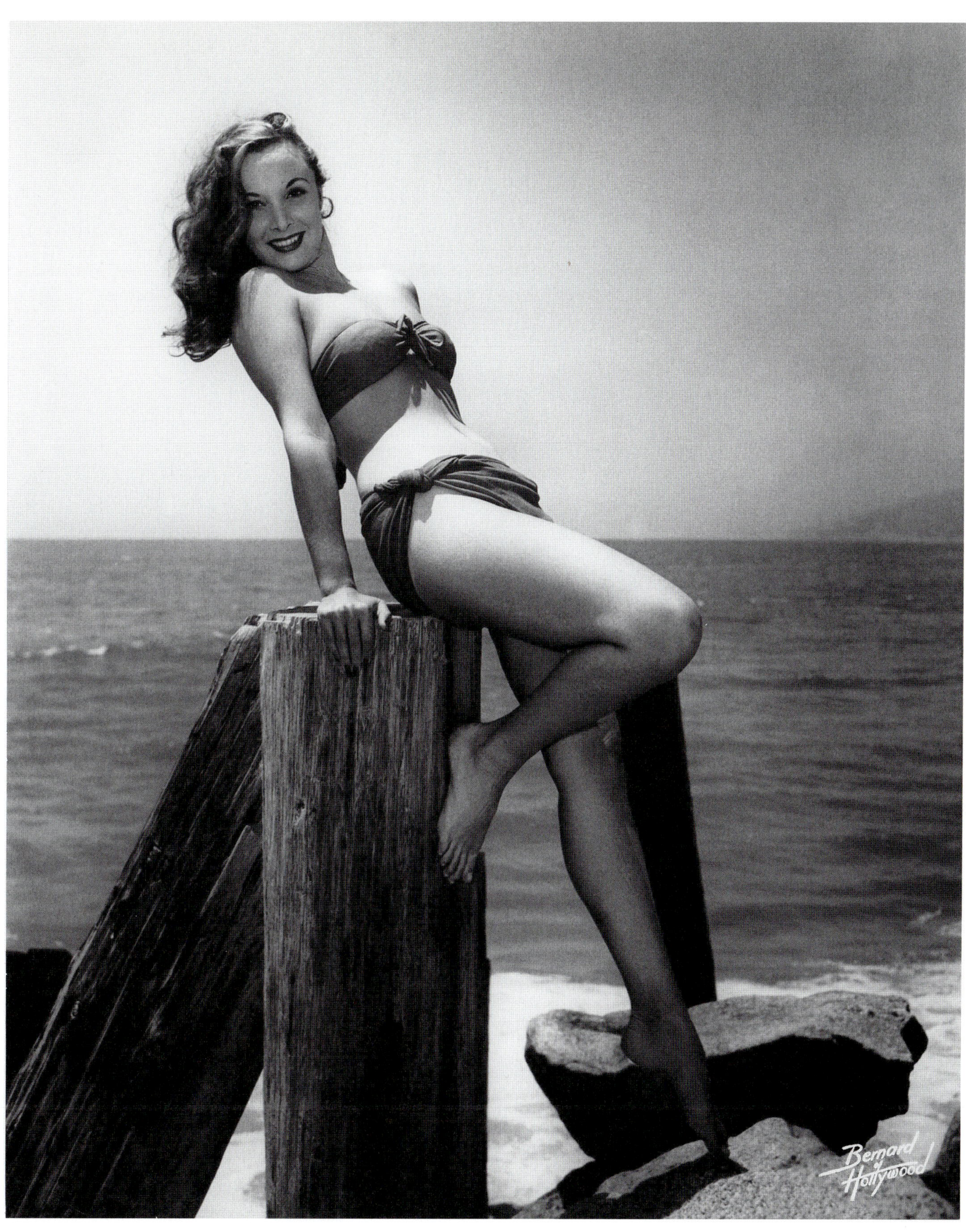

Sea Siren

SIRENENGESANG · LA SIRÈNE

A suntanned body against a bleached surfboard floating on a placid pool makes a striking contrast of tonal values. Ripples, caused by the subject's playing with autumn leaves in the water, slightly interrupt the tranquility of an afternoon siesta. The unusual perspective is obtained by tilting the camera down ninety degrees from a small overhead bridge. 5x7 Ansco view camera with 10 inch Ektar lens, 1/100 second at f/22.

Ein sonnengebräunter Körper auf einem verblichenen Surfboard, das auf einem friedvollen Pool dahintreibt, erzeugt spannende Tonwertabstufungen. Kleine Wellen, die durch das Spiel des Modells mit dem dahintreibenden Herbstlaub ausgelöst werden, beleben die müßige Stimmung einer nachmittäglichen Siesta. Die ungewöhnliche Perspektive wurde dadurch erzielt, daß die Kamera auf einer schmalen Brücke über der Szene um 90 Grad nach unten geschwenkt wurde. 5x7 Ansco view camera mit 10 Zoll Ektar-Objektiv, 1/100 Sekunde bei f/22.

Le corps bronzé, le bois blanchi de la planche et l'eau cristalline offrent des contrastes saisissants. Les ondes provoquées par la main du modèle dans l'eau, jouant avec des feuilles mortes, troublent la tranquillité de cette sieste. Cette perspective inhabituelle est obtenue en inclinant l'objectif de quatre-vingt-dix degrés depuis un petit pont. 5 x 7 Ansco view camera, objectif Ektar 25 cm, 1/100ème de seconde à f/22.

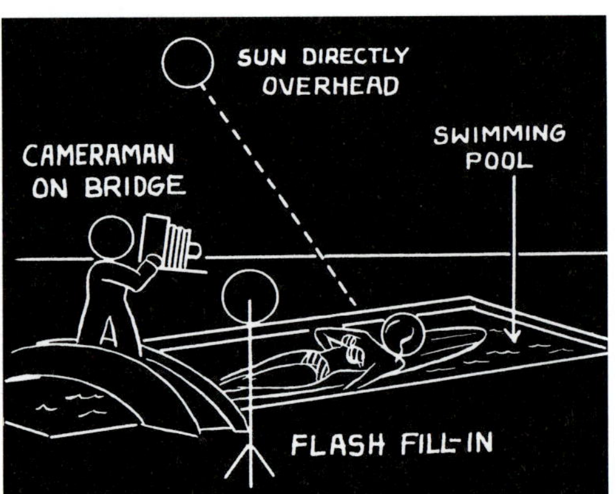

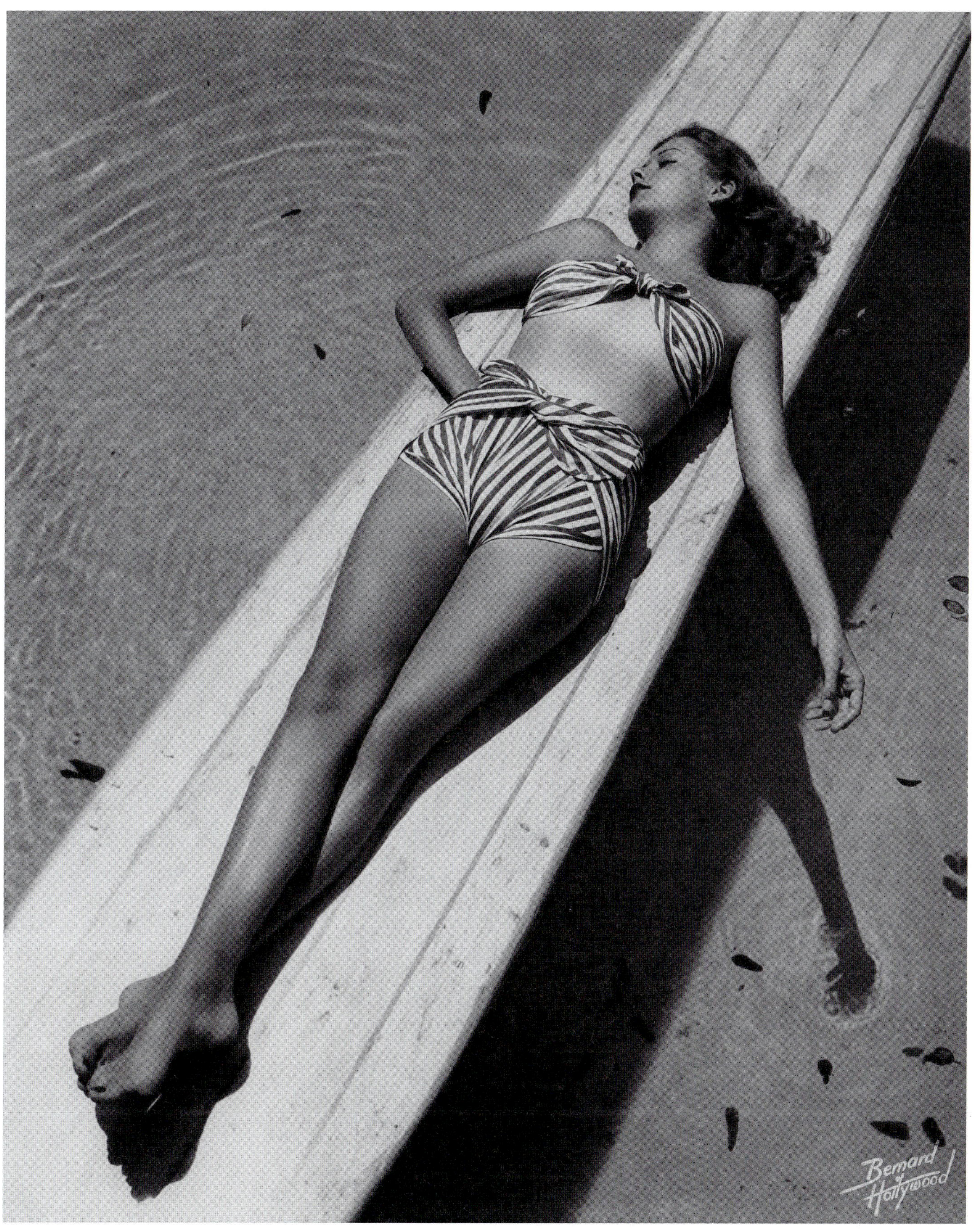

Across the Board

NEPTUNS TOCHTER · LA PLANCHE

The gay and nostalgic atmosphere of the circus is evoked through the use of an old prop in a new way. Side-lighting is emphasized to bring about the sculptural effect. The ball, incidentally, is taped to the toes.

Ein altes Requisit neu eingesetzt, und schon ist eine bunte und nostalgische Zirkusatmosphäre heraufbeschworen. Seitenlicht betont die skulpturale Wirkung. Der Ball ist übrigens mit Klebeband an den Zehen befestigt.

Un accessoire éculé mais utilisé d'une nouvelle façon permet de recréer l'atmosphère gaie et nostalgique du cirque. L'éclairage latéral a été accentué pour donner un effet sculptural. La balle, en fait, est scotchée aux orteils.

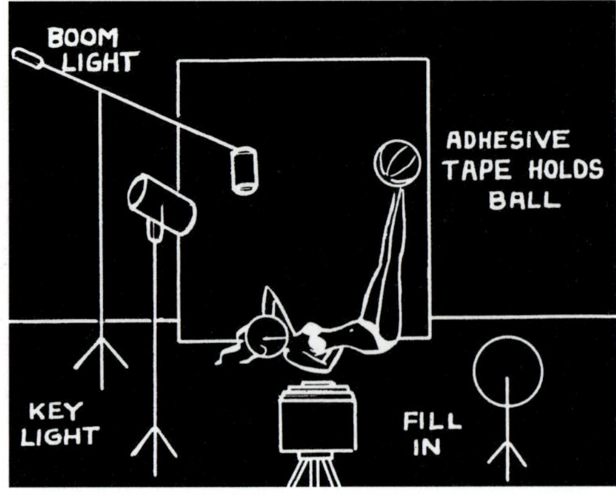

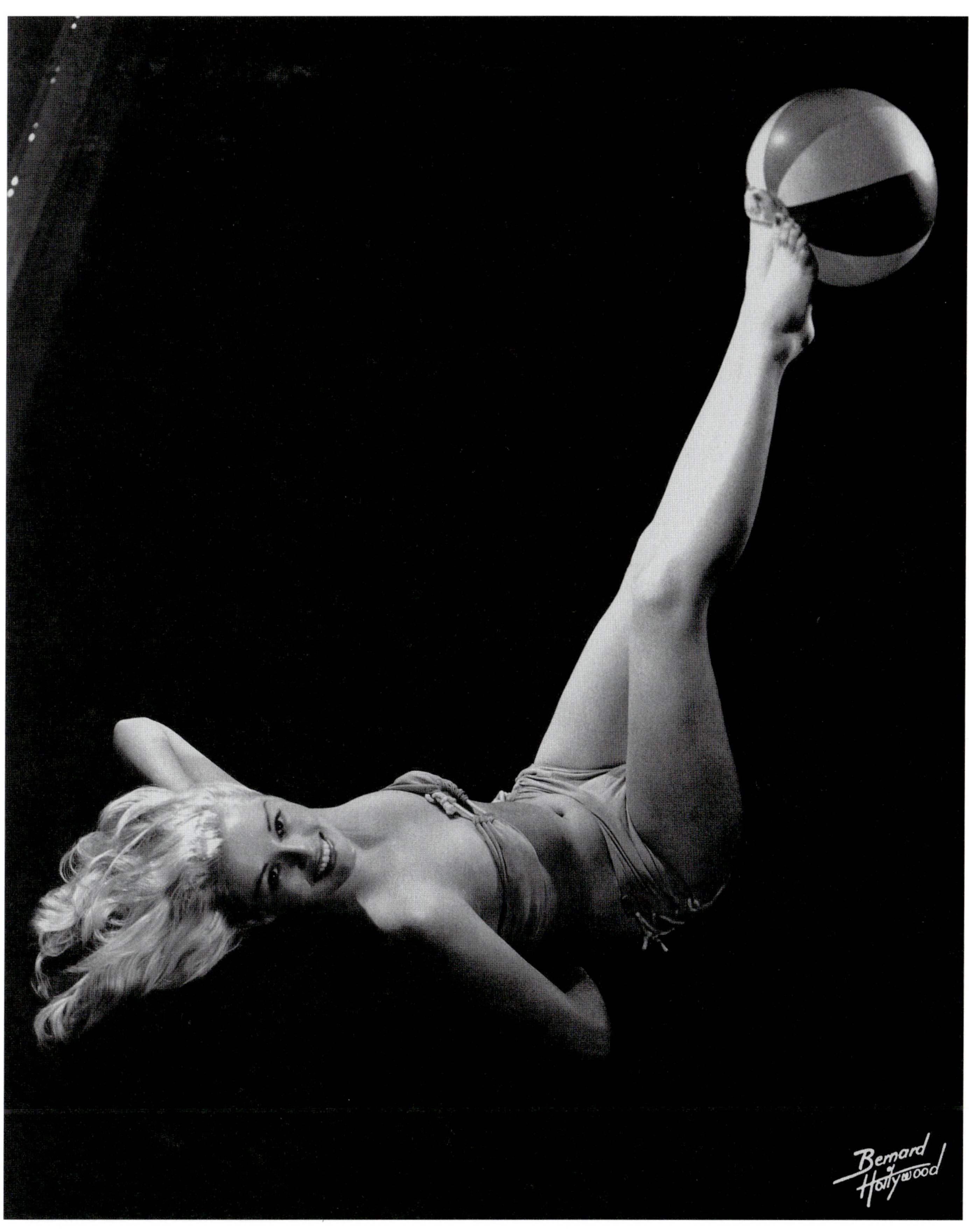

Well Balanced

BALANCEAKT · UNE ENFANT DE LA BALLE

An angelic face, combined with an alluring pose never fails to result in an attention-getting pin-up. The unusually pleasing proportions of the figure give this photograph the free-flowing lines of a drawing. The diagonal composition denotes movement and vitality while the circular prop, offset by the dark area in the upper right provides the ideal element for the creation of this effect. 5x7 Ansco view camera, 1/10 second at f/11.

Ein engelhaftes Gesicht kombiniert mit einer verführerischen Pose garantiert immer ein aufsehenerregendes Pin-Up. Die ungewöhnlich hübschen Proportionen des Modells verleihen dieser Fotografie die fließende Leichtigkeit eines Gemäldes. Die diagonale Komposition suggeriert Bewegung und Vitalität, ein Effekt, der durch das gerundete Requisit, abgehoben von dem dunklen Hintergrund rechts oben, unterstützt wird. 5x7 Ansco view camera, 1/10 Sekunde bei f/11.

La combinaison d'un visage angélique et d'une pose provoquante attire toujours le regard. Les proportions parfaites et harmonieuses de la silhouette donnent à cette photo les lignes fluides d'un dessin. La composition en diagonale évoque le mouvement et la vitalité tandis que l'accessoire circulaire, mis en valeur par le fond sombre dans la partie supérieure droite, contribue parfaitement à créer cet effet. 5x7 Ansco view camera, 1/10ème de seconde à f/11.

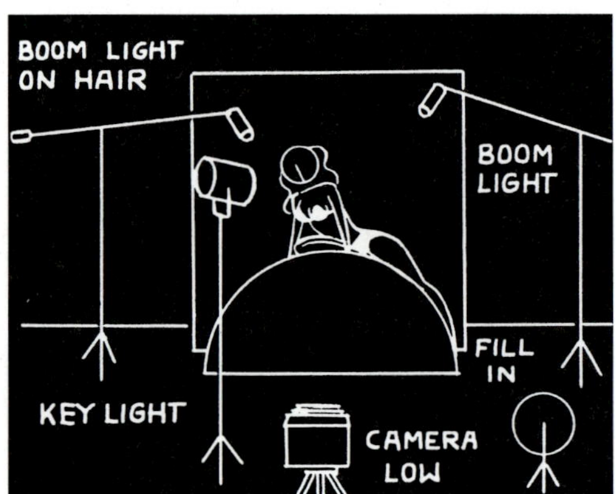

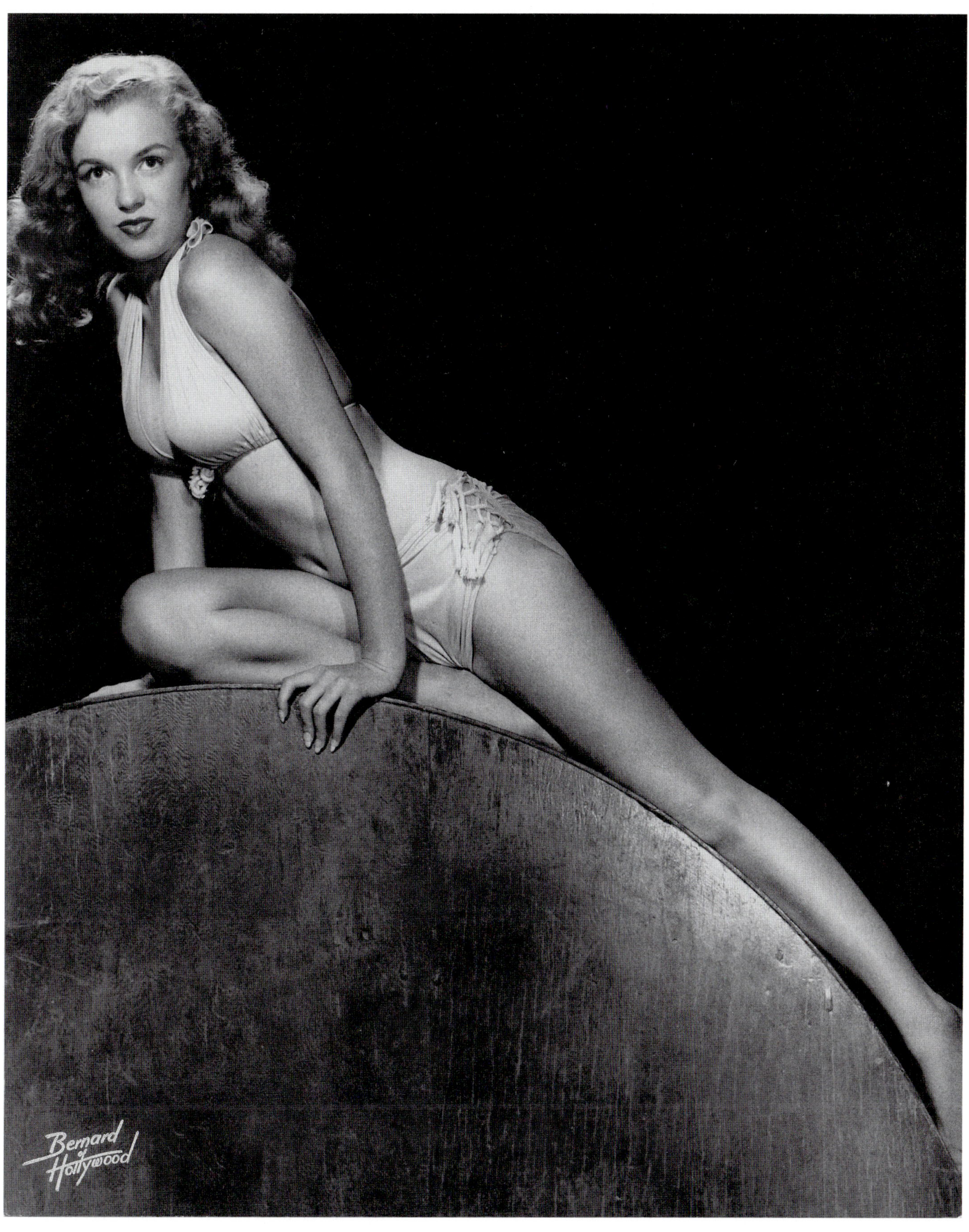

Making the Grade

GRATWANDERUNG · LA QUADRATURE DU CERCLE

That a face can be as effective a pin-up as a shot of the entire figure is demonstrated here. The dynamic element in this study is the feline look in the eyes. The background is purposely thrown out of focus to bring out the head in strong relief.
Auto Graflex, 1/10 second at f/9.

Diese Fotografie demonstriert, daß ein Gesicht ein ebenso gutes Pin-Up-Bild ergeben kann wie eine figürliche Aufnahme. Der katzenhafte Blick des Modells bringt das dynamische Element in diese Studie. Der Hintergrund ist bewußt unscharf aufgenommen, um den Kopf deutlich hervorzuheben.
Auto Graflex, 1/10 Sekunde bei f/9.

Un gros plan de visage peut être aussi efficace qu'une pin-up en pied. Le regard de félin est l'élément dynamique de cette étude. Le fond est délibérément flou afin de faire ressortir le relief du visage. Auto Graflex, 1/10ème de seconde à f/9.

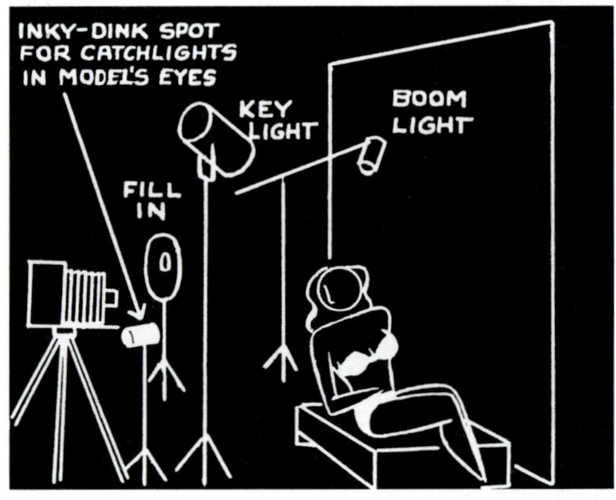

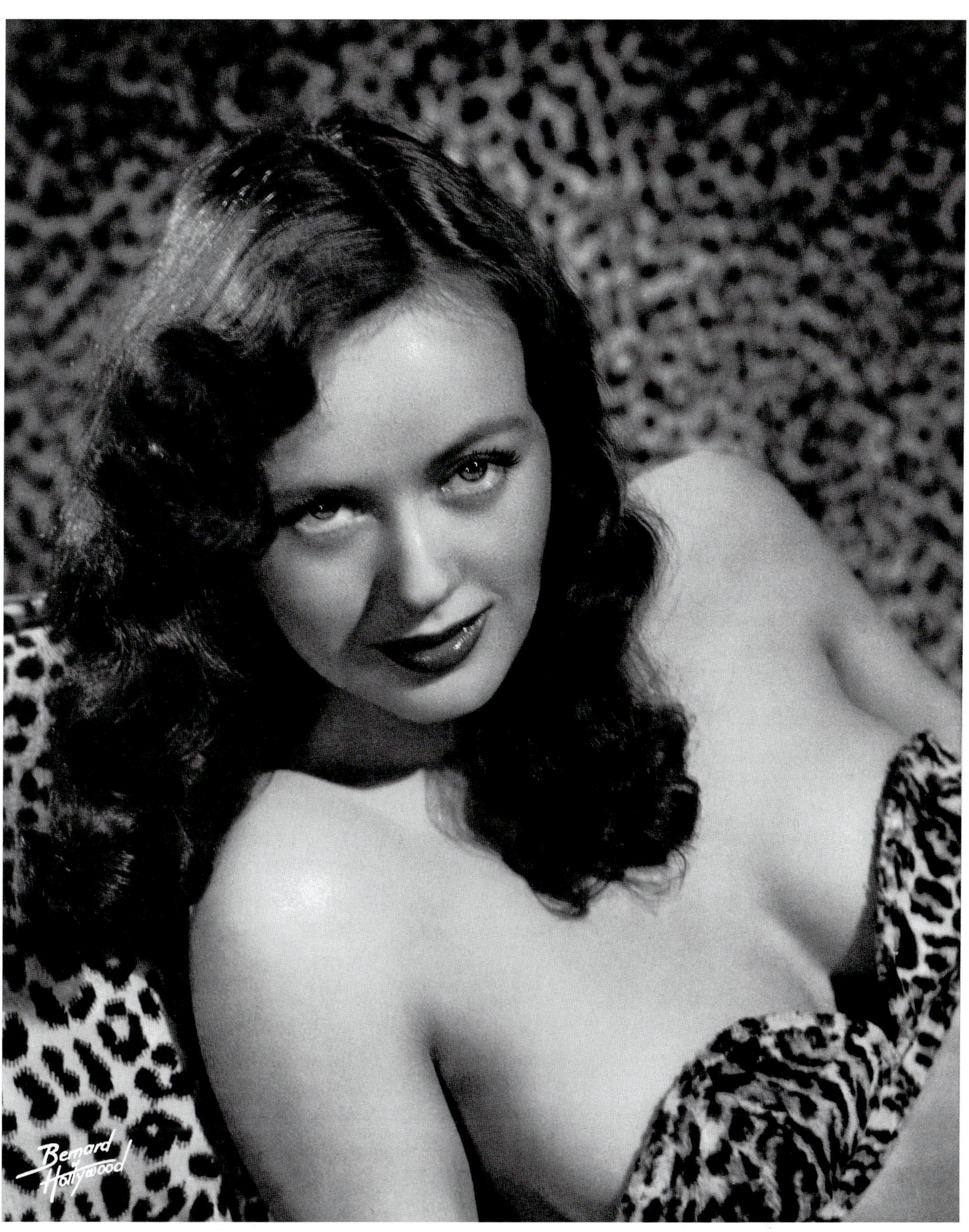

Sultry Savage

WILDKATZE · LA SAUVAGEONNE

Models and Moods

A visiting British journalist recently remarked: "The only women in America who look like the girls in 'Vogue' and 'Harper's Bazaar' are the models in 'Vogue' and 'Harper's Bazaar.'" From the standpoint of the pin-up photographer, may we add: Thank God.

The ideal model for pin-up photography should have a slender, youthful figure; long-legged, but with curves in the right places; not as emaciated as the so-called clothes horses who grace our glossy fashion magazines.

Fortunately for us, the average American girl has as perfect a body as can be found anywhere in the world. This is no accident, but the result of a well-coordinated physical education process, a dieting program and a bathing-suit fashion trend which has given the body back its natural freedom of movement instead of the unhealthy corseting of yesterday.

Statistics are regularly being published in the women's and models' magazines about ideal weights and measurements. The proportions of the female movie stars and starlets, their health and beauty hints as well as the dimensions of the winners of the annual beauty contests are eagerly studied by girls and women all over the country.

Mothers encourage their daughters in this favorite pastime, as they are fully aware of the fact that to become a successful model may be the quickest way to fame and fortune. It may lead to glorification on the stage by master showmen, to glamorization on film and in magazines by ace photographers or illustrators, and – last but not least – to being literally pinned up on the noses of bombers by the globe-girdling Yanks, and thus being proudly flown to the four corners of the earth.

Now suppose that you have found the ideal pin-up model for your photographic field trip. She may be your best girl, or a photogenic neighbor. Discuss your ideas with her in advance, infuse her with your enthusiasm, tell her you intend to create the most breathtaking pictures, to depict her as "the fairest in the Land." There is no model – amateur or professional – who does not fancy she can go one better on Betty Grable or Polka-Dot Chili Williams. Capitalize on this self-assurance by emphasizing that you are on her side, that she inspires you to grow far above your normal work, and she will reward you by all-out cooperation. With touching patience, she will go through all sorts of contortions on dangerous cliffs and mountains, just to be worthy of the occasion – the creation of a delightfully different pin-up.

Modeling is acting, and photography is directing. You have set the stage psychologically through your tactful and enthusiastic behavior, your model is in the right frame of mind ... Now comes the most difficult part: to get the proper mood for the picture. Like a skillful director, you must observe the natural traits of your model, and work from there. Strive to coordinate the expression with the situation, coax your model into emotional projection, because then and only then will you obtain that elusive and alluring quality which makes a pin-up.

There is, of course, no limit to the variety of moods and expressions which you can record with a responsive model. As a general tip: combine a provocative pose with a demure expression. When your artistic imagination and the playful fantasy of your model are synchronized in perfect teamwork, you cannot fail to create pictures which will make your fellowmen stop, look and pin 'em up.

Modell und Stimmung

Ein britischer Journalist bemerkte anläßlich eines Besuches in unserem Land kürzlich: „Die einzigen Frauen in Amerika, die wie die Mädchen in ‚Vogue' oder ‚Harper's Bazaar' aussehen, sind die Models in ‚Vogue' und ‚Harper's Bazaar'." Vom Standpunkt des Pin-Up-Fotografen aus könnten wir hinzufügen: Gott sei Dank.

Das ideale Modell für die Pin-Up-Fotografie sollte eine schlanke, jugendliche Figur haben; es sollte langbeinig sein, aber mit Kurven an den richtigen Stellen, nicht so spindeldürr wie die Kleiderpuppen aus den schicken Modemagazinen.

Zu unserem Glück hat das durchschnittliche amerikanische Mädchen einen Körper, der keine Wünsche offenläßt. Das ist kein bloßer Zufall, sondern das Ergebnis einer gelungenen Kombination aus Leibesertüchtigung, Diätkost und einem Trend in der Bademode, der dem Körper wieder freie Bewegung erlaubt, anstatt ihn wie früher in Korsetts zu zwängen.

In den Frauen- und Modemagazinen werden regelmäßig Statistiken über Idealmaße und Idealgewicht veröffentlicht. Die Maße der weiblichen Filmstars und -sternchen, ihre Gesundheits- und Schönheitstips werden von den Mädchen und Frauen im ganzen Lande ebenso aufmerksam studiert wie die Maße der Schönheitsköniginnen.

Die Mütter unterstützen ihre Töchter bei dieser Lieblingsbeschäftigung, denn sie wissen genau, daß eine Karriere als Fotomodell möglicherweise der schnellste Weg zu Ruhm und Reichtum ist. Vielleicht stehen sie dann schon bald neben internationalen Showgrößen im Rampenlicht, werden selbst zu gefeierten Filmstars und auf Titelblättern von den besten Illustratoren und Fotografen verherrlicht oder fliegen, nicht zu vergessen, an die Bombernasen der überall präsenten Yankees gepinnt, in die entlegensten Winkel der Welt.

Nehmen wir an, Sie haben das perfekte Pin-Up-Modell für Ihre fotografische Exkursion gefunden, vielleicht Ihre Freundin oder eine fotogene Nachbarin. Diskutieren Sie mit ihr vorab Ihre Ideen, lassen Sie den Funken der Begeisterung überspringen, erklären Sie ihr, daß Sie das aufregendste Foto der Welt machen und sie als „die Schönste im ganzen Land" abbilden möchten. Es gibt kein Modell, ob Amateurin oder Profi, das nicht insgeheim überzeugt ist, Betty Grable oder Polka-Dot Chili Williams den Rang ablaufen zu können. Schlagen Sie aus dieser Überzeugung Kapital, indem Sie deutlich machen, daß Sie auf ihrer Seite sind, daß Sie allein von ihr inspiriert sind, weit über sich hinauszuwachsen, und sie wird es Ihnen mit hundertprozentiger Kooperationsbereitschaft danken. Mit rührender Geduld wird sie alle möglichen Verrenkungen auf lebensgefährlichen Klippen und Felsen mitmachen, alles im Dienste des einen hohen Ziels: der Entstehung eines faszinierend anderen Pin-Up-Fotos.

Modellstehen ist Schauspielerei, und fotografieren heißt Regie führen. Sie haben durch ihr taktvolles und enthusiastisches Auftreten die psychologischen Voraussetzungen geschaffen, Ihr Modell ist in der richtigen Stimmung ... Und nun kommt der schwierigste Teil: es gilt die richtige Atmosphäre für die Aufnahme zu finden. Wie ein feinfühliger Regisseur müssen Sie die natürlichen Gaben Ihres Modells herausarbeiten und auf ihnen aufbauen. Bemühen Sie sich, den mimischen Ausdruck mit der Situation in Einklang zu bringen, und drängen Sie Ihr Modell behutsam dazu, eine Emotion auszudrücken, denn dann, und nur dann, entsteht jene schwer definierbare und verführerische Qualität, die ein gutes Pin-Up ausmacht.

Es gibt natürlich keine Einschränkungen hinsichtlich der Stimmungen und Emotionen, in denen man ein aufgeschlossenes Modell ablichten kann. Ein allgemeiner Tip: Kombinieren Sie eine provokante Pose mit einem zurückhaltenden, sittsamen Gesichtsausdruck. Wenn Ihre künstlerische Vorstellungs- und die verspielte Einbildungskraft Ihres Modells zu perfekter Harmonie verschmolzen sind, werden Ihnen wie von selbst Aufnahmen gelingen, die Ihre männlichen Artgenossen erst zum Stehenbleiben, dann zum Hingucken und schließlich zum Pinnen an die Wand animieren werden.

Le choix du modèle et la création d'une ambiance

Un journaliste britannique en visite a remarqué récemment : « Les seules femmes en Amérique qui ressemblent aux mannequins de ‹ Vogue › et de ‹ Harper's Bazaar › sont les mannequins de ‹ Vogue › et de ‹ Harper's Bazaar › ». Et le photographe de pin-up d'ajouter : « Dieu Merci ! »

Le modèle idéal de pin-up doit avoir une silhouette jeune et élancée, avec de longues jambes et des courbes au bon endroit. Rien à voir avec les créatures émaciées, véritables « cintres ambulants », qui illustrent nos revues de mode.

Heureusement pour nous, la jeune américaine moyenne a un corps aussi parfait qu'on peut le souhaiter. Ce n'est pas un hasard mais le résultat d'une éducation physique régulière, d'un régime alimentaire équilibré et d'une mode du maillot de bain qui a redonné au corps sa liberté de mouvement naturelle. Finies les contraintes malsaines du corset de nos grands-mères !

Les magazines féminins publient régulièrement les statistiques de poids et de mensurations idéales de la femme. Les proportions des actrices et des starlettes, leur état de santé et leurs conseils de beauté, tout comme les caractéristiques des lauréates des concours annuels de beauté, sont attentivement étudiés par les lectrices de tout âge à travers le pays.

Les mères encouragent leurs filles à entretenir leur corps, et sont parfaitement conscientes que de réussir comme modèle peut être le chemin le plus court vers la gloire et la fortune. Qui sait ? Leur fille sera peut-être glorifiée par un maître du spectacle, immortalisée sur le grand écran par un grand réalisateur, sublimée dans les pages de revues par de grands photographes ou illustrateurs ou encore, consécration suprême, peinte sur le cockpit d'un bombardier américain afin d'être fièrement exposée aux quatre coins de la planète.

Imaginons que vous ayez trouvé le modèle de pin-up idéal pour votre projet. Ce peut-être votre petite amie ou une voisine photogénique. Discutez de vos idées avec elle, transmettez-lui votre enthousiasme, dites-lui que vous comptez réaliser des images à couper le souffle, que vous allez faire d'elle « la plus jolie fille du pays ». Il n'existe pas de modèle qui ne rêve de supplanter Betty Grable ou Polka-Dot Chili Williams. Profitez de sa confiance pour souligner que vous êtes de son côté, qu'elle vous inspire, et elle vous récompensera par une coopération inconditionnelle. Avec une patience émouvante, elle se pliera à toutes sortes de contorsions sur des falaises dangereuses et des montagnes, uniquement pour se montrer à la hauteur de l'occasion : la création d'une pin-up originale et ravissante.

Le modèle est une actrice et le photographe un metteur en scène. Si vous voulez que votre modèle soit dans le bon état d'esprit, vous devez d'abord planter le décor psychologiquement par une approche diplomate et enthousiaste.

A présent, voici venir la partie la plus difficile : créer l'ambiance appropriée à l'image que vous voulez réaliser. Tel un metteur en scène expérimenté, vous devez chercher les caractères naturels de votre modèle et en faire la base de votre travail. Essayez de faire correspondre l'expression avec la situation, incitez votre modèle à se projeter mentalement, car ce n'est qu'ainsi que vous obtiendrez cette qualité insaisissable et attirante qui fait une vraie pin-up.

Naturellement, il n'y a pas de limites aux moues et aux expressions que l'on puisse obtenir d'un modèle réceptif. Un petit conseil général : associez une pose provoquante avec une expression ingénue. Si votre sens artistique et l'imagination de votre modèle sont synchronisés en un parfait travail d'équipe, vous ne pouvez échouer et vous réaliserez des images qui feront s'arrêter net vos congénères, les feront écarquiller les yeux, puis les accrocher au mur.

Harmonious and rhythmic interplay of high and low key nuances helps to create a luminescent tableau treatment in this embodiment of grace and beauty. The staging and draping of such sheer material entails painstaking effort. Texture lighting with the aid of three spots is applied to reveal the silky detail of the gown and to silhouette the body.

Ein harmonisches und rhythmisches Zusammenspiel heller und dunkler Schattierungen hilft, diese Verkörperung von Grazie und Schönheit als luminöses Tableau in Szene zu setzen. Die Inszenierung und der Faltenwurf eines so hauchdünnen Materials wie Seide erfordert höchste Sorgfalt. Die Ausarbeitung der feinen Strukturen mit Hilfe dreier Spots enthüllt jedes Detail des Gewandes und zeichnet die Konturen des Körpers nach.

Le jeu harmonieux et rythmé entre les nuances fortes et douces permet de créer un effet luminescent sur cette incarnation de la grâce et de la beauté. La mise en scène et l'éclairage ont nécessité de gros efforts. Trois spots mettent en valeur les textures, révélant le soyeux du plissé de la robe et faisant se détacher la silhouette du modèle.

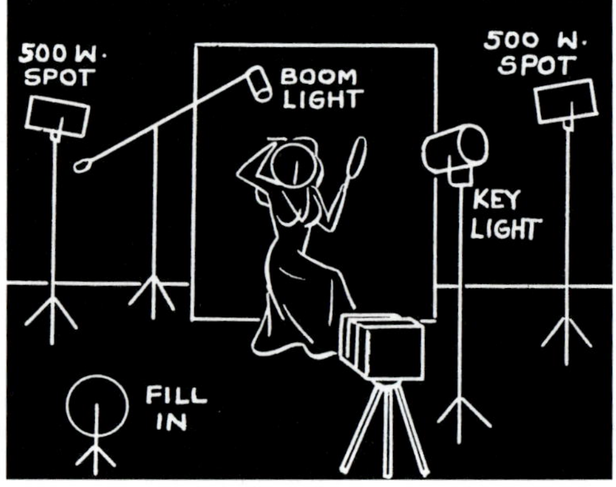

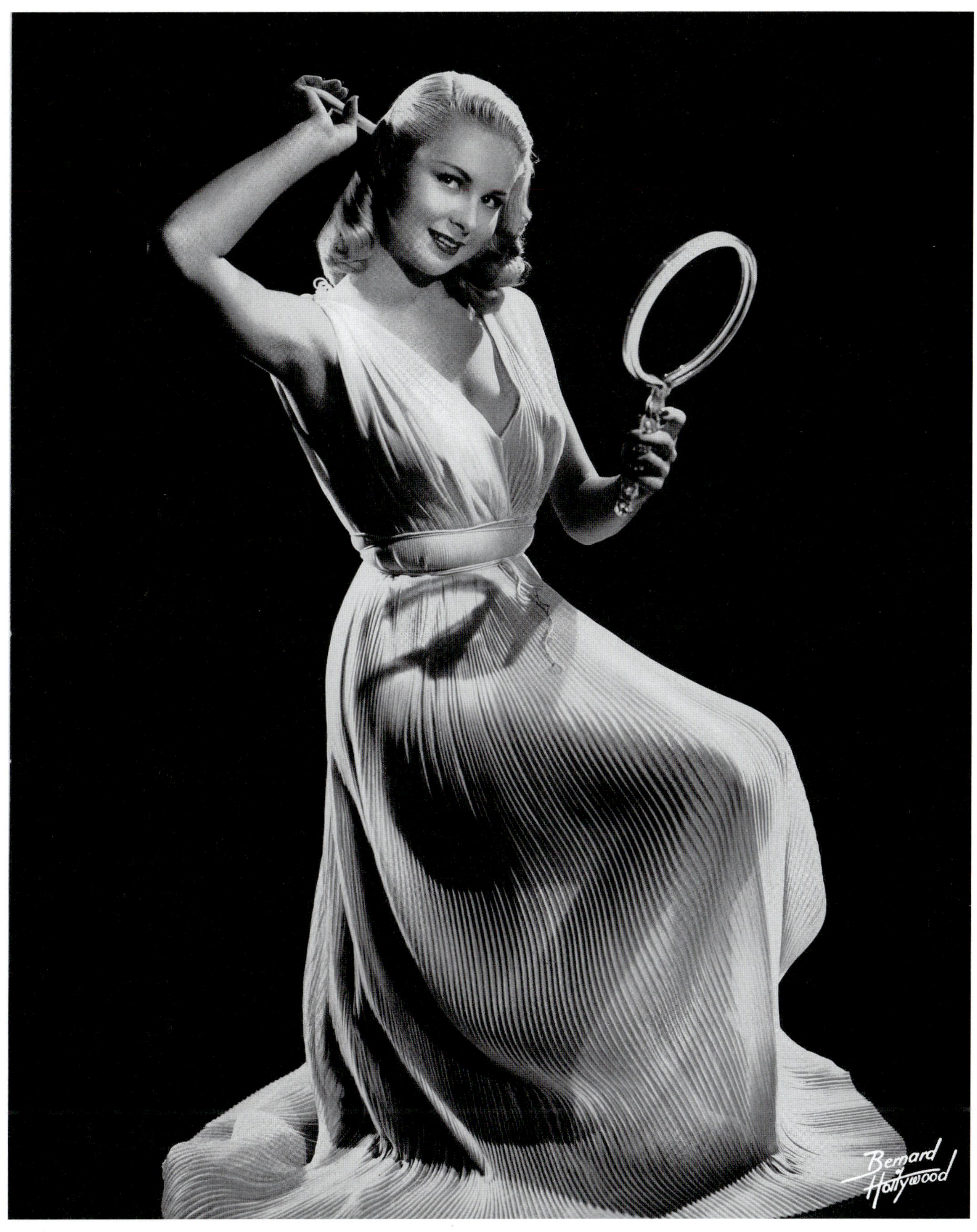

Nocturne

George Petty's famed drawing with its unforgettable caption, "When you lost your yacht, something within me died," is translated here for the camera by judicious use of model and props. The sculptural lighting quality is achieved by strong spot lighting from the side with a boom light thrown very close to the hair. A small stage, covered with velvet, makes it possible for the model to pose with relative ease. 1/5 second at f/16.

George Pettys berühmtes Bild mit dem unvergeßlichen Titel „Als du deine Yacht verloren hast, starb auch ein Stück von mir" wird hier durch den durchdachten Einsatz von Modell und Requisiten in das Medium der Fotografie überführt. Die stark modellierende Ausleuchtung wird durch ein scharfes Spotlicht von der Seite und ein Galgenlicht auf das Haar erzielt. Eine kleine, mit Samt bezogene Bühne erlaubt es dem Modell, diese schwierige Pose relativ bequem einzubehalten. 1/5 Sekunde bei f/16.

Le célèbre dessin de George Petty et son inoubliable légende (« Quand tu as perdu ton yacht, quelque chose en moi s'est éteint ») se traduit ici par une utilisation judicieuse du modèle et des accessoires. L'effet sculptural est obtenu par un spot de perche puissant placé de côté et orienté très près des cheveux. Une petite estrade, tapissée de velours, permet au modèle de poser dans un confort relatif. 1/5ème de seconde à f/16.

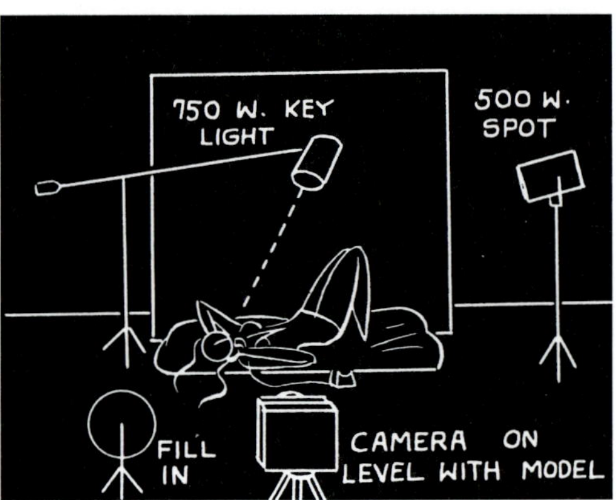

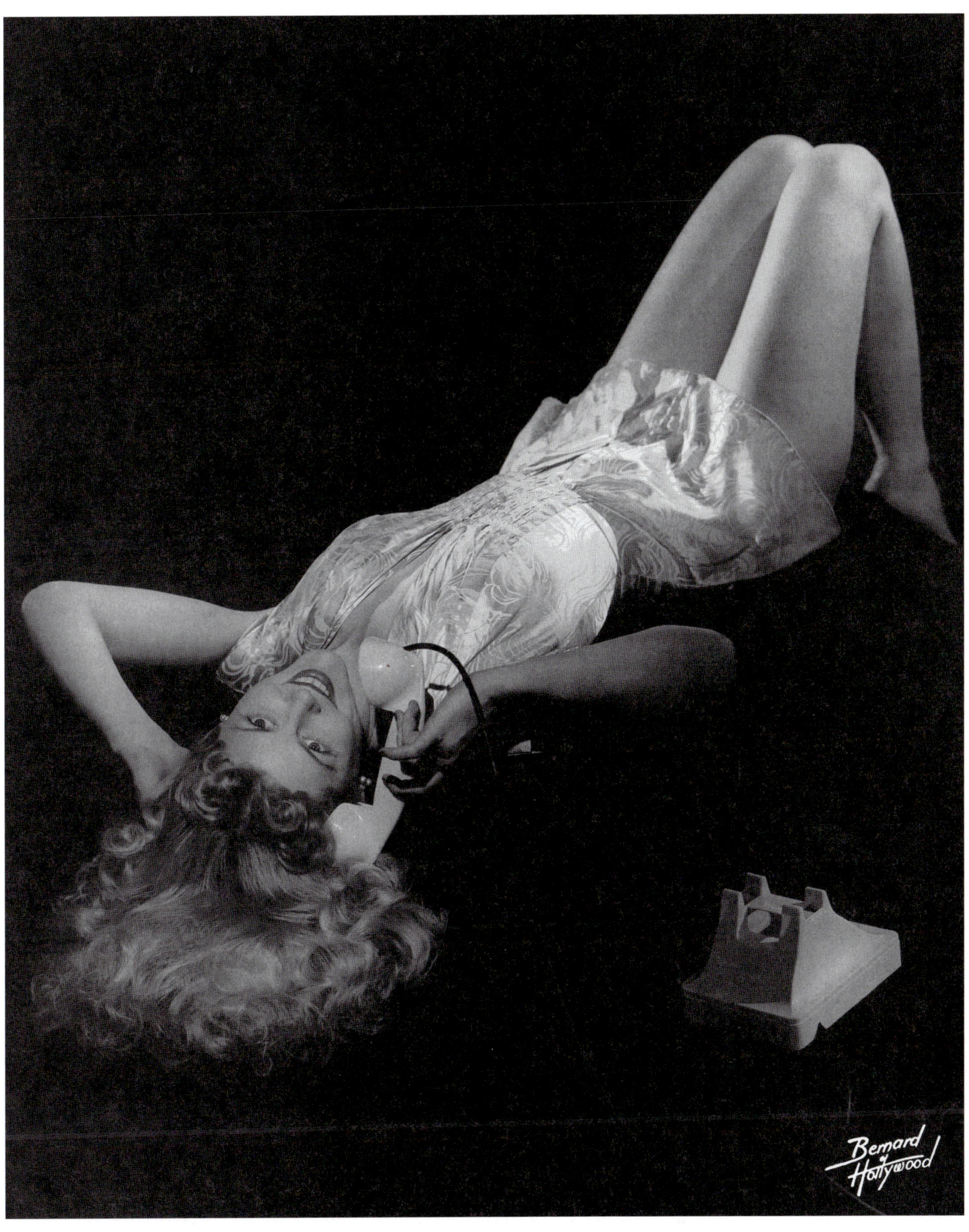

Hollywood Calling

HOLLYWOOD IN DER LEITUNG · HOLLYWOOD EN LIGNE

All the exhilaration, fun and frolic of a ski run are mirrored in this close-up of an imaginative winter scene. This is a convincing illustration for the prime compositional rule: "less is more." The mind of the viewer will automatically supplement the rest of the figure and scenery. This "outdoor" shot was made in the studio in front of a painted cloud background with a fan blowing on the hair.

Diese Nahaufnahme einer phantasievollen Winterszene fängt die ganze Ausgelassenheit und gute Laune einer Skiabfahrt ein. Ein überzeugendes Beispiel für die wichtigste Kompositionsregel: „Weniger ist mehr.“ Der Betrachter wird sich den Rest der Figur und die Szenerie automatisch hinzudenken. Diese „Außenaufnahme“ wurde im Studio vor einem gemalten Wolkenhintergrund aufgenommen. Ein Ventilator bewegte das Haar.

Toute la trépidation et le plaisir d'une descente à ski sont restitués dans ce gros plan d'une jolie skieuse. C'est là l'illustration convaincante de l'une des premières règles de la composition : « Inutile d'en rajouter ! ». L'esprit du spectateur reconstitue automatiquement le reste de la scène et du décor. Cette prise de vue « en extérieur » a été réalisée en studio devant une toile de fond peinte et avec un ventilateur pour créer l'illusion du vent dans les cheveux.

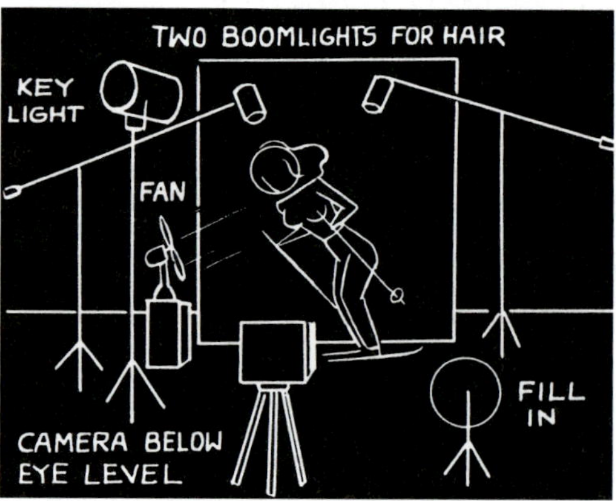

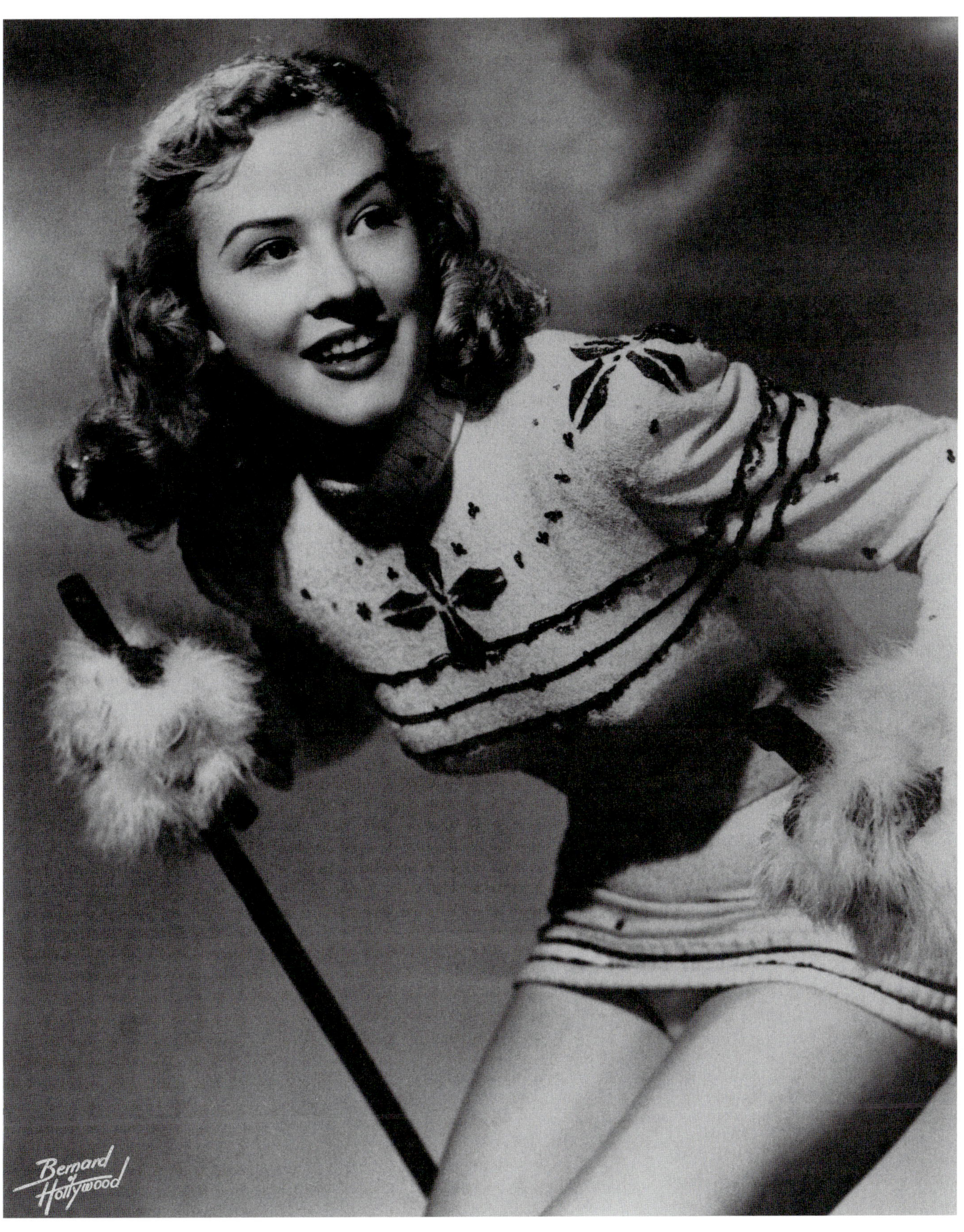

Winter Joy

WINTERFREUDEN · LES JOIES DE L'HIVER

The simplest of settings, when used imaginatively, can provide an effective pictorial background. The composition suggests itself with the stacked bales of hay, and the sitting position injects a static element in keeping with summer sun loafing down on the farm. The exposure was made at 1/100 second at f/22 with a K-2 filter.

Erfindungsreich ins Bild gesetzt, kann auch der einfachste Schauplatz einen wirkungsvollen Hintergrund liefern. Der Bildaufbau drängt sich bei den aufgestapelten Heuballen wie von selbst auf; die sitzende Position bringt ein statisches Element hinein, das so recht zum Müßiggang in der ländlichen Sommerhitze paßt. Die Aufnahme wurde mit 1/100 Sekunde bei f/22 mit einem K-2-Filter gemacht.

Le décor le plus simple, s'il est utilisé avec un peu d'imagination, peut offrir un fond des plus évocateurs. La composition est construite par l'empilement des balles de foin et la position assise du modèle ajoute un élément statique qui renforce l'idée d'un soleil invitant à paresser dans les champs. Exposition : 1/100ème de seconde à f/22 avec un filtre K-2.

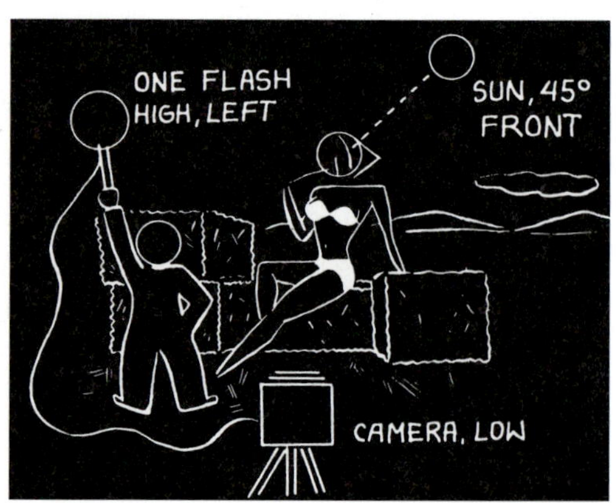

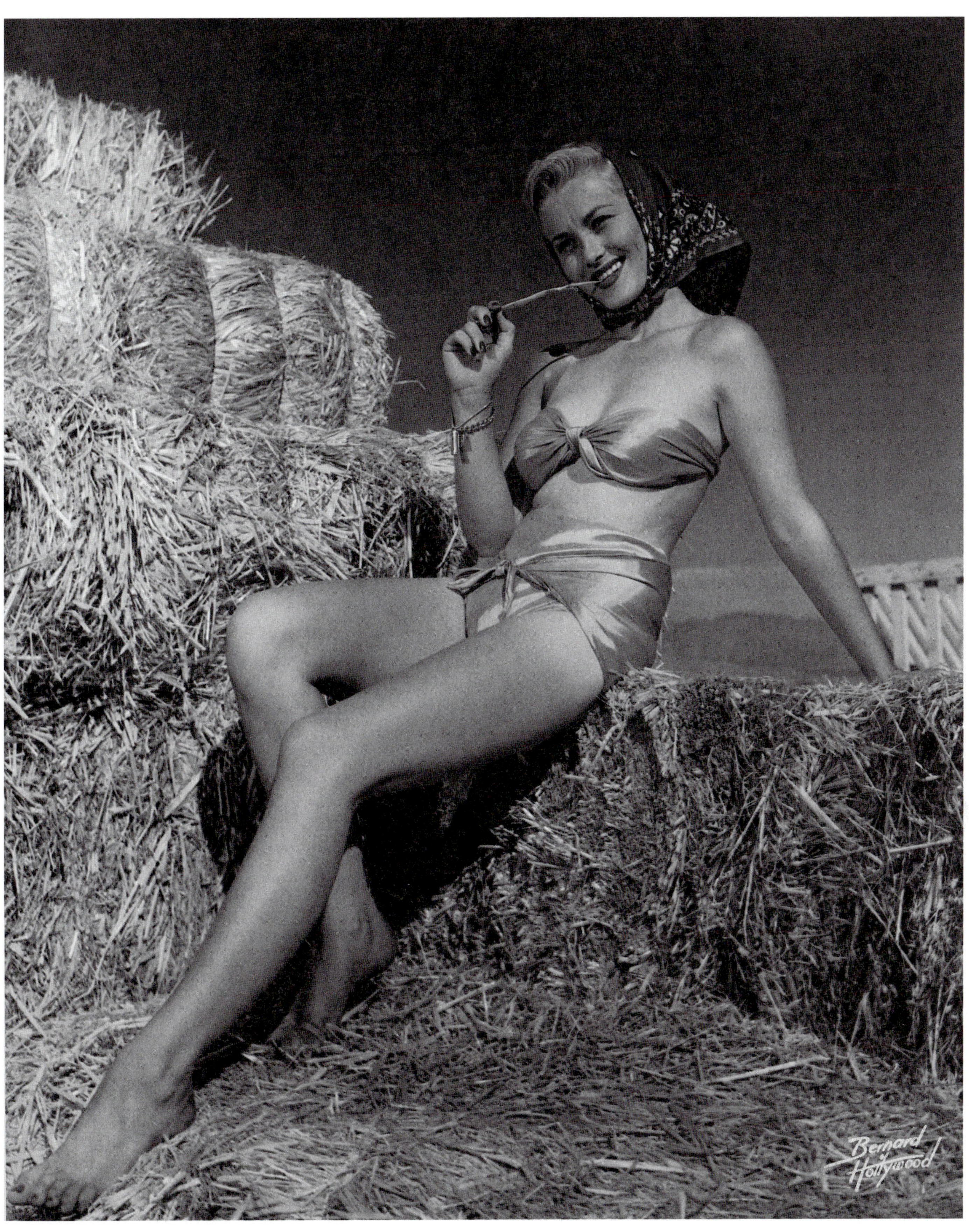

Summer Harvest

STROHFEUER · LA MOISSON

This inviting welcomette beckons to the lure of the islands … to sailing, surfing and spear-fishing in the land of the leis. The background lighting is subdued to increase the contrast between the fair complexion of the honey-blonde model and the similar hue of the bamboo.

Vom Zauber Hawaiis erzählt diese lockende Schöne … vom Segeln, Surfen und Fischen im Südseeparadies. Die Hintergrundbeleuchtung ist gedämpft, um den Kontrast zwischen dem hellen Teint des honigblonden Modells und den ähnlichen Tonwerten des Bambushintergrundes zu verstärken.

Cette jeune beauté des îles nous convie aux charmes des tropiques … La voile, le surf et la pêche à la lance sur la terre des dieux. La lumière du fond a été atténuée pour accroître le contraste entre le teint clair du modèle aux cheveux couleur de miel et le ton similaire des bambous.

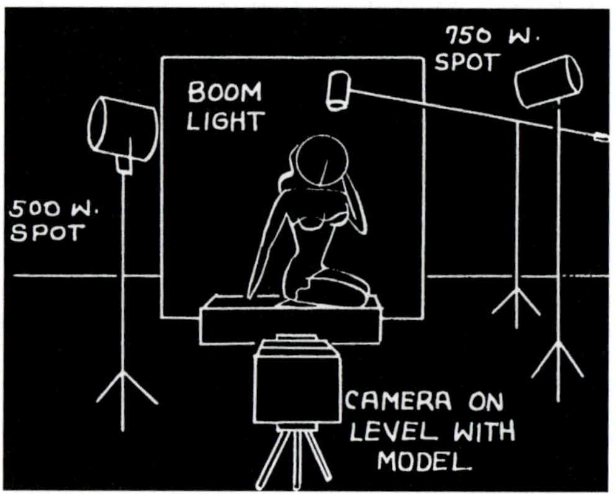

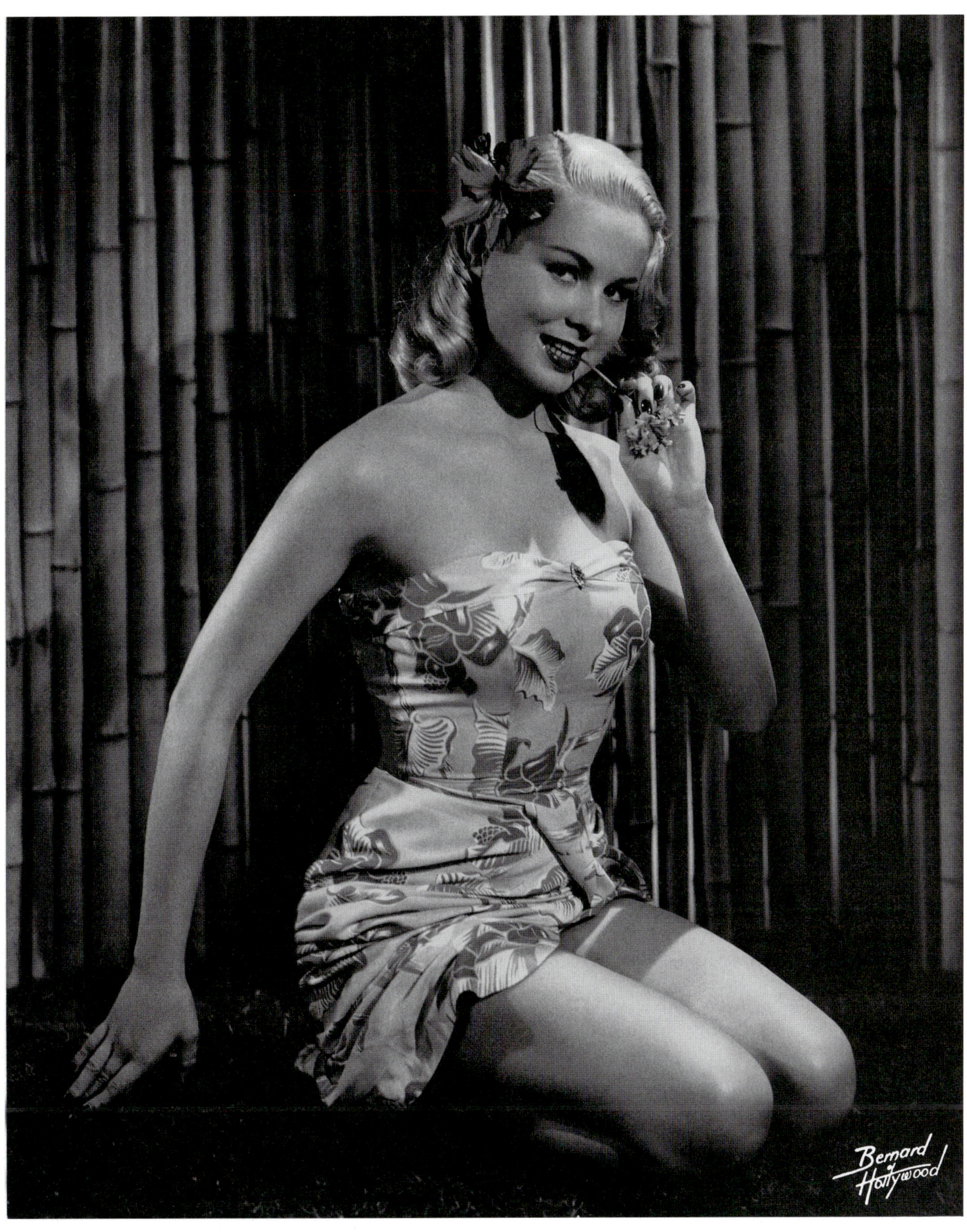

Island Dressing

MAL SEHN, KAPITÄN · PARFUM DES ÎLES

The impact of a pin-up placed in a bedroom setting depends largely on the choice of the model. While the illustrator is able to create a type or personality with a few strokes of pencil or brush, the photographer must find a living counterpart to fit the desired characterization. 5x7 Ansco view camera with 10 inch Ektar lens, 1/10 second at f/11.

Die Wirkung eines Pin-Ups in einer Schlafzimmerkulisse hängt wesentlich von der Wahl des Modells ab. Während der Illustrator mit ein paar Pinsel- oder Bleistiftstrichen einen Typ oder eine Persönlichkeit erschaffen kann, muß der Fotograf ein Modell finden, das dem gewünschten Typ entspricht. 5x7 Ansco view camera mit 10 Zoll Ektar-Objektiv, 1/10 Sekunde bei f/11.

L'impact d'une pin-up dans sa chambre à coucher dépend en grande partie du choix du modèle. Si l'illustrateur peut brosser une personnalité en quelques coups de crayon ou de pinceau, le photographe doit trouver un modèle qui correspond au personnage recherché. 5x7 Ansco view camera, objectif Ektar 25 cm, 1/10ème de seconde à f/11.

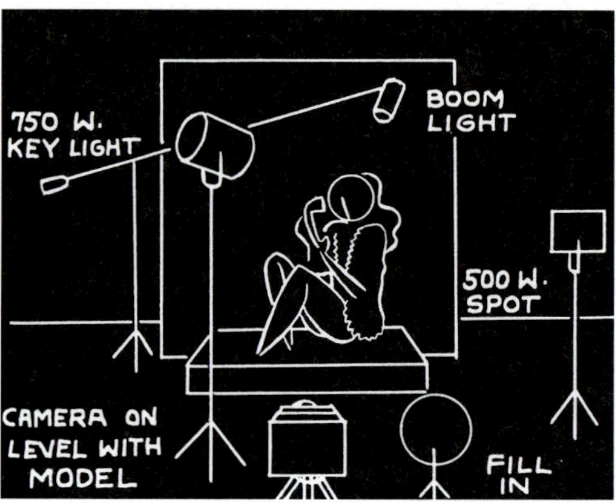

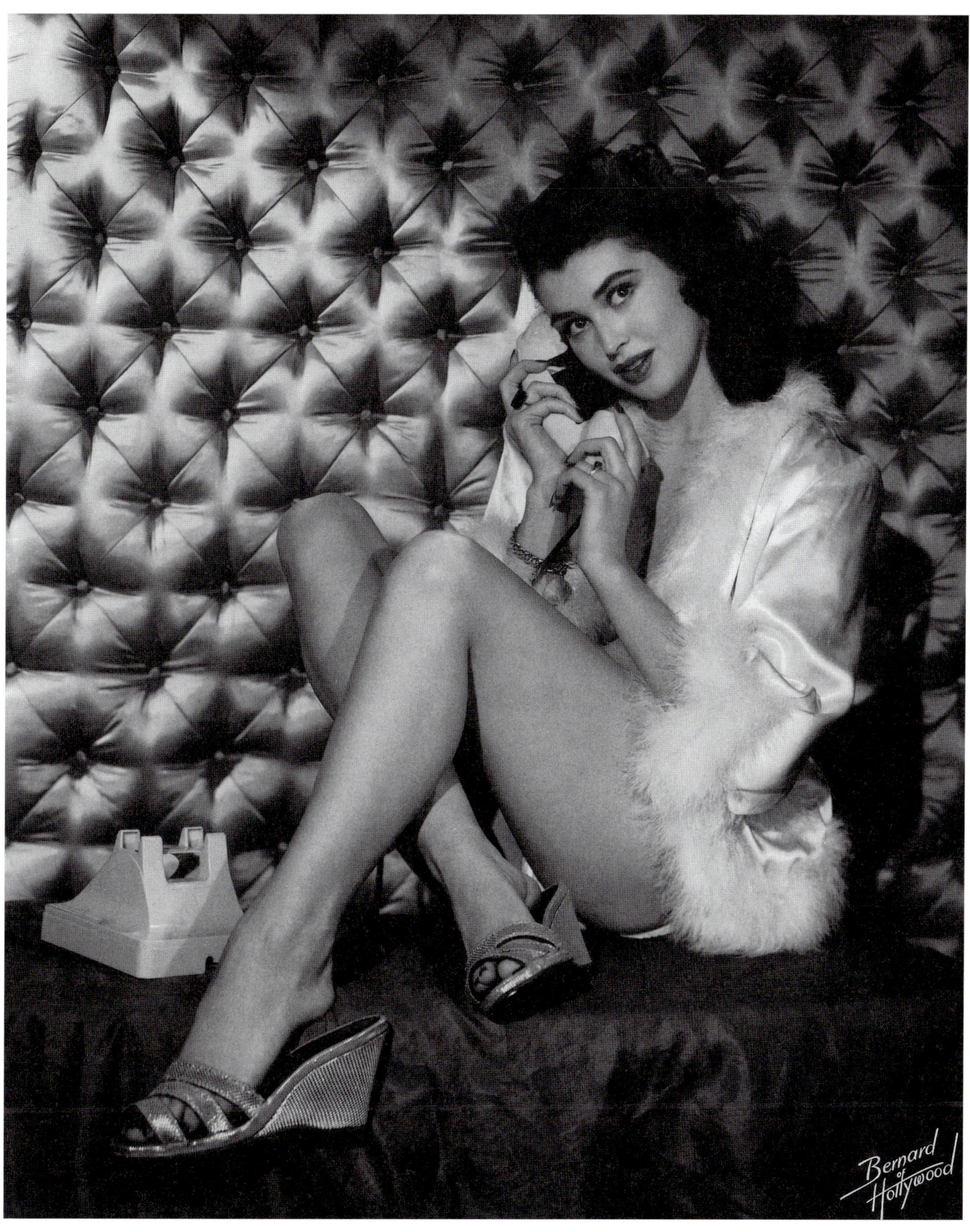

Good Connection

BITTE NICHT AUFLEGEN! · PAS DE FRITURE SUR LA LIGNE

The atmosphere of a wharf is projected right into the studio by the use of a few nautical props. The perfection of the model's legs is accentuated by subdued back and side lighting which leaves them in partial shadow. A spotlight on the white backdrop adds further emphasis.

Mit ein paar nautischen Requisiten wird die Atmosphäre einer Anlegestelle ins Studio geholt. Die tadellosen Beine des Modells werden durch weiches Gegen- und Seitenlicht betont, das die Beine teilweise im Schatten läßt. Ein Spotlicht auf den weißen Hintergrund setzt zusätzliche Akzente.

L'atmosphère d'un quai a été restituée en studio grâce à quelques accessoires nautiques. La perfection des jambes du modèle est soulignée par un éclairage doux venant de l'arrière et du côté, les laissant dans une ombre partielle. Un spot dirigé sur le fond blanc accentue encore l'effet.

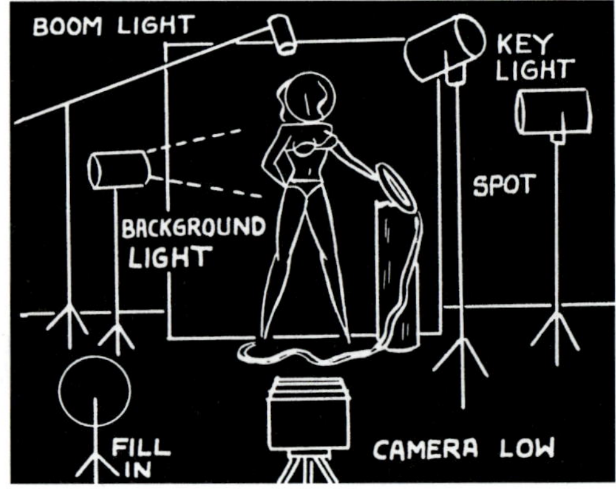

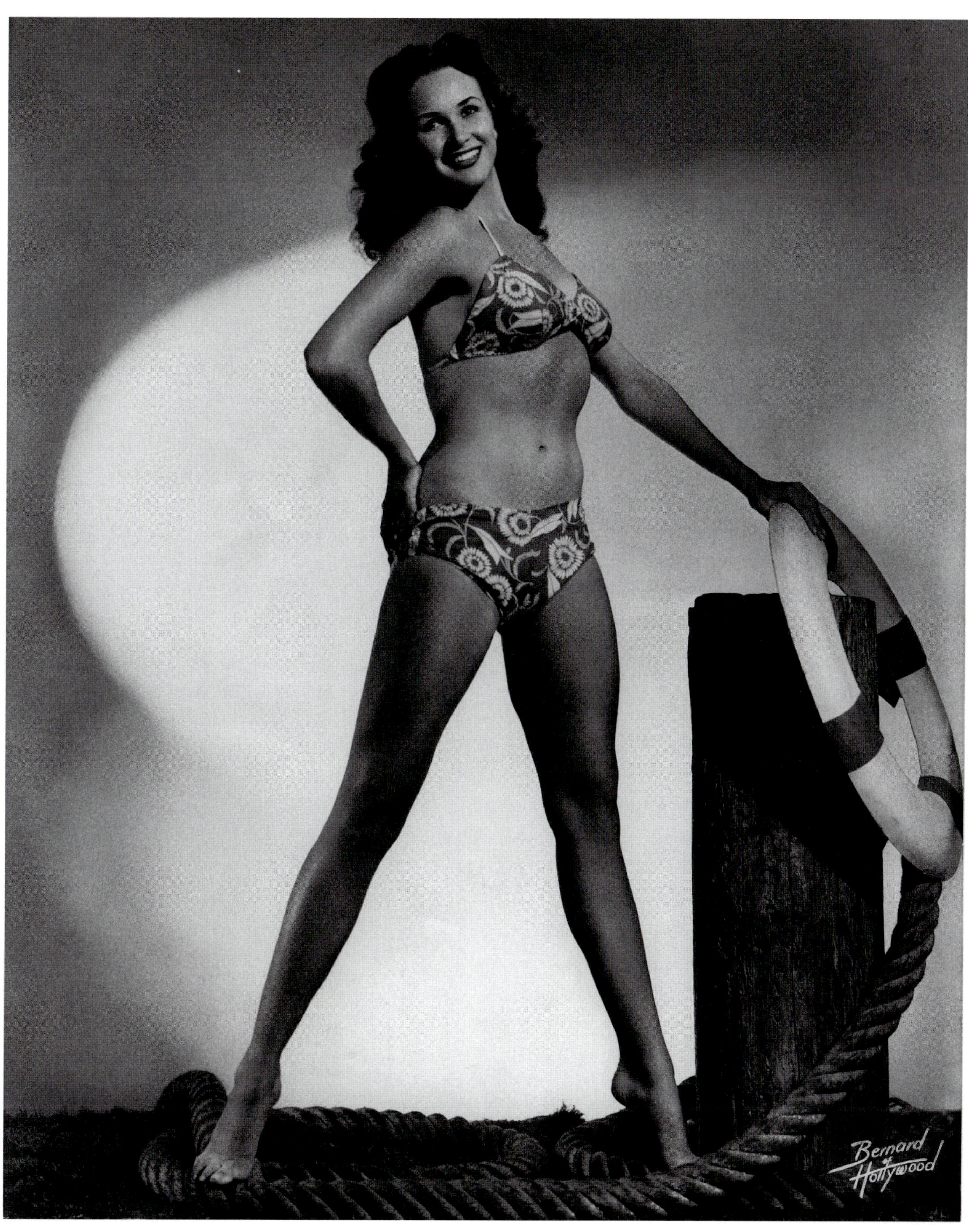

Figurehead

GALIONSFIGUR · FIGURE DE PROUE

Pert, carefree and vivacious is the mood caught in this Nevada ranch location shot. It has a lasting pin-up quality without any special camera tricks. Shot at eye-level with the sun high, and flash fill-in.

Eine heitere, sorglose und muntere Stimmung ist in dieser auf einer Ranch in Nevada entstandenen Aufnahme eingefangen. Sie hat eine unvergängliche Pin-Up-Qualität, ohne daß besondere Kameratricks vonnöten waren. Aus Augenhöhe bei hochstehender Sonne und mit zusätzlichem Aufhellblitz aufgenommen.

Cette prise de vue réalisée dans un ranch au Nevada dégage une atmosphère d'espièglerie, d'insouciance et de joie de vivre. C'est une véritable pin-up qui n'a pas besoin d'effets spéciaux. Prise de face avec le soleil au zénith et un flash comme source secondaire.

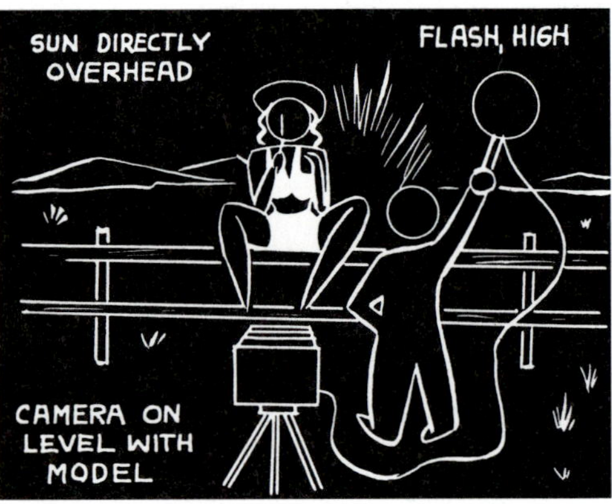

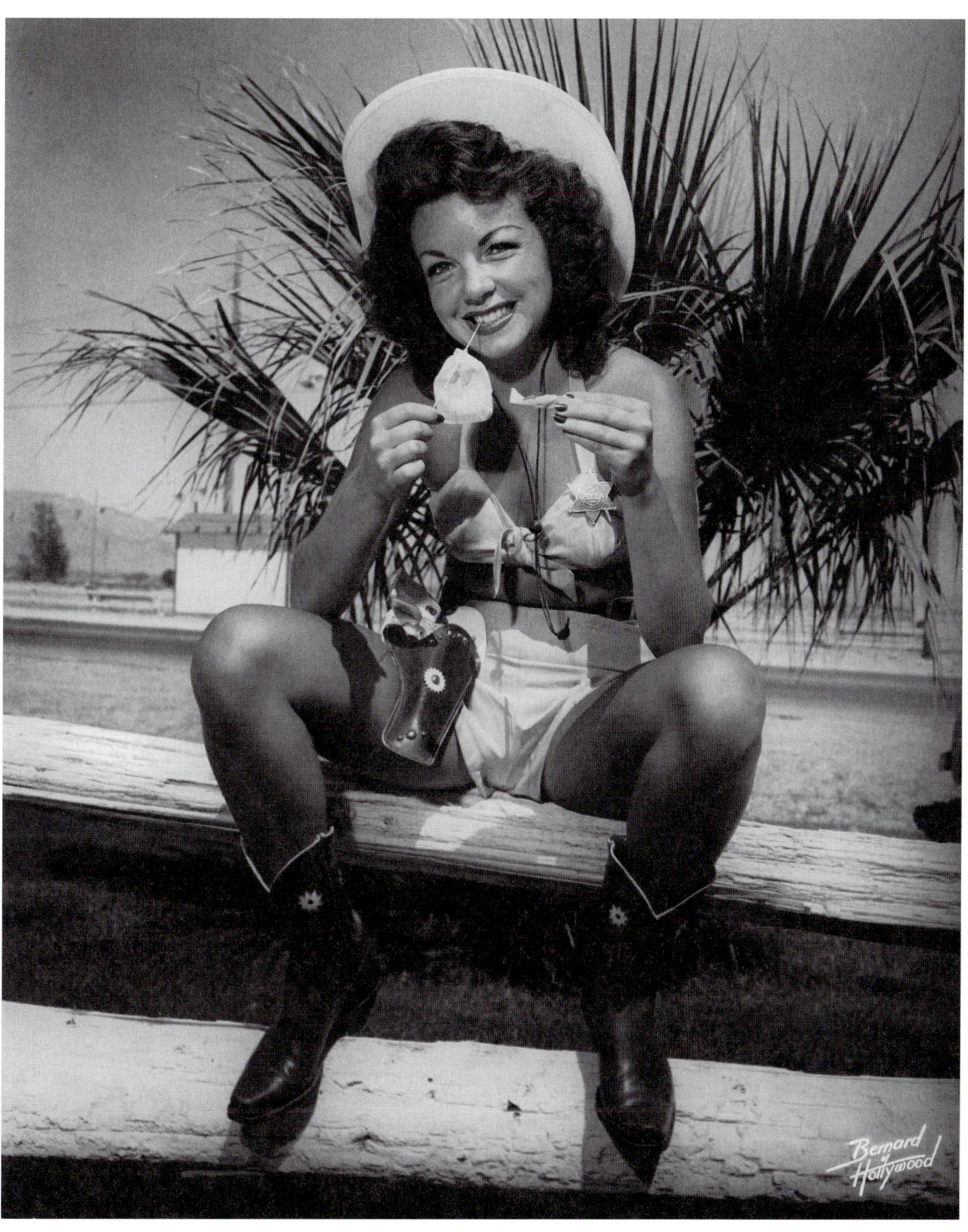

Sitting Pretty

HALLO, COWBOY! · LA COWGIRL

Here an amusing effect is created by combining the suave, sophisticated facial expression of the typical high-type fashion model with the pose and figure of a pin-up cutie. This shot was taken at high noon which accounts for the modeling in the face and strong shadows over the entire body. The white sand acts as a reflector, giving a luminous shadow.

Hier wird ein amüsanter Effekt erzielt, indem der reservierte und kultivierte Gesichtsausdruck des typischen, eleganten Mannequins mit der Pose und Figur einer Pin-Up-Schönen kombiniert wird. Das Foto wurde zur Mittagszeit aufgenommen, was die Modellierung des Gesichtes und die harten Schatten auf dem gesamten Körper erklärt. Der weiße Sand wirkt wie ein Reflektor und hellt die Schatten auf.

Ici, on a créé un effet amusant en associant l'air sophistiqué et hautain d'un mannequin de mode avec la pose et la silhouette d'une pin-up. La prise de vue a été réalisée à midi, d'où les ombres contrastées sur le visage et le corps. Le sable blanc fait office de réflecteur, donnant une ombre lumineuse.

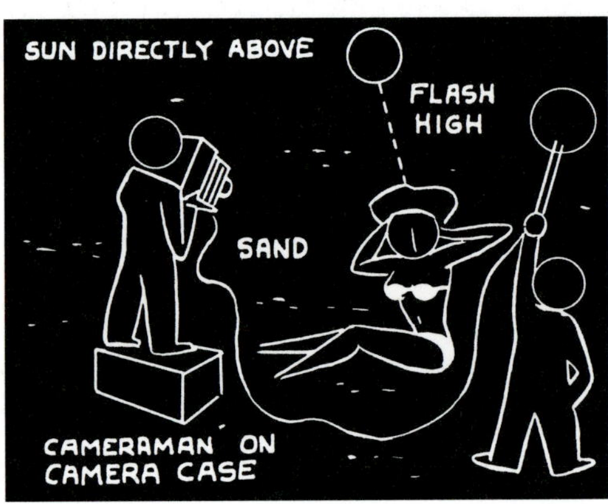

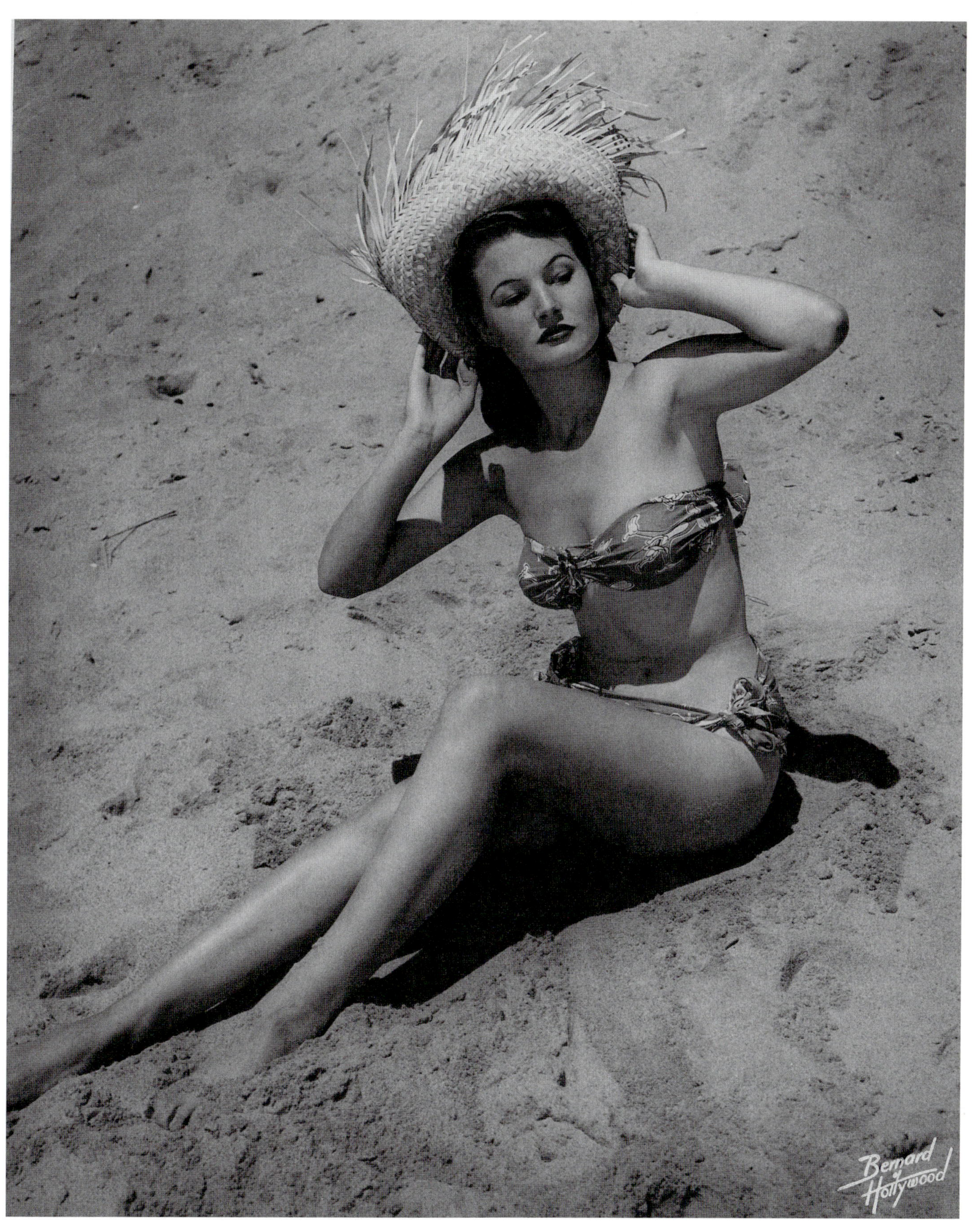

Body and Soil

DÜNENLANDSCHAFT · CORPS ET ÂME

Like floating on a cloud any Sunday morning in a cool, California pool! Taken at high noon when the steeple roof of a house threw the weird shadows which, broken up by the water ripples, create an abstract prismatic pattern. 1/200 second at f/22, with flash fill-in.

Dahinschweben wie auf einer Wolke – ein Sonntagmorgen in einem kühlen Pool irgendwo in Kalifornien. Das Foto wurde zur Mittagszeit aufgenommen, als der Dachfirst eines nahestehenden Hauses diesen eigenwilligen Schatten warf. Auf dem leicht gekräuselten Wasser schuf er ein abstraktes Prismenmuster. 1/200 Sekunde bei f/22 mit Aufhellblitz.

Elle semble flotter sur un nuage. Ce pourrait être n'importe quel dimanche matin dans une piscine fraîche de Californie ! La photo a été prise à midi, lorsque le toit abrupt de la maison projetait des ombres étranges, brisant les ondes sur l'eau, créant un effet abstrait de prisme. 1/200ème de seconde à f/22, avec flash.

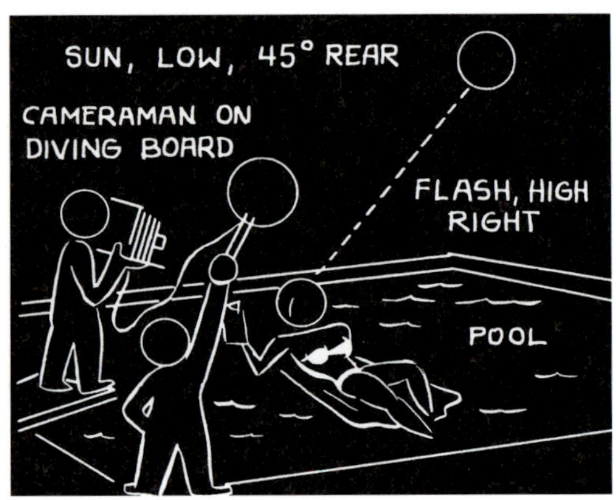

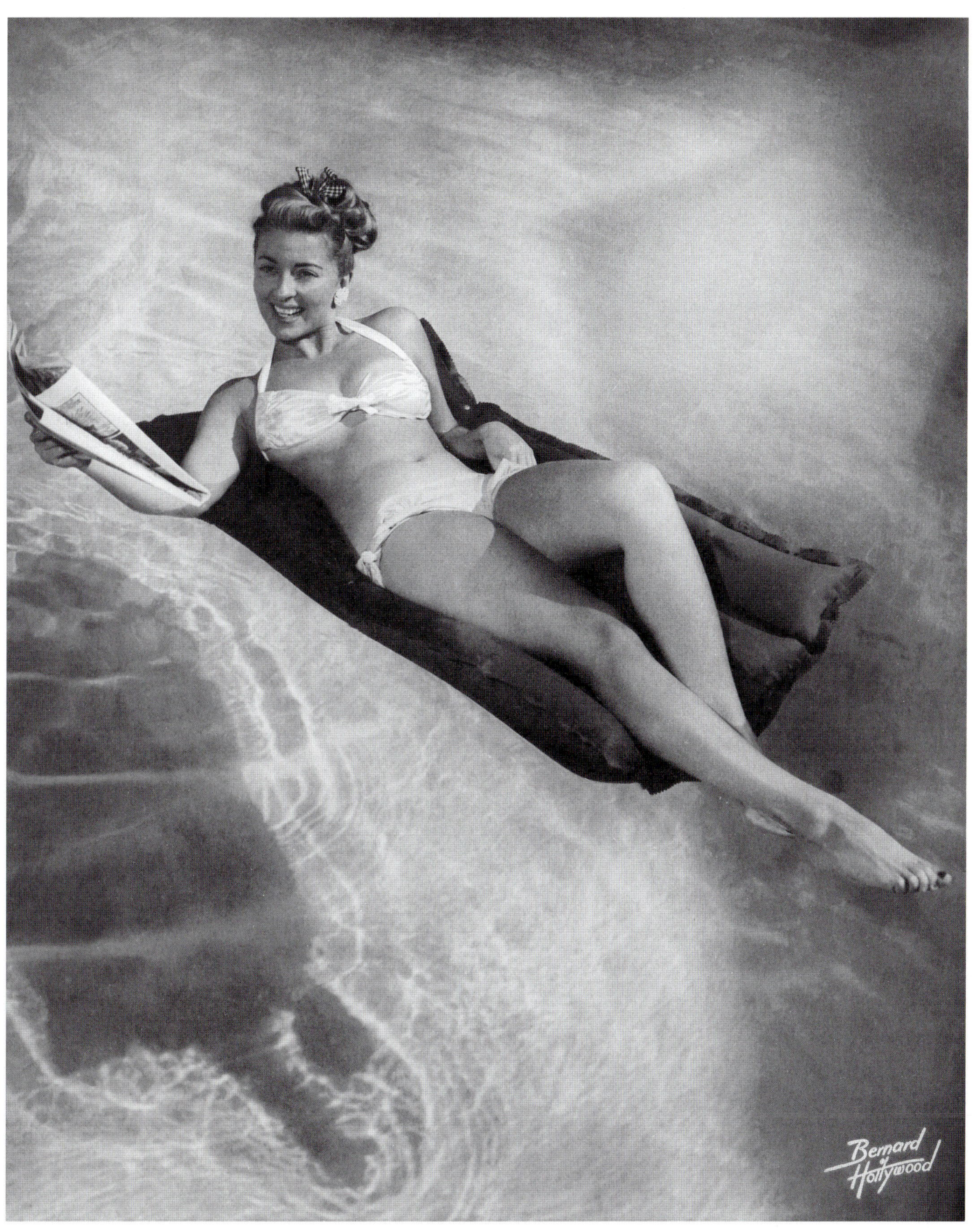

Lighter than Air

SCHWERELOS · PLUS LÉGÈRE QUE L'AIR

The picture and that on Page 85 of the same model on a commercial hosiery assignment hardly filled the bill for the manufacturer. They both resulted, however, in piquant pin-ups. This studio shot should have been focussed only on the legs, but what portrait photographer could ignore such a bright facial expression! 5x7 Ansco view camera with 10 inch Ektar lens, 1/5 second at f/16, Super Panchro-Press Type B film.

Diese Fotografie und die desselben Modells auf Seite 85 entstanden während einer Fotosession für einen Strumpffabrikanten und dürften wohl kaum den Vorstellungen des Auftraggebers entsprochen haben. Als Pin-Ups sind sie jedoch ausgesprochen pikant. Diese Atelieraufnahme hätte sich eigentlich nur auf die Beine konzentrieren sollen, doch welcher Porträtfotograf könnte dieses reizende Gesicht ignorieren? 5x7 Ansco view camera mit 10 Zoll Ektar-Objektiv, 1/5 Sekunde bei f/16, Super Panchro-Press Type B-Film.

Cette image et celle de la page 85 (avec le même modèle) furent rejetées par le fabriquant de bas qui les avaient commandées. Elles sont toutefois devenues de piquantes pin-up. La photo aurait dû se concentrer davantage sur les jambes, mais quel portraitiste aurait pu résisté à une si jolie expression! 5x7 Ansco view camera, objectif Ektar 25 cm, 1/5ème de seconde à f/16, pellicule Super Panchro-Press Type B.

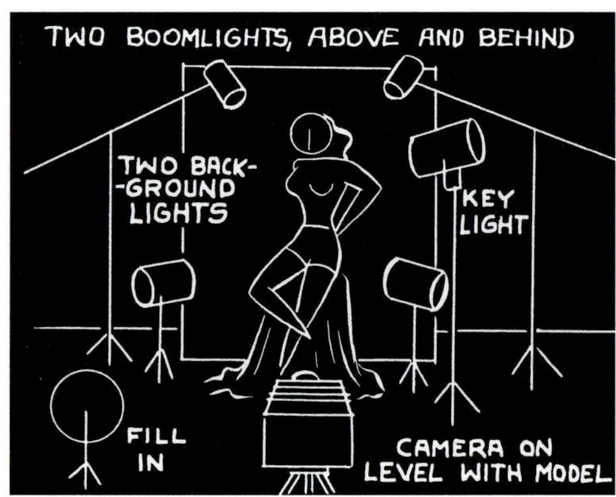

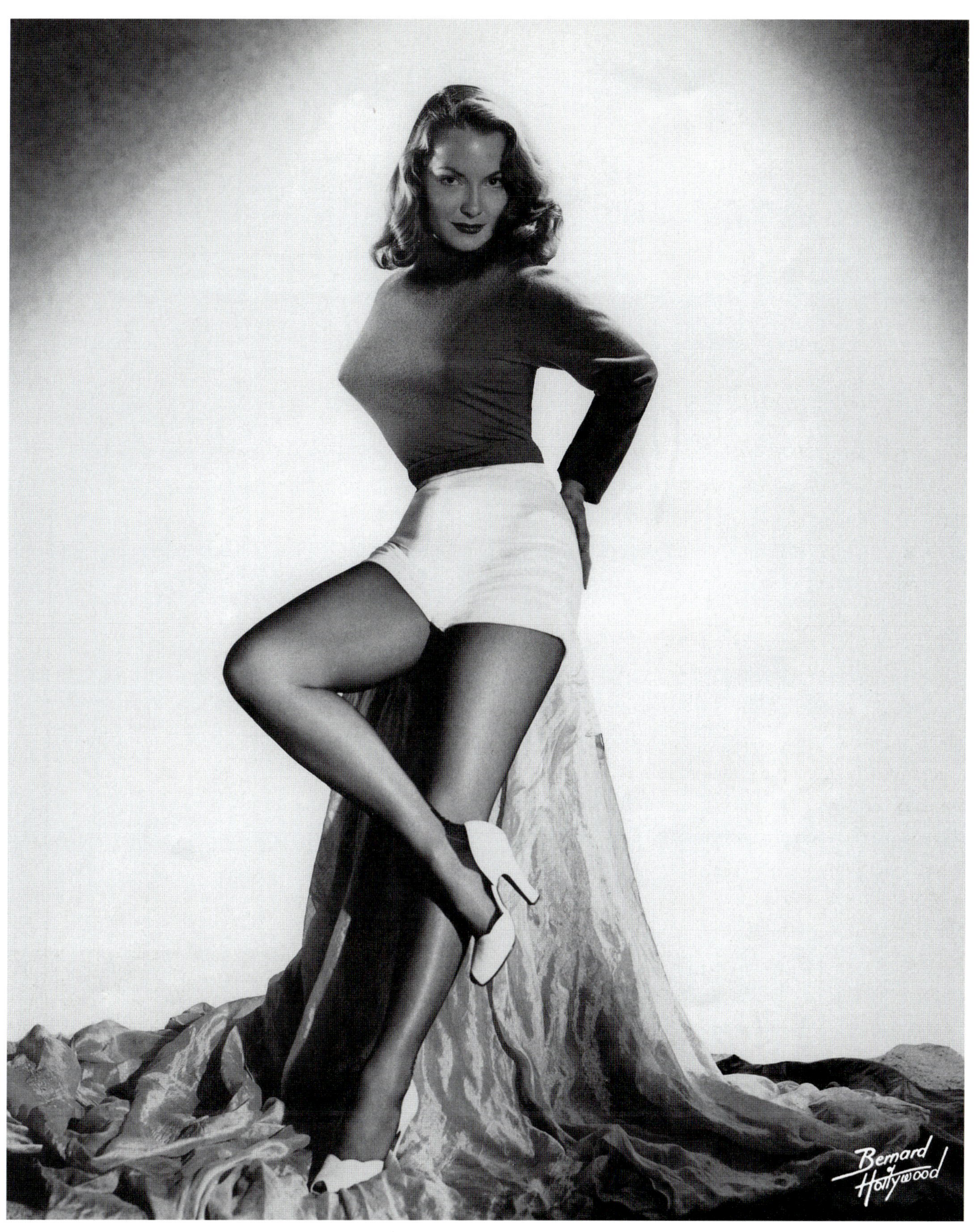

Design for Loving

ZUM ANBEISSEN · CONÇUE POUR L'AMOUR

This is a perfect example of the "posed-candid" technique, where a seemingly off-guard moment is frozen after a pre-studied bit of action. 4x5 Speed Graphic, 1/20 second at f/22, Super Panchro-Press Type B film.

Dies ist ein perfektes Beispiel für die Technik des „inszenierten Schnappschusses", bei der ein scheinbar zufälliger Moment in einem vorher einstudierten Bewegungsablauf eingefroren wird. 4x5 Speed Graphic, 1/20 Sekunde bei f/22, Super Panchro-Press Type B-Film.

C'est là un exemple parfait d'« instantané posé », où une situation longuement répétée à l'avance doit donner l'impression d'avoir été prise sur le vif. 4x5 Speed Graphic, 1/20ème de seconde à f/22, pellicule Super Panchro-Press Type B.

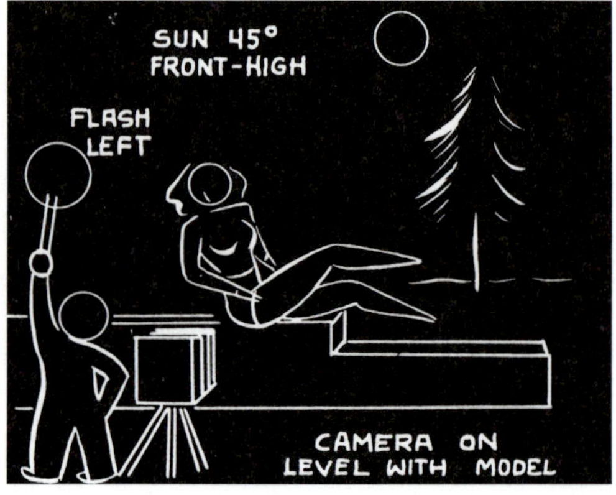

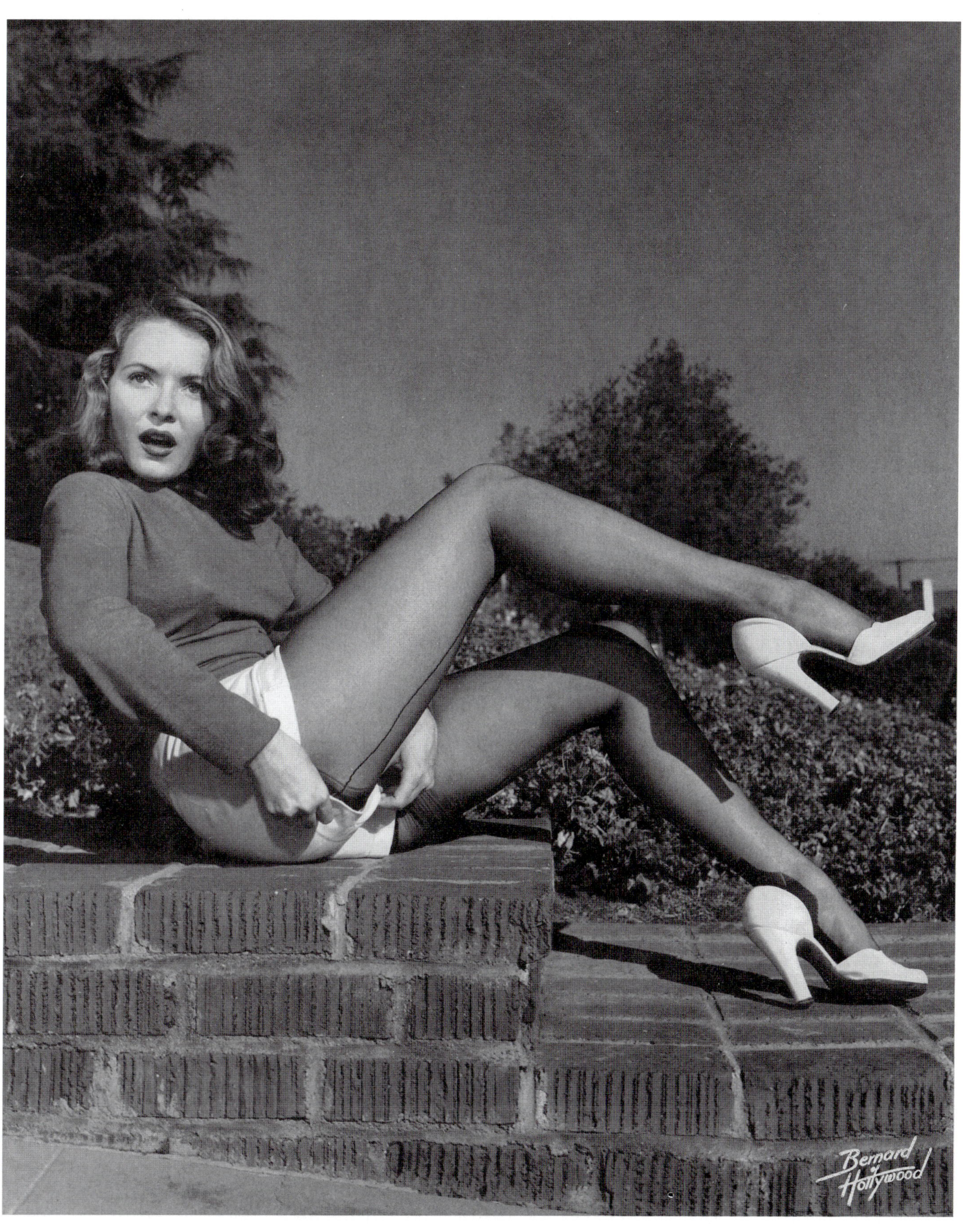

Quick Adjustment

KLEINE KORREKTUREN · PETIT RAJUSTEMENT

A simple Indian headdress provides an ornamental frame for this rhythmic composition. Three dimensional quality is produced by strong backlighting of the feathers and balanced front lights for even modeling. Shot with 5x7 Ansco view camera with 10 inch Ektar lens, 1/10 second at f/11.

Ein einfacher indianischer Kopfschmuck gibt dieser dynamischen Komposition den ornamentalen Rahmen. Die dreidimensionale Wirkung wird durch ein kräftiges Gegenlicht auf die Federn und sparsam dosiertes Vorderlicht erreicht. Aufgenommen mit einer 5x7 Ansco view camera mit 10 Zoll Ektar-Objektiv, 1/10 Sekunde bei f/11.

Une simple coiffe indienne fournit un cadre ornemental à cette composition rythmée. L'effet tridimensionnel est obtenu en éclairant fortement les plumes par derrière et en équilibrant la luminosité grâce à des lumières frontales. 5x7 Ansco view camera, objectif Ektar 25cm, 1/10ème de seconde à f/11.

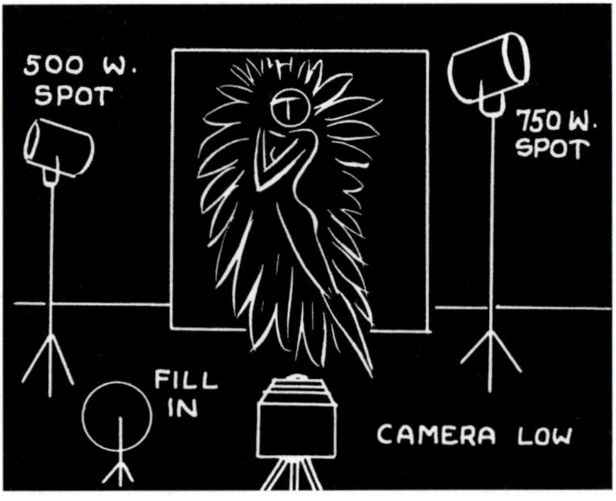

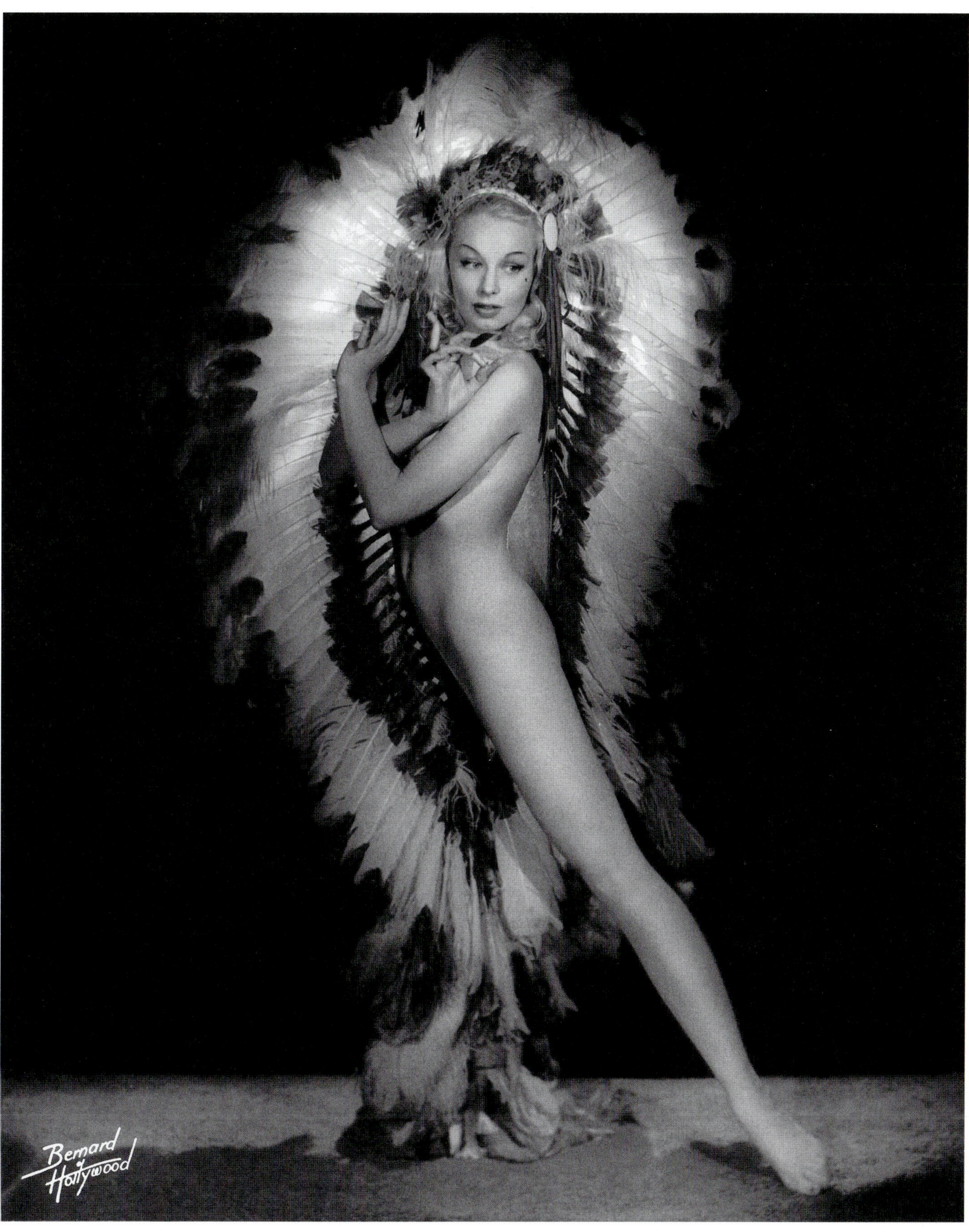

Early American

AUF DEM KRIEGSPFAD · LA SQUAW

Costuming and Background

A few months ago, a famous French actress startled the Hollywood publicity and camera brigade with a firm, French-accented "No cheesecake, pleeze!" As she alighted from the train, she went on lecturing: "In our country, women don't have to take off their clothes in order to look sexy." To the frustrated camera boys, such a pronunciamento must have sounded strange, coming as it did from a lady whose country has been hailed as the birthplace of the Folies Bergères and the Bikini Suit.

Before the Hollywood press agents had had a chance to recover from that shock, another French import upset their equilibrium afresh. This lady defied her countrywoman by barnstorming the United States with a plunging neckline that made Dior look like a fumbling beginner, and exposing her legs to as many cameramen as cared to photograph them. The reticence of other members of her sex she explained very simply by "Sour Grapes."

When ladies battle so gallantly, a gentleman can hardly afford to remain a fence sitter. We could dodge the issue, of course, by pointing out that the question of whether "it is better to conceal than to reveal" is thousands of years old, and has found many answers, according to changing tastes. Even the old Greeks could not decide whether they liked the garments of their goddesses short and trim, or long and free-flowing. Diana and Juno, the leading exponents of the different styles, have both had their legions of worshipers over the centuries.

The author is inclined to side with the school which leaves something to the imagination. A nude will exude less sex appeal than a cleverly costumed pin-up, because the latter invites visual audience participation. The most alluring pin-up of a motion picture star is the famed picture of Rita Hayworth in a negligee. Requests for copies, from World War II until this very day, have run into astronomical figures.

At any rate, the question of proper costuming is of the utmost importance for the outcome of your pictures. Make your model your partner in this enterprise – girls are very often both skillful and imaginative when it comes to making their own costumes out of scraps of material. By discussing your ideas with them in advance, you will avoid possible embarrassment when you pull out of your prop box an assortment of ties hastily converted into a Bikini Suit. Bear in mind that your costume must suit the individuality of your model. Not every girl would or should slip into a French bathing suit – which is by no means standard equipment for a pin-up, as too many photographers seem to think. Strive for originality in costuming, and you will have one more attention-getting factor on your side.

Last, but not least, comes your background. It can make or break the picture – it can be either the most eye-appealing decoration for your pin-up queen, or it can be so disturbing and distracting that it kills all compositional quality.

When you work with studio props and backgrounds, see that the model is comfortably posed against them, otherwise strain instead of ease will result.

Out-of-doors, we have an abundance of the most beautiful natural backgrounds. The mountains, seashores, lakes and deserts of this great continent form a never-ending scenic wonderland. You don't need Aladdin's lamp to find it – it's everywhere.

In the interest of good pictorial composition you should use just that segment of nature which best complements the human figure.

As the pictures in this book show, this might be a tree trunk, a piling, a wave or a rock formation, an iron chair or a plain backdrop. What the great German painter Max Liebermann said about the art of painting: "Malen ist weglassen" (to paint is to omit), is equally true of photography. Blend the outline of the human figure rhythmically into the curves of nature, and you will have mastered the prime rule of good composition: to integrate the divergent parts into one complete harmony.

Kleidung und Hintergrund

Vor ein paar Monaten brüskierte eine berühmte französische Schauspielerin die vollzählig erschienene Riege der PR-Leute und Fotografen Hollywoods mit den Worten: „No cheesecake, pleeze!" Als sie aus dem Zug stieg, fuhr sie belehrend fort: „In meinem Land müssen sich Frauen nicht ausziehen, um sexy auszusehen." Für die frustrierten Fotografen muß sich dieser Aufruf seltsam angehört haben, kam er doch von einer Dame, deren Land immerhin als Geburtsstätte der Folies Bergères und des Bikinis gerühmt wird.

Kaum hatten sich die Presseagenten Hollywoods von diesem Schock erholt, brachte sie ein anderer französischer Import erneut aus dem Gleichgewicht. Diese Dame nun strafte ihre Landsmännin Lügen, indem sie mit einem schwindelerregend tief ausgeschnittenen Dekolleté, das Dior wie einen linkischen Anfänger aussehen ließ, durch die Staaten tourte und jedem, der eine Kamera umhängen hatte, ihre Beine enthüllte. Die Zurückhaltung gewisser Geschlechtsgenossinnen tat sie schlicht als „Neid der Besitzlosen" ab.

Wenn Damen so galant die Klingen kreuzen, kann ein Gentleman kaum untätiger Zaungast bleiben. Wir können uns natürlich mit dem dezenten Hinweis begnügen, daß der Streit darüber, ob verhüllen besser als enthüllen ist, so alt ist wie die Menschheit selbst und jeweils nach dem herrschenden Geschmack entschieden wurde. Schon die alten Griechen konnten sich nicht einigen, ob sie die Gewänder ihrer Göttinnen kurz und knapp oder lang und fließend bevorzugten. Diana und Juno, die führenden Vertreterinnen dieser entgegengesetzten Stile, hatten beide über die Jahrhunderte hinweg zahllose Verehrer.

Der Verfasser neigt eher zu jener Fraktion, die noch etwas der Vorstellungskraft überlassen will. Ein nacktes Pin-Up wird weniger Sex-Appeal verströmen als ein geschickt herausgeputztes, läßt dieses doch der Phantasie des Betrachters noch Spielraum. Das verführerischste Filmstar-Pin-Up ist das berühmte Bild von Rita Hayworth im Negligé. Die Nachfrage danach ist seit dem Zweiten Weltkrieg bis heute in astronomische Höhen geklettert.

Auf jeden Fall ist die Wahl der richtigen Kleidung von größter Bedeutung. Machen Sie Ihr Modell zu Ihrer Komplizin bei diesem Unterfangen – Mädchen sind äußerst einfallsreich, aus einigen Fetzen Stoff ein originelles Kostüm zu kreieren. Unterbreiten Sie ihr bereits im Vorfeld Ihre Ideen, um Enttäuschungen vorzubeugen, wenn Sie unvermittelt aus Ihrer Requisitenkiste ein paar hastig zum Bikini umfunktionierte Halstücher herausziehen. Vergessen Sie nie, daß das Kostüm die Persönlichkeit des Modells unterstreichen muß. Nicht jedes Mädchen will oder sollte in einen „französischen Badeanzug" schlüpfen, der keineswegs die Standardbekleidung für Pin-Ups ist, auch wenn viele Fotografen dies zu glauben scheinen. Bemühen Sie sich um eine originelle Garderobe, und Sie werden einen weiteren Blickfang auf Ihrer Seite haben.

Nicht zu vergessen ist der Hintergrund. Damit steht und fällt das Bild: er kann entweder einen traumhaften Rahmen für Ihre Pin-up-Königin abgeben oder aber so störend sein, daß er Ihre sorgfältige Komposition ruiniert.

Wenn Sie mit Studiorequisiten und Hintergründen arbeiten, achten Sie darauf, daß das Modell dabei eine bequeme Haltung einnehmen kann. Andernfalls wirkt das Ergebnis verkrampft.

Im Freien bieten sich uns schöne natürliche Kulissen in Hülle und Fülle. Die Berge, Küsten, Seen und Wüsten unseres wunderbaren Kontinents halten ein unerschöpfliches Reservoir traumhafter Szenerien bereit. Es bedarf nicht Aladins Wunderlampe, sie zu finden – sie sind überall.

Im Interesse einer guten Bildkomposition sollten Sie nur das aus der Natur benutzen, was die Wirkung der menschlichen Gestalt optimal unterstützt.

Wie die Bilder in diesem Buch veranschaulichen, kann das ein Baumstamm sein, ein Holzpfahl, eine Welle oder eine Felsformation, ein Stahlrohrstuhl oder auch ein neutraler Hintergrund. Was der große deutsche Künstler Max Liebermann über die Malerei sagte, gilt in gleichem Maße für die Fotografie: „Malen ist Weglassen". Lassen Sie die menschliche Silhouette harmonisch mit den Linien der Natur verschmelzen, und Sie haben die wichtigste Regel für einen gelungenen Bildaufbau beherzigt: die verschiedenen Teile müssen sich in perfekter Harmonie verbinden.

Costumes et arrière-plans

Il y a quelques mois, une célèbre actrice française a prit de court les agents de publicité et les photographes d'Hollywood en annonçant fermement: « Pas question que je pose en pin-up! » Tout en descendant du train, elle a poursuivi: « Dans mon pays, les femmes n'ont pas besoin d'ôter leurs vêtements pour être sexy!» Pour les paparazzis frustrés, c'était un commentaire surprenant de la part d'une dame venant du pays qui avait inventé les Folies Bergères et le bikini!

Avant que les agents de presse n'aient eu le temps de se remettre de leur choc, une autre Française vint de nouveau les déconcerter. Cette dernière défia ses compatriotes en quadrillant les Etats-Unis avec un décolleté vertigineux à côté duquel les créations de Dior paraissaient être les élucubrations d'un débutant et en exhibant ses jambes à tous ceux qui étaient disposés à les photographier. La réticence des autres membres de son sexe, expliqua-t-elle, était simplement « de la fausse pudeur ».

Comment un gentlemen pourrait-il rester insensible à un tel feu croisé entre de jolies dames? Naturellement, nous pourrions éluder la question en répondant que « Faut-il couvrir ou dévoiler? » est une question vieille comme le monde à laquelle on a déjà proposé de multiples réponses selon les goûts et les époques. Même les Grecs de l'Antiquité n'arrivaient à décider s'ils préféraient leurs déesses en tuniques courtes et raides, ou en robes longues et flottantes. Diane et Junon, les principales tenantes de ces deux styles, ont chacune eut leurs légions de fidèles au fil des siècles.

Personnellement, je pencherais plutôt pour l'école qui préfère laisser quelque chose à l'imagination. Un nu dégage moins de sex-appeal qu'une pin-up judicieusement vêtue, car cette dernière suscite la participation visuelle du spectateur. La pin-up de cinéma la plus réussie est sans conteste la célèbre photo de Rita Hayworth en négligé. Depuis la Seconde Guerre mondiale, son tirage a atteint des chiffres astronomiques.

Quoi qu'il en soit, le choix de la bonne tenue est essentiel pour la réussite de vos photos. Associez votre modèle à cette aventure: les filles redoublent d'imagination et de créativité quand il s'agit de se faire un costume à partir d'un rien. Discutez préalablement avec elle de votre projet, cela vous évitera de vous ridiculiser en sortant de votre boîte d'accessoires un bikini miteux fait avec une série de cravates nouées à la hâte. N'oubliez pas que le costume doit convenir à la personnalité du sujet. Toutes les filles n'accepteront pas et ne devraient pas accepter d'enfiler un bikini, qui, d'ailleurs, n'est absolument pas l'accessoire indispensable de la pin-up, contrairement à ce que semblent croire de nombreux photographes. Trouvez un costume original et vous aurez ainsi un facteur de plus pour attirer l'attention.

Dernier détail et non des moindres: le décor. Il peut sauver ou tuer une image, mettre en valeur votre pin-up ou être dérangeant et déconcentrant au point d'anéantir la qualité de la composition.

Lorsque vous travaillez avec des accessoires et des fonds de studio, veillez à ce que votre modèle soit confortablement installé ou le résultat final aura un effet artificiel.

Pour ce qui est des extérieurs, ce vaste continent vous offre une gamme inépuisable de superbes arrière-plans naturels. Inutile d'aller chercher des décors à l'autre bout de la planète, il y en a partout autour de vous.

Pour une bonne composition, n'utilisez que la partie du décor naturel qui complète le mieux la silhouette du modèle.

Comme le montrent les photos rassemblées dans ce livre, il peut s'agir d'un tronc d'arbre, d'un pilier, d'une vague, d'un rocher, d'une chaise de jardin ou d'une simple toile de fond. Ce qu'a déclaré le grand peintre allemand Max Liebermann sur l'art de la peinture « Peindre, c'est omettre », vaut également pour la photographie. Faites en sorte que la silhouette de votre modèle épouse les lignes naturelles de la nature et vous aurez déjà en main la règle principale de la composition : intégrer les parties divergentes en une harmonie complète.

A pretty girl and a cute doll are always a sure-fire combination for an effective pin-up. Simple props and basic lighting prove that elaborate staging is unnecessary in creating an appealing result. 1/5 second at f/16.

Ein hübsches Mädchen und eine niedliche Puppe sind immer eine todsichere Kombination für ein wirkungsvolles Pin-Up. Einfache Requisiten und eine klare Lichtführung beweisen, daß es keiner aufwendigen Inszenierung bedarf, um ein ansprechendes Ergebnis zu erzielen. 1/5 Sekunde bei f/16.

Une jolie fille et une poupée amusante sont une combinaison gagnante pour une pin-up réussie. Ces accessoires simples et cet éclairage conventionnel prouvent qu'une mise en scène sophistiquée n'est pas indispensable pour obtenir un résultat attrayant. 1/5ème de seconde à f/16.

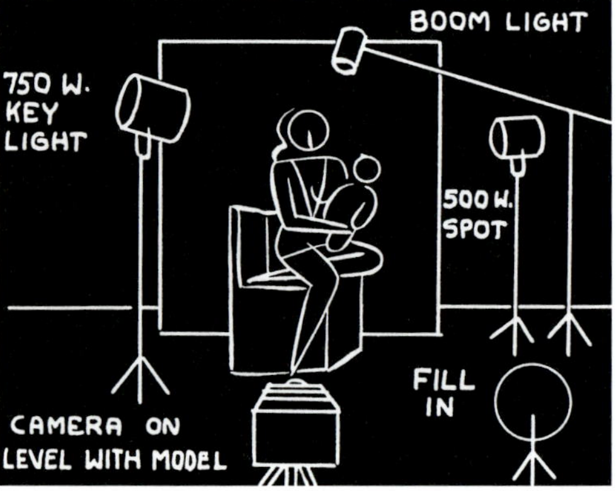

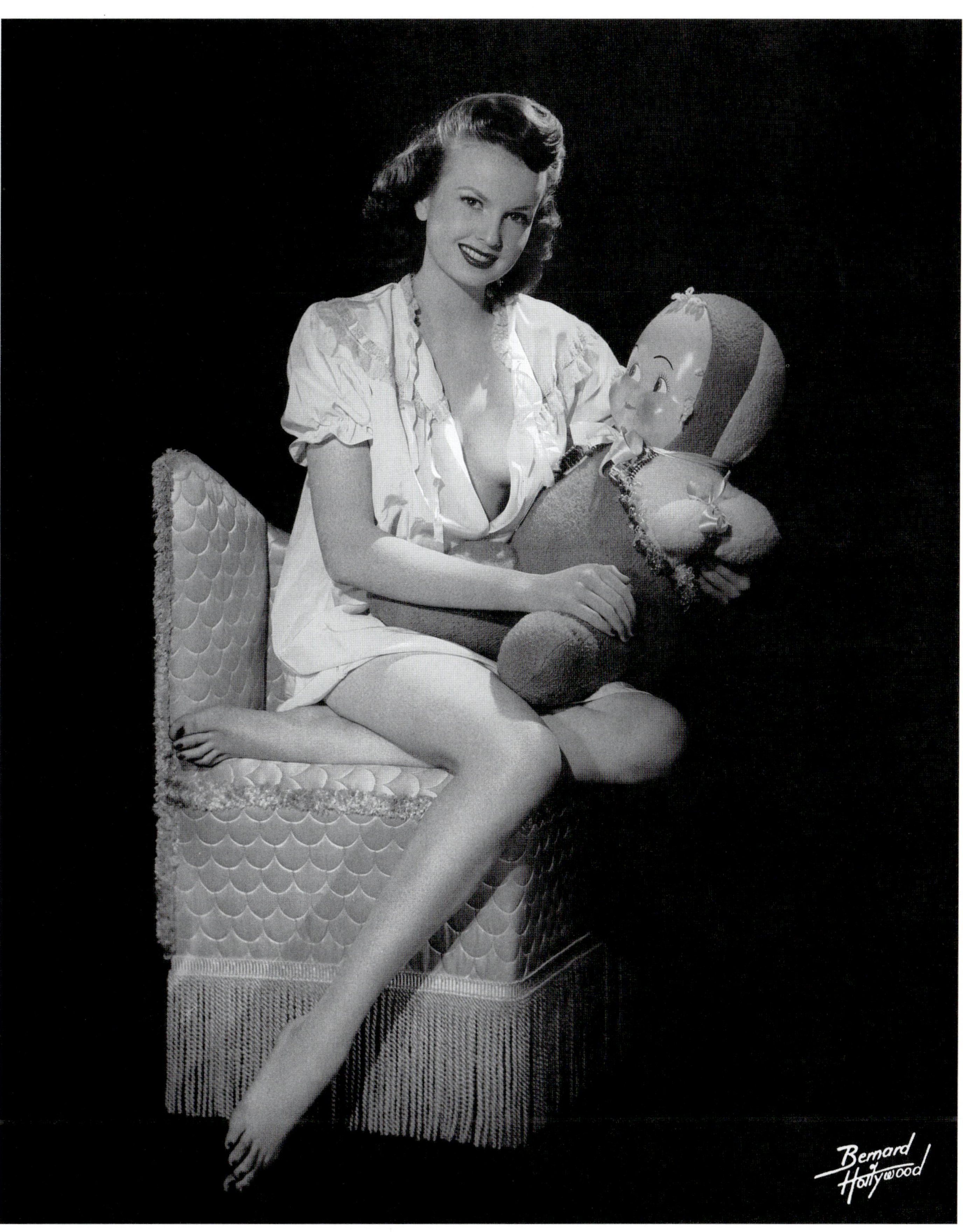

Pretty Baby

BABY DOLL · PRETTY BABY

This innocent little study personifies the playfulness of a coy high school sweetie in any corner drug store back home. Spot staging with a stool and dixie cup serves to create the right atmosphere without any distracting elements. 5x7 Ansco view camera, Panchro-Press Type B, 1/5 second at f/16.

Diese unschuldige kleine Studie personifiziert die Verspieltheit eines scheuen High-School-Häschens, wie man es im Drugstore um die Ecke trifft. Die sparsame Inszenierung mit einem Hocker und einem Pappbecher als Requisiten schafft die richtige Atmosphäre ohne ablenkende Elemente. 5x7 Ansco view camera, Panchro-Press Type B-Film, 1/5 Sekunde bei f/16.

Cette petite étude traduit le caractère mutin et faussement modeste d'une jeune adolescente comme on en voit au comptoir de tous les drugstores du pays. Deux spots, un tabouret, un verre et une paille suffisent pour créer la bonne ambiance sans avoir besoin d'en rajouter. 5x7 Ansco view camera, pellicule Panchro-Press Type B, 1/5ème de seconde à f/16.

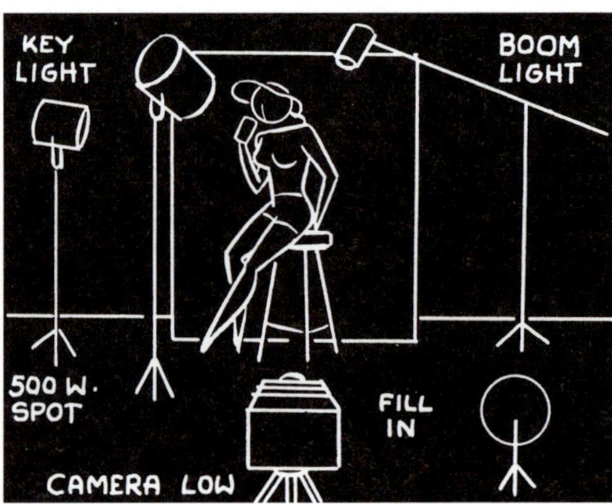

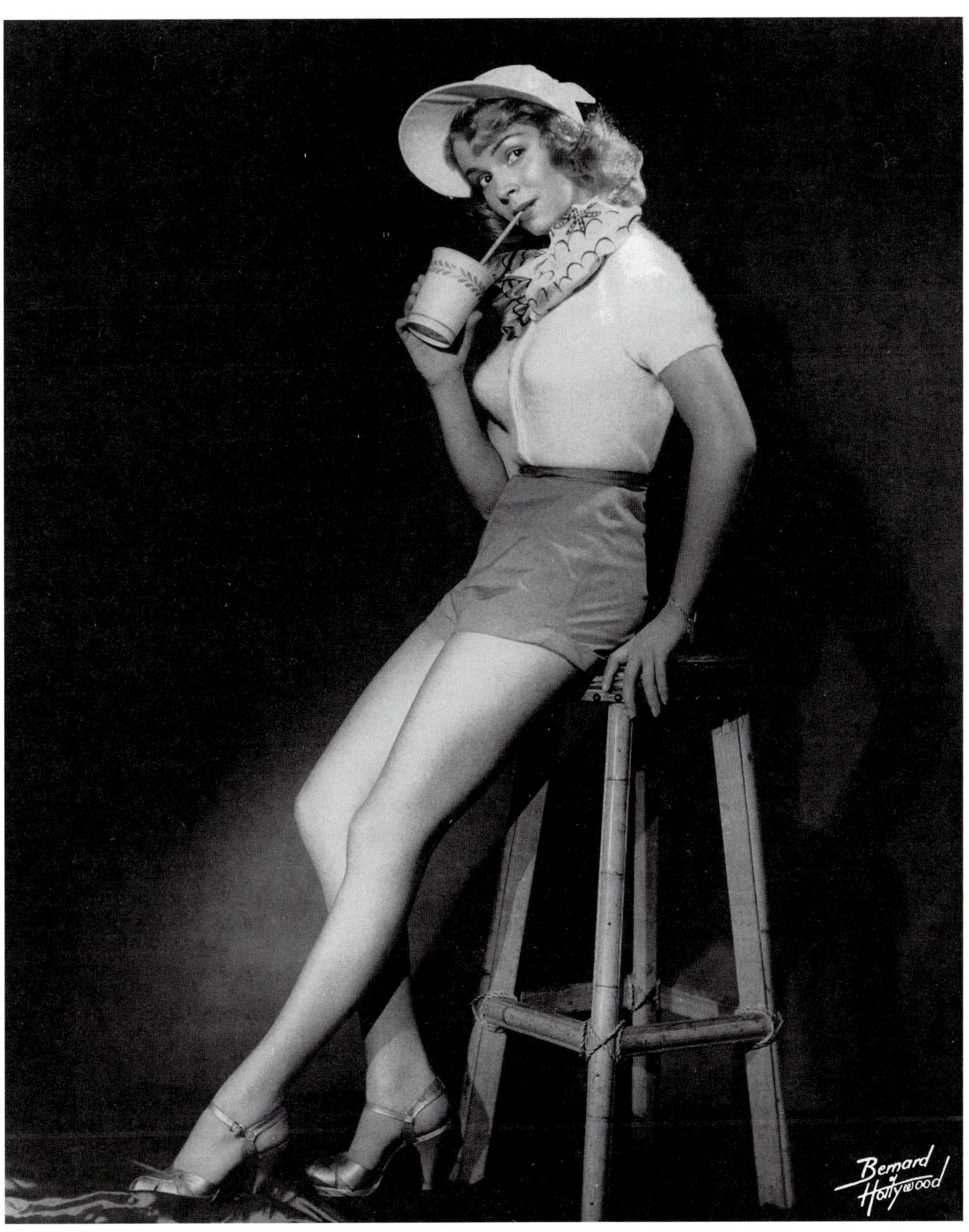

A Sip in Time

KLEINE ERFRISCHUNG · TOUT SUCRE TOUT MIEL

The sensuousness of a ballet mermaid is captured in the use of silk mesh stockings against a rocky cove. The seeming incongruity of comb and mirror is purposely introduced in this modern version of Lorelei.

Seidene Netzstrümpfe in einer felsigen Bucht bringen die ganze Sinnlichkeit einer Ballettnixe zum Ausdruck. Die scheinbar deplazierten Accessoires Spiegel und Kamm sind dieser modernen Version der Lorelei mit Bedacht hinzugefügt worden.

La sensualité de cette sirène ballerine est évoquée par la juxtaposition des bas résilles et de la crique rocheuse. L'incongruité apparente du peigne et du miroir a été introduite exprès dans cette version moderne de la Lorelei.

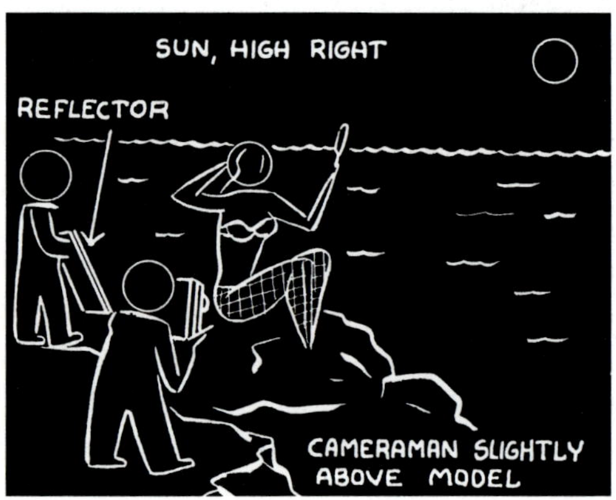

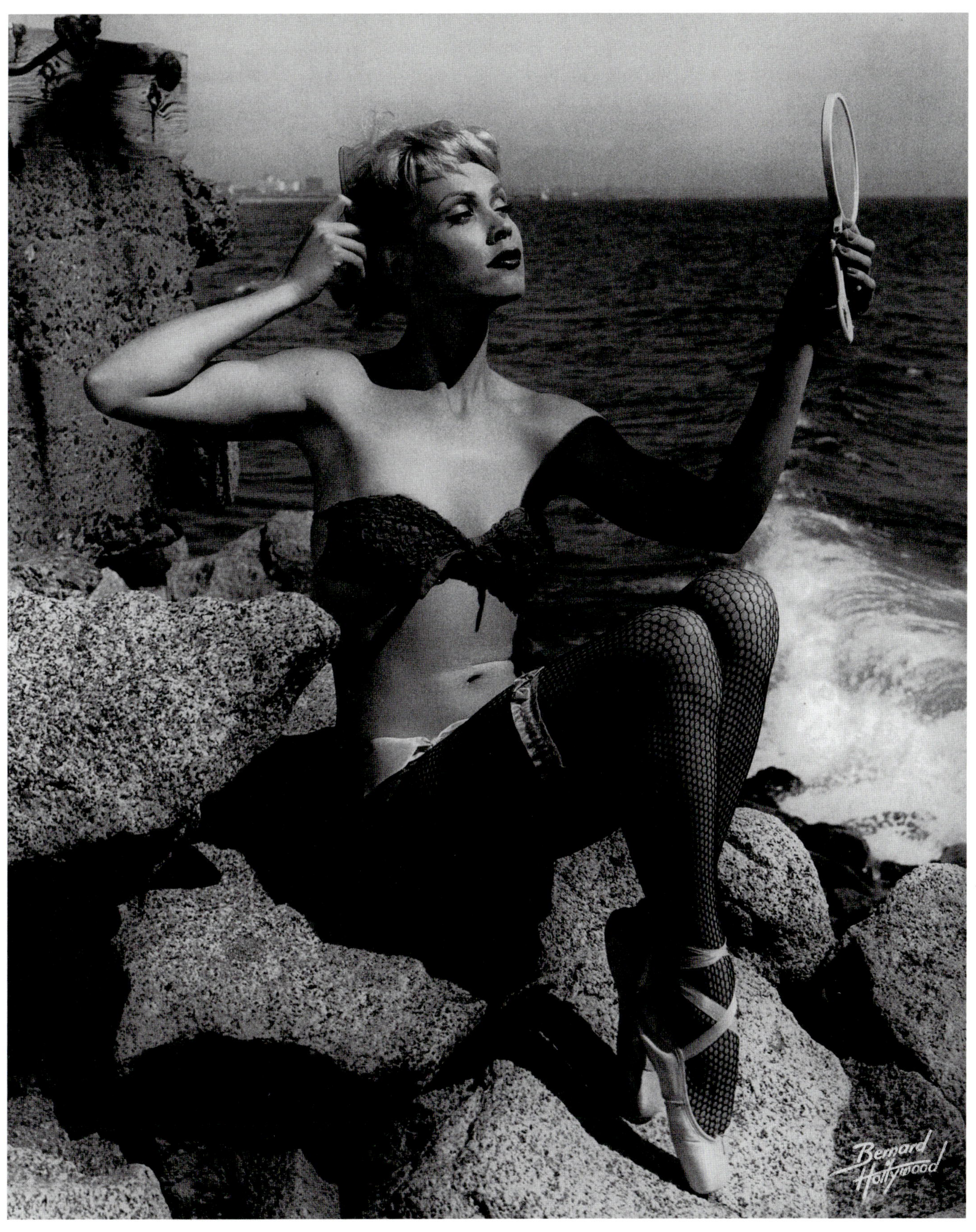

Lorelei

The eerie atmosphere of this picture is due to a desert sandstorm, just before the sun went down. The flowing rhythm of the body blends with the wind-swept grasses and shrubs in the background. The relatively brilliant illumination was produced through a close flash fill-in with one diffuser. 4x5 Speed Graphic, 1/200 second at f/20, K-2 filter, Superpan Press.

Ein Sandsturm kurz vor Sonnenuntergang schuf die gespenstische Atmosphäre dieses Bildes. Die fließende Bewegung des Körpers harmoniert mit den windgepeitschten Grasbüscheln des Hintergrundes. Die relativ helle Beleuchtung wurde durch einen Aufhellblitz mit Diffusor aus kurzer Entfernung erreicht.
4x5 Speed Graphic, 1/200 Sekunde bei f/20, K-2-Filter, Superpan Press-Film.

Prise lors d'une tempête de sable juste avant le coucher du soleil, cette image dégage une atmosphère irréelle. Le rythme fluide du corps se fond dans les herbes et les buissons couchés par le vent en arrière-plan. La lumière assez brillante a été produite par un flash supplémentaire équipé d'un diffuseur. 4x5 Speed Graphic, 1/200ème de seconde à f/20, Filtre K-2, pellicule Superpan Press.

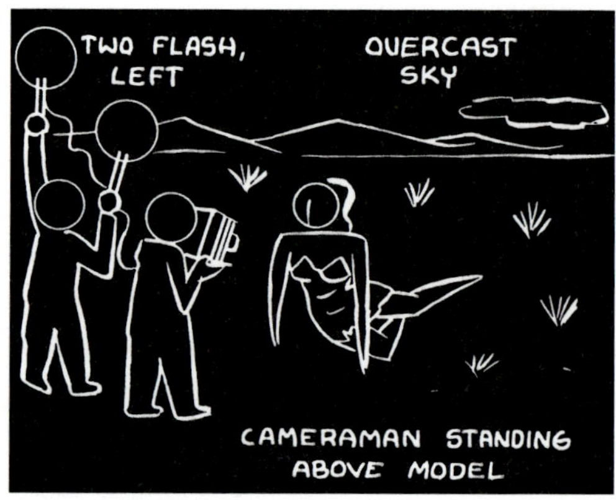

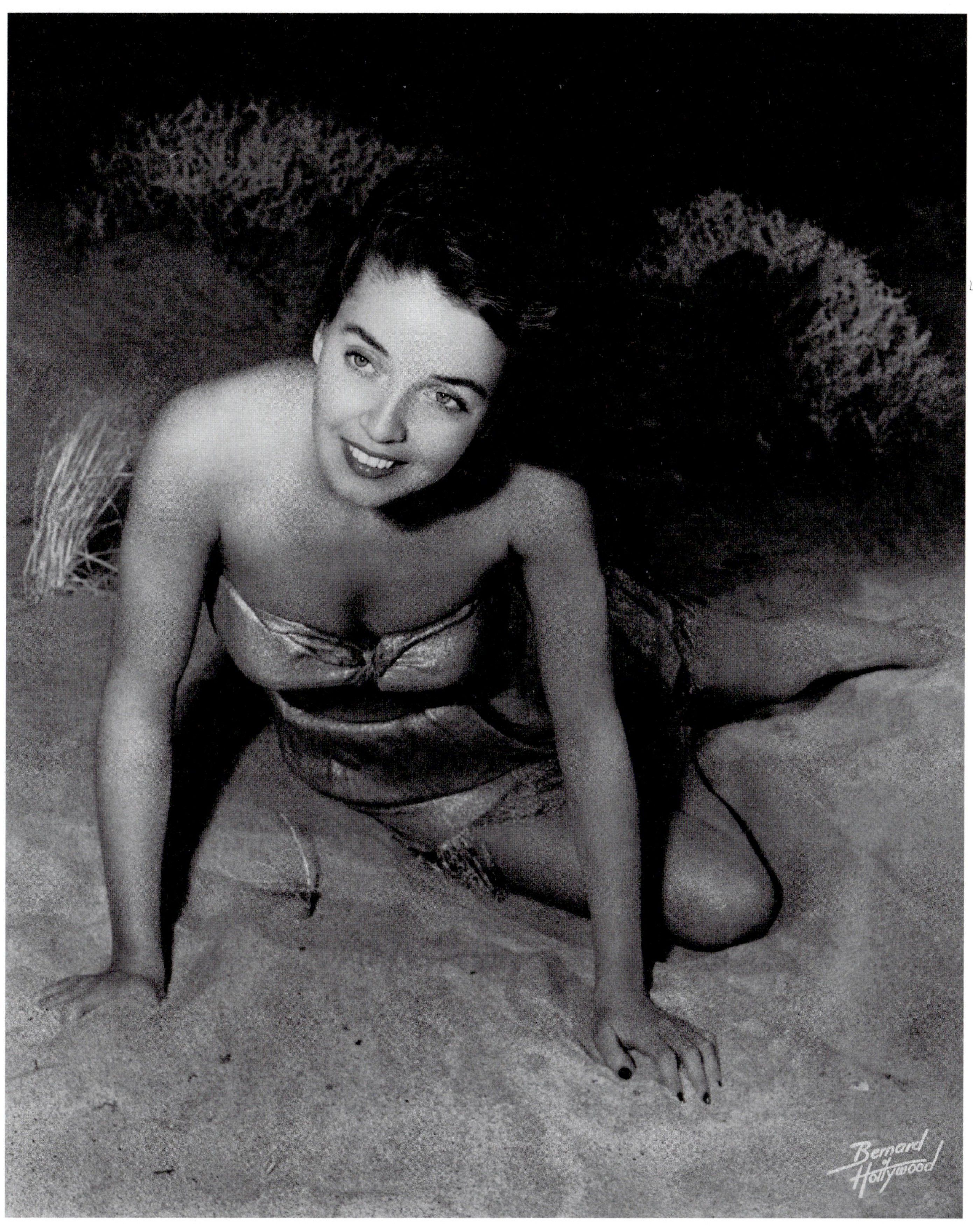

Trade Winds

STURMWARNUNG · VENT DE SABLE

Vacation mood, sunshine, clear skies and smooth sailing! Depth of focus was increased by placing the model midway on the pier, leaving sufficient space to lead into the picture and separate the far horizon from the foreground. Polaroid filter cuts out undesirable reflection, and graduates the tonal scale of the sky. 1/100 second at f/18, Superpan Press.

Ferienstimmung, Sonnenschein, blauer Himmel und spiegelglatte See! Die Schärfentiefe wurde verstärkt, indem das Modell in der Mitte des Piers plaziert wurde, so daß genügend Raum blieb, die Bildführung zu gestalten und den fernen Horizont deutlich vom Vordergrund abzuheben. Polarisationsfilter verhindern unerwünschte Spiegelungen und beeinflussen die Abstufungen des Himmels. 1/100 Sekunde bei f/18. Superpan Press-Film.

Une ambiance de vacances, un ciel dégagé et une mer calme! La profondeur de champ a été augmentée en plaçant le modèle sur une jetée, laissant suffisamment d'espace pour attirer le regard au centre de l'image et séparer la ligne d'horizon du premier plan. Un filtre Polaroïd élimine les reflets indésirables et nuance la gamme tonale du ciel. 1/100ème de seconde à f/18, pellicule Superpan Press.

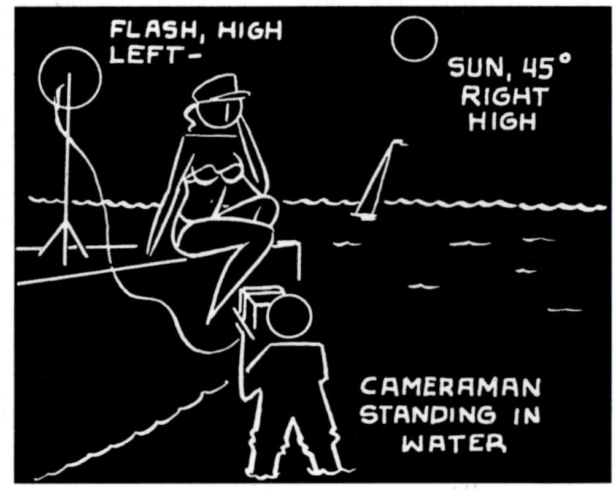

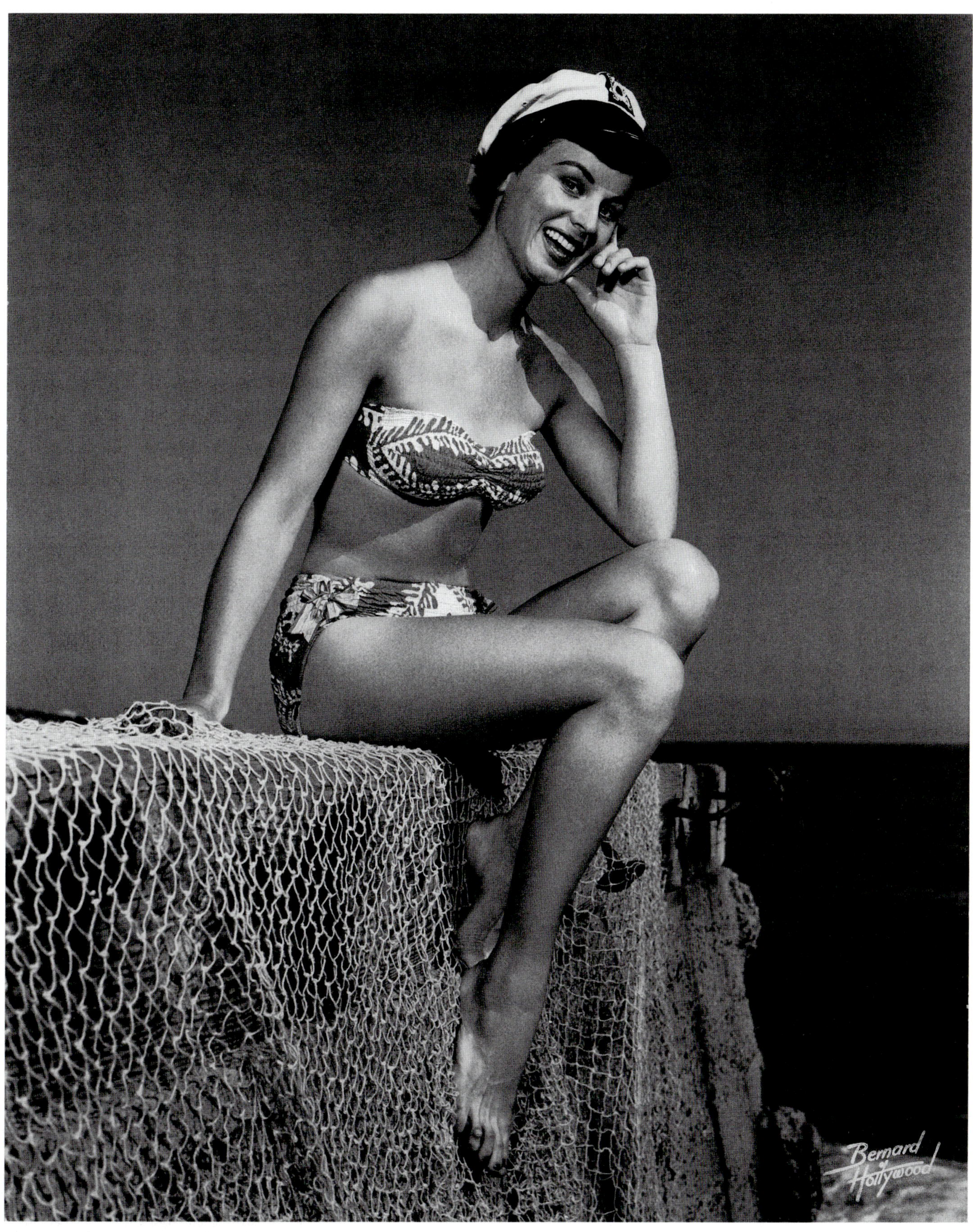

Net Result

INS NETZ GEGANGEN · DANS LES FILETS

Fishing scenes being pin-up favorites, the theme merits this second treatment of a saucy angler. Diagonal arrangement on a vertical studio pile injects feeling of movement. Note: The careful posing of leg, reel with rope in diametrically opposites gives compositional balance. Side rim lighting; two spots and one hair light with one senior spot as main light and a 500 watt projection flood as fill in. 1/10 second at f/11.

Da Angelszenen ein Lieblingsmotiv der Pin-Up-Fotografie sind, hier ein weiteres Bild einer flotten Anglerin. Die diagonale Ausrichtung auf dem vertikalen Pfosten vermittelt das Gefühl von Bewegung. Man beachte: das durchdachte Arrangement von Bein und Angelrute, die in entgegengesetzte Richtungen weisen, verleiht der Komposition Balance. Streiflicht, zwei Spots, ein Akzentlicht auf dem Haar, ein Oberlicht als Hauptlicht und ein 500 Watt-Flutlicht zur Aufhellung. 1/10 Sekunde bei f/11.

Les scènes de pêche étant particulièrement prisées des créateurs de pin-up, le thème méritait cette seconde version de la pêcheuse coquine. Une pose en diagonale sur un pilier vertical en studio donne la sensation de mouvement. On remarquera la disposition minutieuse de la jambe, formant un angle droit avec la cane à pêche, tandis que la corde est placée parallèlement à cette dernière afin d'équilibrer la composition. L'éclairage latéral permet de faire ressortir la silhouette : deux petits spots sur les cheveux, un gros spot comme source principale et un autre de 500 Watt comme source secondaire. 1/10ème de seconde à f/11.

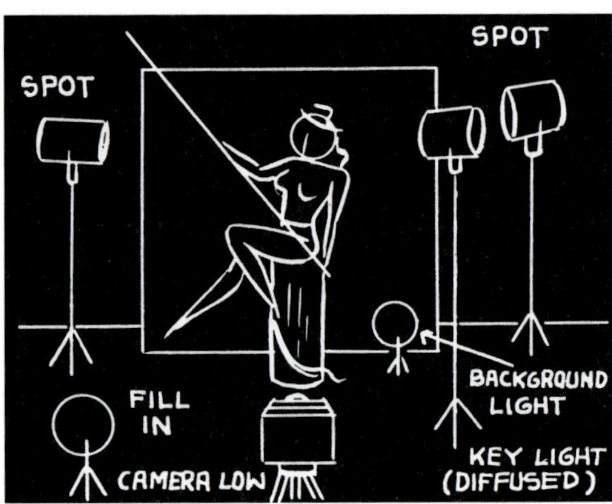

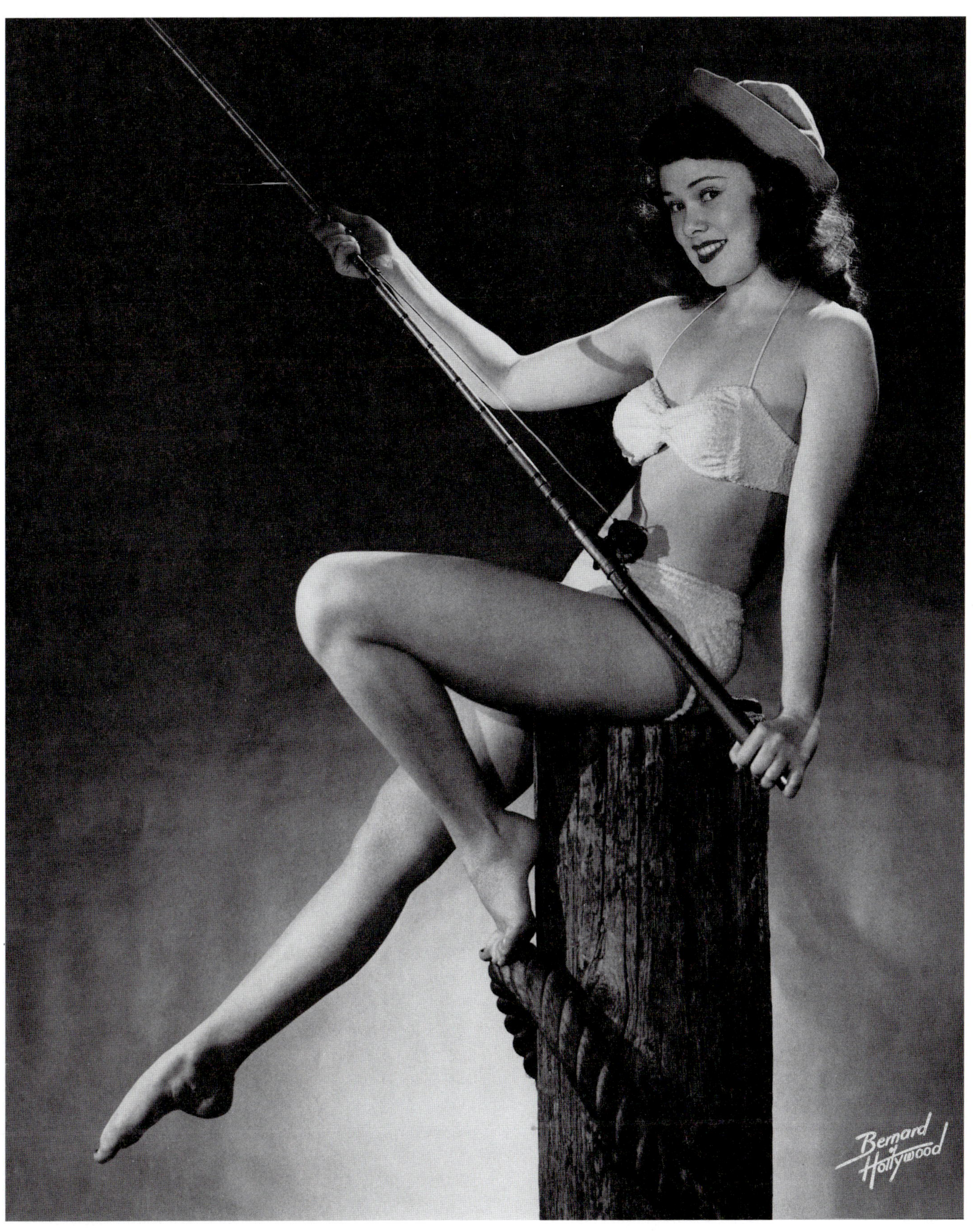

Hook, Line and Sinker

PETRI HEIL! · ÇA MORD !

A symphony of lights and shadows, the whole photographic tonal scale of blacks and whites, is recorded in this composition. The abstract shadow on the background injects an impressionist element which lends itself to a variety of interpretations. Texture-lighting, produced by spotlights from each side, brings out the three-dimensional quality of the figure. The diaphragm was stopped down to f/22 for sharpness.

Eine Symphonie aus Licht und Schatten, alle Abstufungen zwischen schwarz und weiß finden sich in diesem Bild. Der abstrakte Schatten auf dem Hintergrund verleiht dem Bild ein impressionistisches Element, das vieldeutige Interpretationen zuläßt. Eine klare Modellierung durch Spotlichter von beiden Seiten betont die Dreidimensionalität der Gestalt. Um eine maximale Schärfe zu erzielen, wurde bei f/22 abgeblendet.

Une symphonie d'ombres et de lumière. Toute la gamme tonale photographique des noirs et des blancs est enregistrée dans cette composition. L'ombre abstraite en arrière plan ajoute un élément impressionniste qui se prête à diverses interprétations. L'éclairage, produit par des spots placés de chaque côtés, fait ressortir la texture des matière et la qualité tridimensionnelle de la silhouette. Le diaphragme a été réglé sur f/22 pour une plus grande netteté.

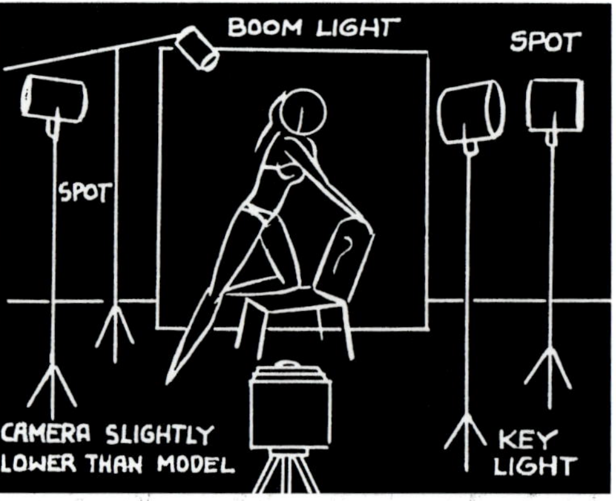

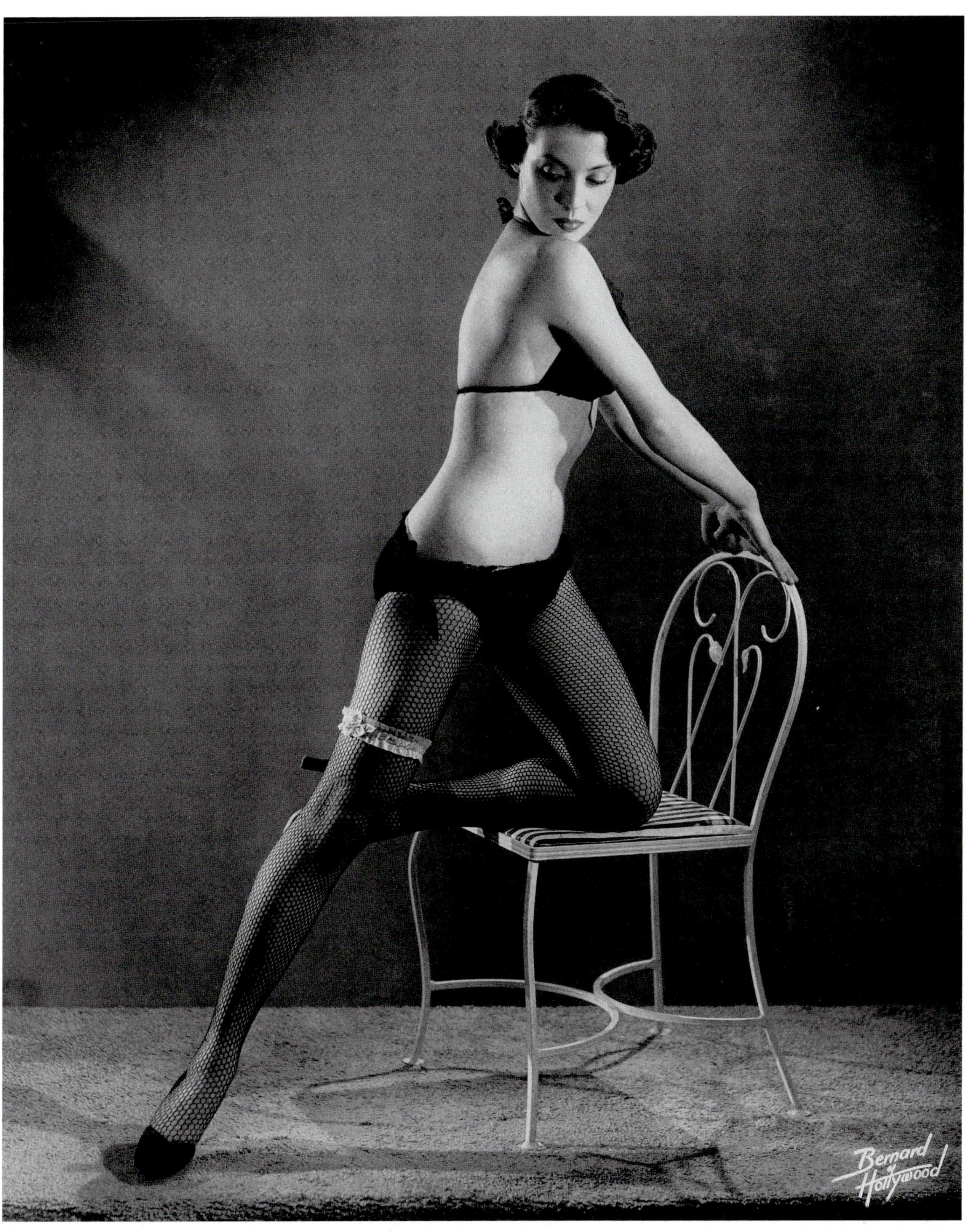

Black Magic

SCHWARZE MAGIE · MAGIE NOIRE

Deliberately provocative is this extreme pose which manages to capture something of the spirit of the *Folies Bergères*. A low camera angle accentuates the long-limbed beauty of the dancer. 4x5 Speed Graphic, strobe lights as back, side and key lighting.

Diese gewagte Pose, die etwas vom Geist der „Folies Bergères" atmet, ist bewußt provokant angelegt. Ein niedriger Kamerastandpunkt betont die langen Beine der Tänzerin. 4x5 Speed Graphic, Strobolight als Streif-, Seiten- und Hauptlicht.

Délibérément provoquante, cette pose extrême parvient à restituer un peu l'esprit des Folies Bergères. Un objectif placé bas accentue la longueur des jambes de la danseuse. 4x5 Speed Graphic, projecteurs stroboscopiques comme éclairage par derrière, latéral et principal.

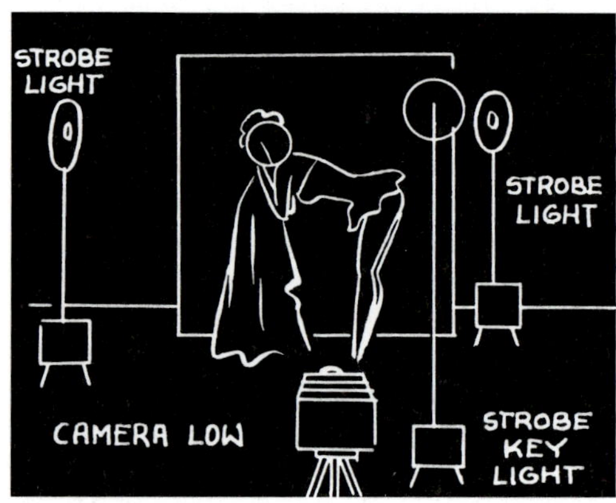

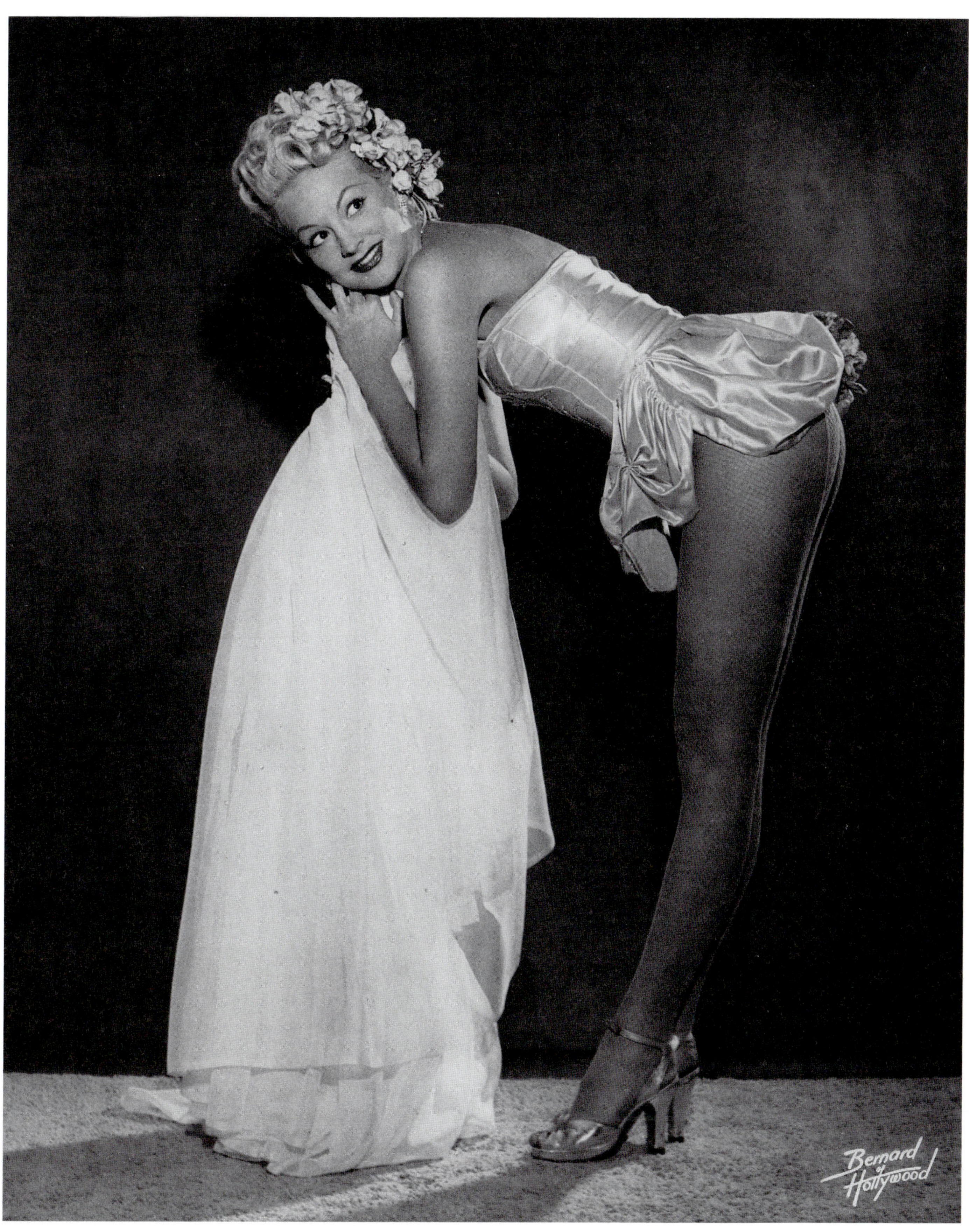

Wedding Belle

HOCHZEITSGLOCKEN · VIVE LA MARIÉE !

As fresh and exhilarating as an ocean breeze, this picture was achieved by posing the body of the model in an S-curve formation against an appropriate background. Full advantage is taken of side lighting by the sun using flash fill-in with diffusing screen. 1/100 second at f/22, K-2 filter.

Die S-förmige Pose des Modells vor einem passenden Hintergrund ließ eine Aufnahme entstehen, die frisch und belebend wie eine Meeresbrise wirkt. Die hochstehende Sonne spendete das Seitenlicht, zusätzlich wurde ein Aufhellblitz mit Reflexwand benutzt. 1/100 Sekunde bei f/22, K-2-Filter.

Fraîche et revigorante comme une brise marine, cette image a été obtenue en plaçant le corps du modèle en S contre un fond approprié. Un flash avec écran diffuseur permet de tirer le profit maximum du soleil latéral. 1/100ème de seconde à f/22, filtre K-2.

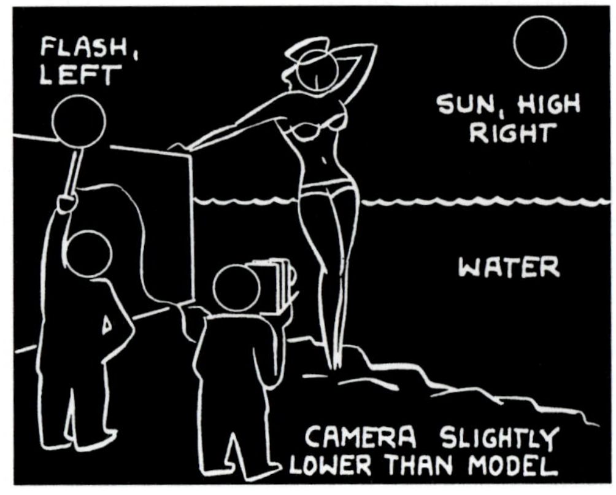

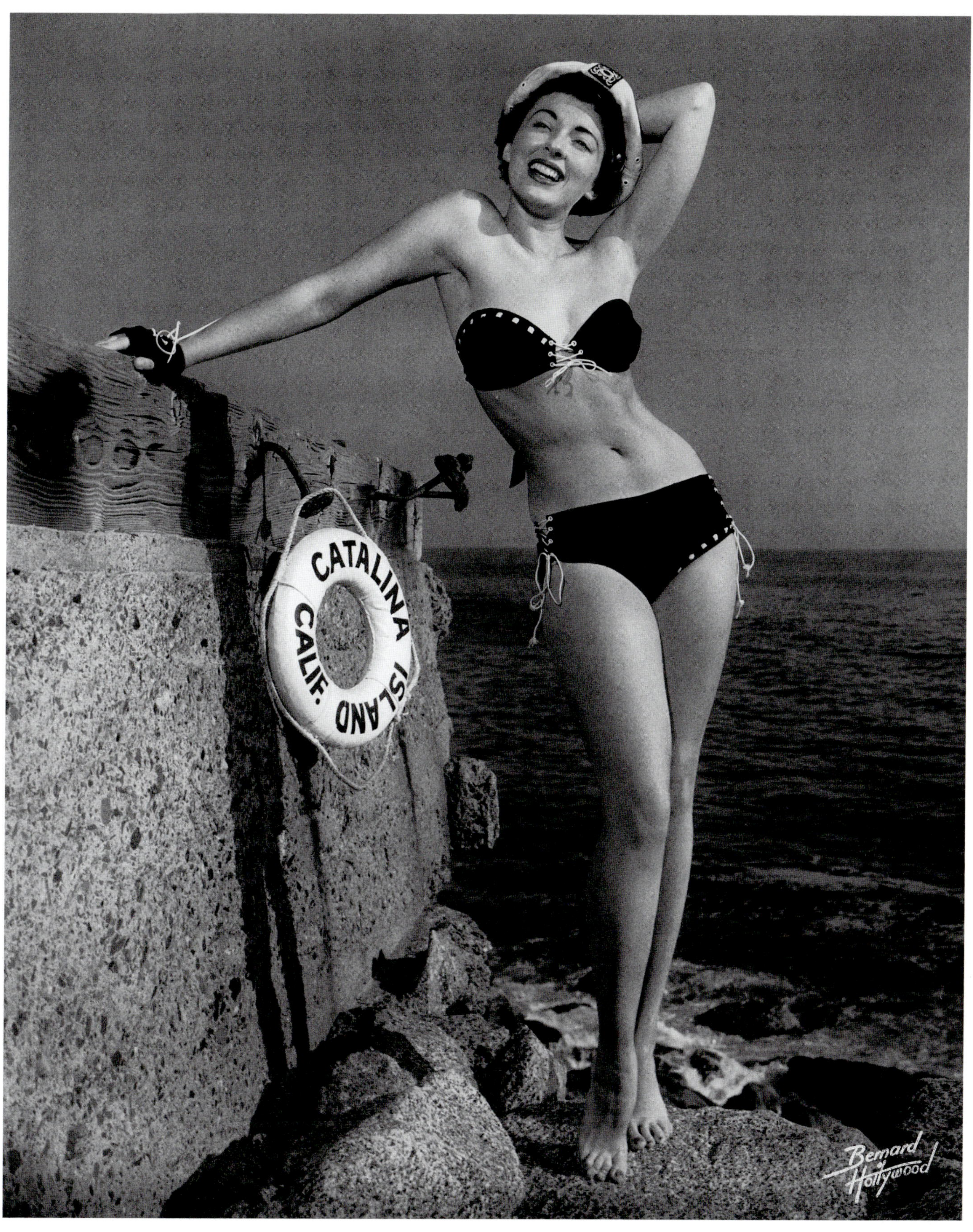

Man Overboard

MANN ÜBER BORD! · UN HOMME À LA MER

A commercial assignment for sun-tan lotion results in this appealing pin-up. Although the figure dominates the composition, the misty canyon background affords the desirable pictorial elements. This is a striking example of the "posed-candid" technique in which the action is carefully rehearsed and then frozen at the most characteristic moment.

Dieses hübsche Pin-Up entstand bei Werbeaufnahmen für eine Sonnencreme. Obwohl das Modell im Mittelpunkt der Komposition steht, liefert das dunstverhangene Tal als Hintergrund doch die erwünschten malerischen Elemente. Dies ist ein treffendes Beispiel für die Technik des „inszenierten Schnappschusses", bei der die Bewegung sorgfältig einstudiert und dann in der charakteristischsten Phase eingefroren wird.

Cette commande d'une publicité pour une marque d'ambre solaire a débouché sur une charmante pin-up. Bien que le personnage domine la composition, le canyon perdu dans la brume en arrière-plan constitue un excellent élément pictural. C'est là un exemple frappant de la technique d'« instantané posé » où l'action est soigneusement répétée puis figée en une attitude caractéristique.

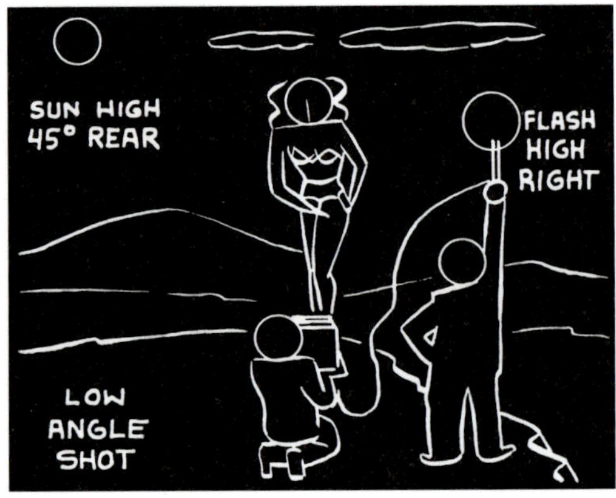

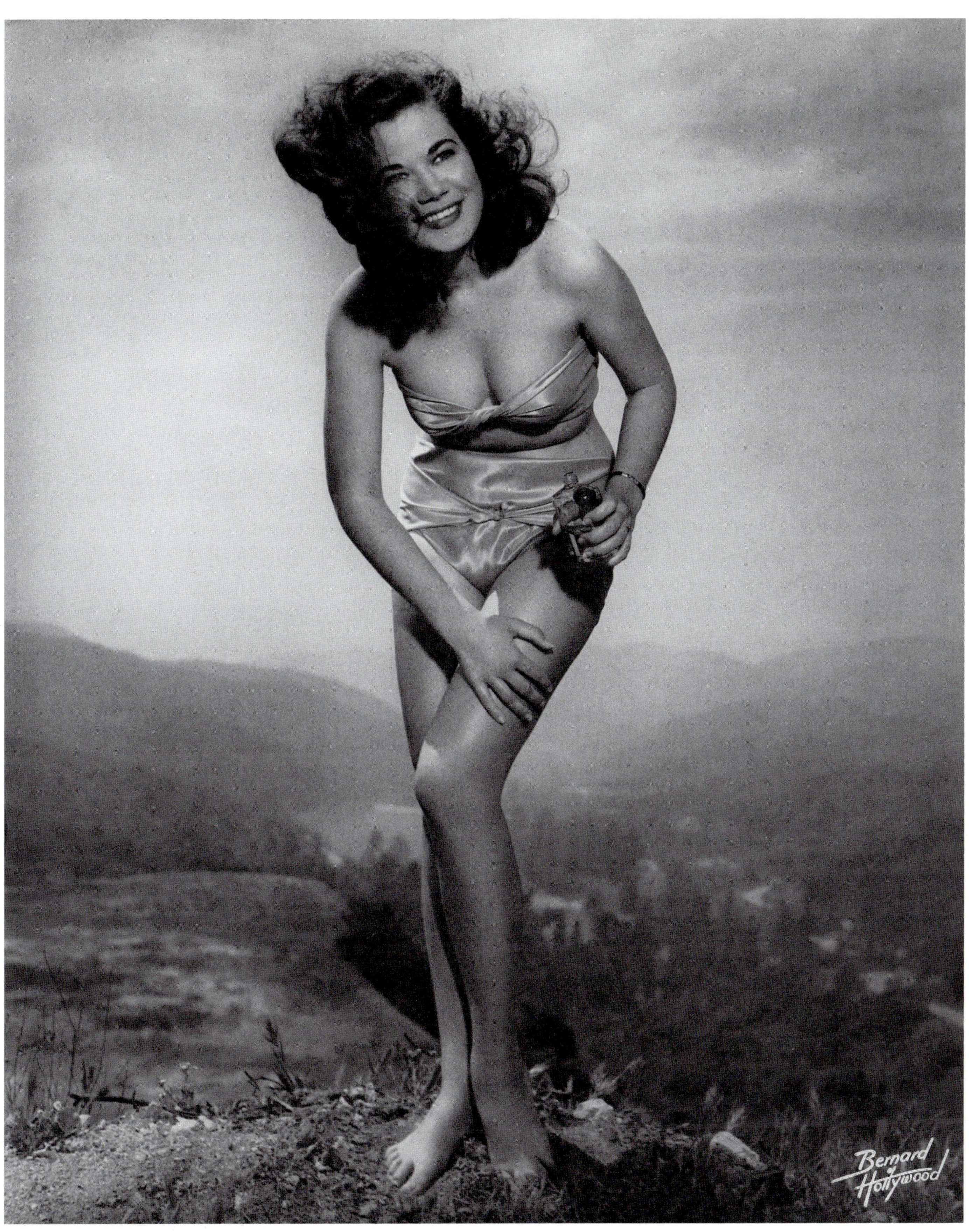

Slow Burn

SONNENANBETERIN · ÉCRAN TOTAL

Fresh, sweet and as American as apple pie is this natural blonde beauty. The choice of a hassock as the only prop gives a feeling of motion to the study and underlines the subject's genuine cheerfulness and vitality.

Diese naturblonde Schönheit wirkt frisch, süß und so amerikanisch wie ein Doughnut. Das runde Sitzkissen als einziges Requisit verleiht dieser Studie eine gewisse Dynamik und unterstreicht die ungekünstelte Fröhlichkeit und Vitalität des Modells.

Une jolie blonde fraîche, charmante et typiquement américaine. Le choix d'un pouf rond comme seul accessoire donne une impression de mouvement et souligne la gaieté naturelle et la vitalité du modèle.

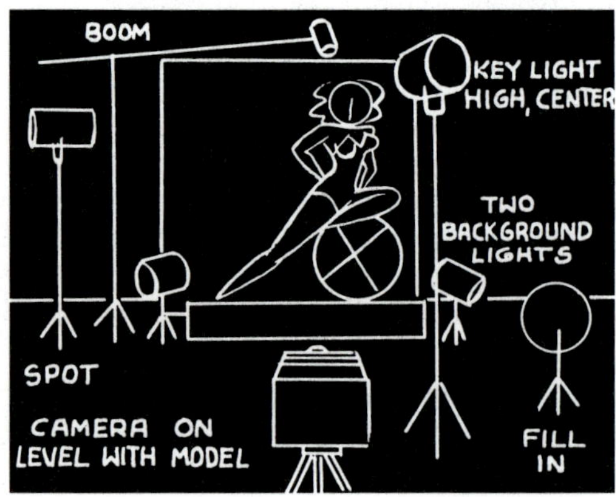

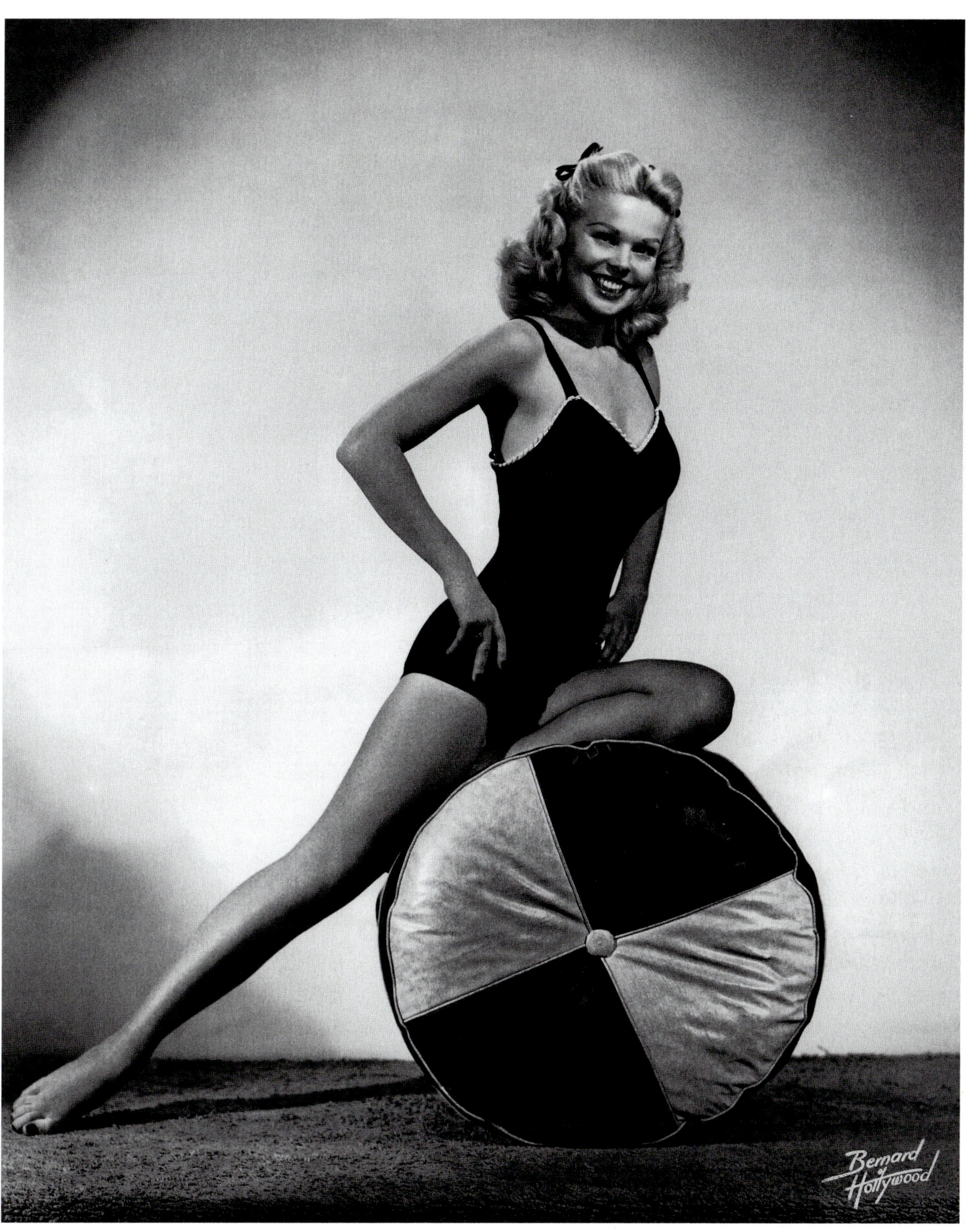

Rolling Along

EINE RUNDE SACHE · PIERRE QUI ROULE …

Costuming introduces a humorous element into an otherwise routine assignment, thus producing a diverting pin-up. The flirtatious expression and nonchalant posture go well with the French atmosphere it suggests. A spotlight, diagonally thrown arcross the background, serves to bring out the figure. 1/10 second at f/11, Triple S Pan. 12 mins. in DK 50.

Die Kostümierung gibt dieser ansonsten nicht ungewöhnlichen Arbeit den richtigen Pfiff und macht aus ihr ein amüsantes Pin-Up. Der kokette Ausdruck und die nonchalante Pose passen gut zu der französischen Atmosphäre. Ein Spotlicht fällt diagonal auf den Hintergrund und hebt die Silhouette hervor. 1/10 Sekunde bei f/11, Triple S Pan-Film, entwickelt in 12 Minuten in DK 50.

Ici, le costume introduit un élément humoristique dans cette photo traditionnelle de pin-up. L'expression coquine et la pose nonchalante du modèle conviennent bien à l'ambiance à la française que l'image veut suggérer. Un spot éclairant le fond en diagonale permet de faire ressortir la silhouette. 1/10ème de seconde à f/11, pellicule Triple S Pan 12 min. en DK 50.

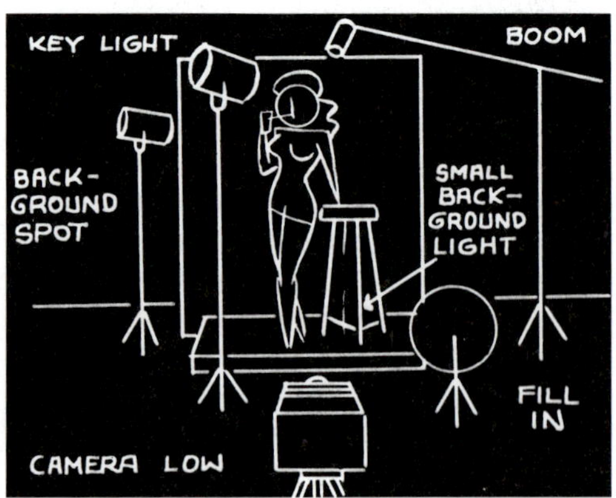

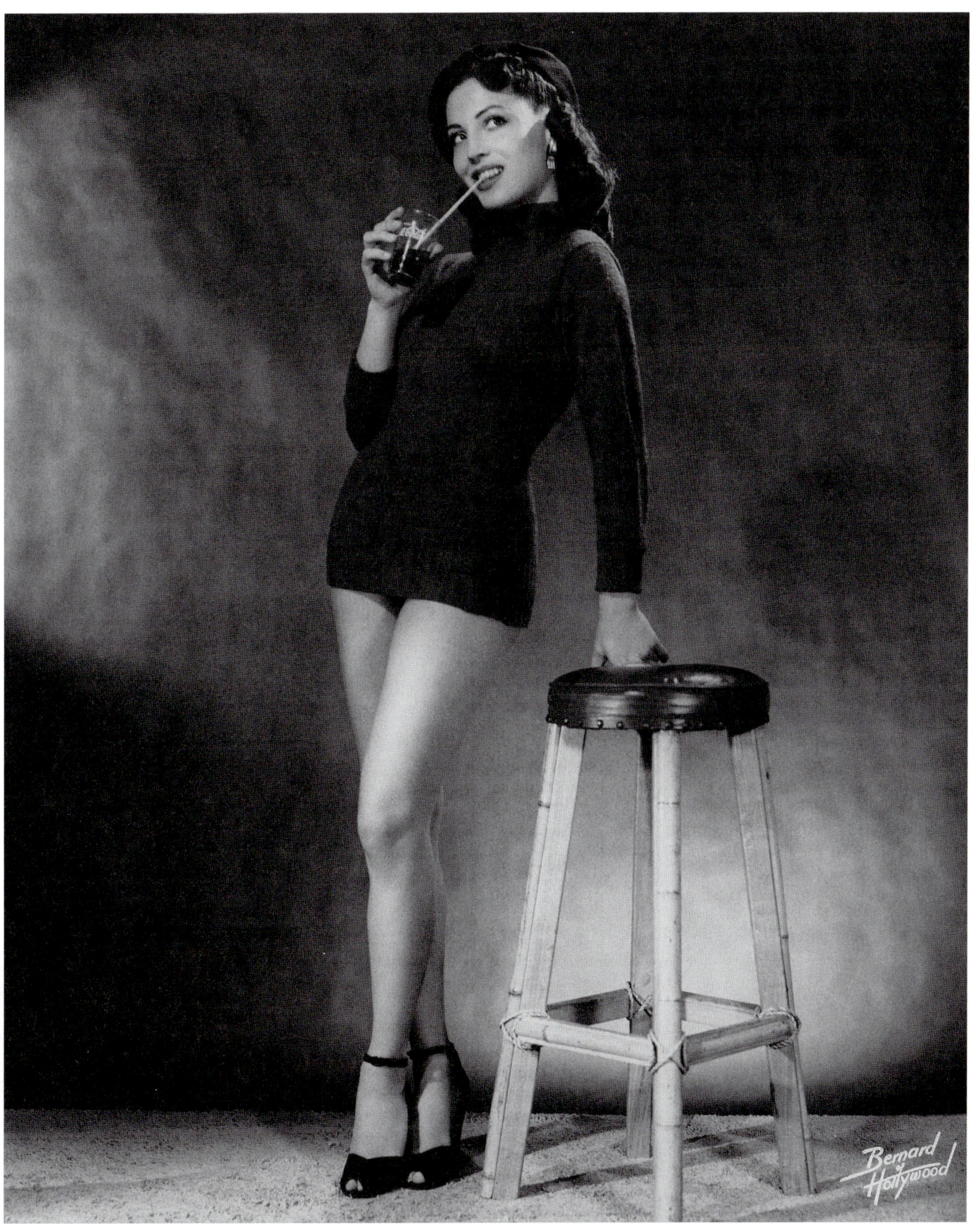

Cola-Coquette

COLA-COQUETTE · SAINT-GERMAIN-DES-PRÉS

The most dramatic visual impact is always transmitted by a close-up as every motion picture director knows. Here the viewer is inescapably brought face to face with the subject's personal magnetism. This is one picture that says more than a thousand words, so why add another.

Wie jeder Filmregisseur weiß, haben Nahaufnahmen immer die stärkste visuelle Wirkung. Von Angesicht zu Angesicht kann sich der Betrachter der Ausstrahlung des Modells nicht entziehen. Dies ist eins der Bilder, die mehr sagen als tausend Worte. Warum also ein weiteres verlieren?

Comme le sait tout réalisateur de cinéma qui se respecte, rien de tel qu'un gros plan pour obtenir un puissant effet dramatique. Ici, le spectateur ne peut échapper au puissant magnétisme du modèle. L'image parle d'elle-même, alors inutile d'en rajouter.

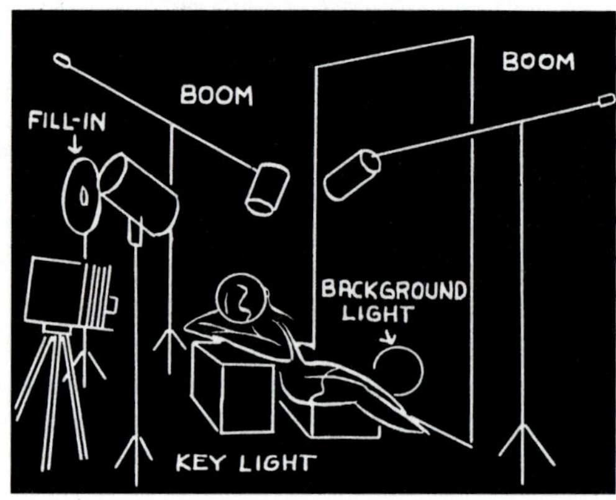

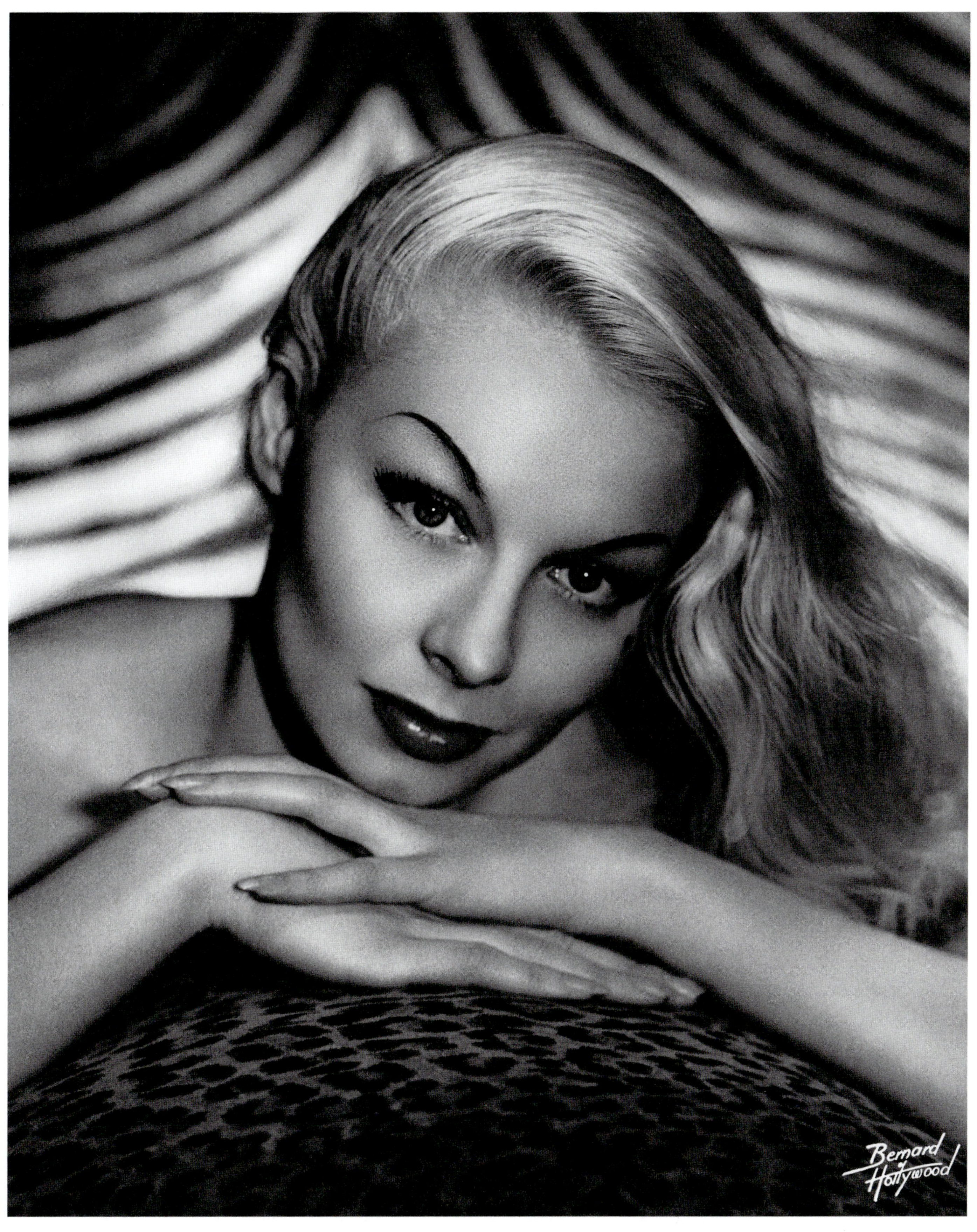

Bewitching and Bewildering

MAGISCHE BLICKE · L'ENSORCELEUSE

Illustration versus Photography

The very word pin-up implies that this is a picture meant to be pinned up and looked at for a long time without the spectator getting tired of it. The art directors of the big calendar companies impress these requirements upon their illustrators. Of course these lucky fellows are in an enviable position when it comes to the glamorization of the subject. They can photograph the living model and then improve upon nature at will. A Vargas or a Petty can elongate legs and bend them in impossible positions without getting wrinkles in the stomach or decreasing the head size.

The photographer has to use a few tricks of his own in order to achieve a similar effect.

The best method to elongate the figure without getting the head too small is to choose a low camera angle and have the model bend forward slightly from the waist up. Photographers using view cameras with tilt and swing backs should make full use of these adjustments, as this method is preferable to the elongation process of tilting the easel in printing. The latter technique entails the danger of distorting the face while attempting to elongate the lower part of the body. However, no matter how skillful the photographer is, he will never be able to take the same "poetic license" in perspective and composition as the brush-and-pen artist.

On the other hand, the photographic pin-up has more realism and therefore greater immediacy for the spectator. He knows *this* girl exists, while the calendar cutie is often the product of a colorful imagination.

While keeping the differences of the two techniques in mind, the photographer can learn a great deal from a comparative study of the different styles of the famous calendar artists.

A short analysis reveals that Vargas is the exponent of the long-stemmed American beauty with a sultry and exotic look; he is the illustrative counterpart of the late Florenz Ziegfeld. From my personal acquaintance with Vargas, I happen to know that for all the exotic impact of his finished drawings, he prefers the natural, wholesome American girl as his working model.

Petty tends to depict the urbane, flapper-type glamor doll who seems to be forever perched on luxurious furnishings with the inevitable white telephone in her dainty hands.

Moran and Armstrong seem to favor the All-American girl – vivacious and saucy, slightly mischievous but irresistibly cute – in short, the kind of girl who can brighten up the drab atmosphere of a machine shop, a business office, a lonely sailor's cabin, or a foxhole.

Whatever their variations in style, they all are past masters in the glorification of the American girl. Study their best-selling calendars, and then don't slavishly imitate, but use them as a guide to make *your own* original pin-ups.

Illustration kontra Fotografie

Schon das Wort Pin-Up verweist darauf, daß es um ein Foto geht, das aufgehängt werden und über einen langen Zeitraum auch aufgehängt bleiben soll, ohne daß der Betrachter seiner überdrüssig wird. Die Artdirektoren der großen Kalenderverlage halten ihre Illustratoren nachdrücklich dazu an, dem gerecht zu werden. Natürlich haben diese Glückspilze einen beneidenswerten Vorteil, wenn es darum geht, ihr Motiv glamourös erscheinen zu lassen. Sie können das Modell aus Fleisch und Blut abfotografieren und dann die Natur nach Gutdünken verbessern.

Der Fotograf hingegen muß in die Trickkiste greifen. Will man etwa die Beine verlängern, ohne daß der Kopf dabei zu klein wird, sollte man eine niedrige Kameraperspektive wählen. Das Modell muß seinen Oberkörper dann leicht nach vorne beugen. Lichtbildkünstler, die eine Fachkamera mit verschwenkbarem Rückteil benutzen, sollten von dieser Vorrichtung beherzt Gebrauch machen. Diese Methode ist dem Schwenken des Vergrößerungskopfes beim Vergrößern unbedingt vorzuziehen, da sonst die Gefahr besteht, das Gesicht zu verzerren, wenn man die untere Körperhälfte zu verlängern versucht. Aber wie versiert der Fotograf auch immer arbeiten mag, er wird bei Perspektive und Bildkomposition nie die „künstlerische Freiheit“ eines Malers und Zeichners genießen.

Auf der anderen Seite besitzt das fotografische Pin-Up einen größeren Realismus und wirkt daher auf den Betrachter unmittelbarer. Er weiß, daß dieses Mädchen tatsächlich existiert, während die Kalenderschönheit oft nur das Produkt einer lebhaften Phantasie ist.

Ein Fotograf kann viel lernen, wenn er die verschiedenen Stile der berühmten Kalenderillustratoren miteinander vergleicht.

Ein solcher Vergleich zeigt, daß Vargas die langbeinige Schönheit mit heißblütigem, exotischem Look bevorzugt. Aus meiner eigenen Bekanntschaft mit ihm weiß ich, daß er trotz der unbestritten exotischen Wirkung seiner Werke doch das bodenständige amerikanische Mädchen als Modell schätzt.

Petty setzt eher auf das urbane, unkonventionelle Glamourgirl, das stets auf luxuriösen Sesseln thront und unweigerlich einen weißen Telefonhörer in der zierlichen Hand hält.

Moran und Armstrong scheinen das All-American Girl zu favorisieren – lebhaft und neckisch, etwas frech, aber unwiderstehlich süß, kurz gesagt, die Sorte Mädchen, die die eintönige Atmosphäre einer Maschinenhalle, eines Büros, einer einsamen Seemannskajüte oder eines Schützengrabens aufheitern kann.

Welchem Typ sie auch immer den Vorzug geben, alle sind sie Großmeister in der Verherrlichung des amerikanischen Mädchens. Studieren Sie ihre auflagenstarken Kalender, aber imitieren Sie dann nicht sklavisch, sondern benutzen Sie diese als Leitfaden, um Ihre ganz eigenen Pin-Ups zu gestalten.

Illustration contre photographie

Le terme « pin-up » implique que l'image est destinée à être punaisée quelque part et admirée pendant longtemps sans qu'on s'en lasse. Les directeurs artistiques des grands éditeurs de calendriers rappellent sans cesse ce principe à leurs illustrateurs. Naturellement, ces derniers ont la chance de pouvoir retoucher leurs sujets. Ils sont libres de photographier leur modèle puis d'améliorer la nature à loisir. Un Vargas ou un Petty, par exemple, peuvent allonger les jambes et les fléchir dans des positions impossibles sans faire plisser le ventre ou faire apparaître la tête trop petite.

Pour obtenir un effet similaire, le photographe, lui, doit avoir recours à quelques stratagèmes.

La meilleure méthode pour allonger une silhouette sans que la tête ne paraisse trop petite, c'est de choisir un angle de vue bas et de demander au modèle d'incliner légèrement le buste en avant. Les photographes utilisant un appareil avec viseur pouvant s'incliner et pivoter sur un axe devraient exploiter au maximum ces possibilités, cette technique étant préférable au processus d'élongation par l'inclinaison du margeur au moment du tirage. Ce dernier présente le risque de déformer le visage en voulant trop étirer la partie inférieure du corps. Toutefois, aussi doué le photographe soit-il, il ne disposera jamais de la même liberté dans la perspective et la composition que l'artiste travaillant avec des pinceaux et des crayons.

D'un autre côté, la pin-up photographique est plus réaliste et présente donc un caractère plus immédiat pour celui qui la regarde. Celui-ci sait que la fille en question existe vraiment, alors que la belle de calendrier n'est souvent que le fruit d'une imagination débridée.

Tout en conservant cette différence fondamentale à l'esprit, le photographe amateur apprendra beaucoup en comparant les différents styles des illustrateurs de calendriers.

Une rapide analyse révèle que Vargas est le chantre de la beauté fatale à longues jambes, sensuelle et exotique. Il est à l'illustration ce que Florenz Ziegfeld était à la revue. Ayant personnellement connu Vargas, je sais qu'en dépit de l'aspect sophistiqué de ses dessins, il préfère utiliser comme modèles de jolies filles naturelles, pleines de santé, à la beauté typiquement américaine.

Petty, lui, dépeint plutôt la jeune citadine émancipée et glamour, qui semble être éternellement perchée sur le coin d'un meuble luxueux, tenant entre ses mains délicates l'inévitable téléphone blanc.

Moran et Armstrong ont une nette préférence pour l'Américaine type, vive et espiègle, légèrement coquine et au charme irrésistible, le genre de fille capable d'égailler l'atmosphère glauque de n'importe quel atelier d'usine, bureau, cabine de marin solitaire ou baraque à soldats.

Quelque soit leur style, ils sont tous passés maîtres dans l'art de glorifier la jeune Américaine. Etudiez bien leurs calendriers, mais ne vous contentez pas de les copier. Utilisez-les comme guides pour créer vos propres pin-up originales.

Composition and Lighting

At a recent photographers' convention, a distinguished lecturer on composition used the painting of an old master to illustrate his theories on the "poetry of composition." Pointing to innumerable spider-web-like diagrams which ran all over the painting, he informed us: "It has taken me years to figure out the dynamic symmetry of this picture, but now at last I have gained the certainty of why it is a masterpiece." Wiping his brow, he added, candidly: "Of course, it is only a hypothesis."

In other words, he might be dead wrong.

Even if he had been right, however, his theories would almost certainly have been news to the original painter, who several centuries ago relied on his creative genius without benefit of geometry.

To some extent, the same is true for photography. Because of the nature of the medium, however, it is far easier to achieve "dynamic symmetry" with a camera.

Basically, composition is the organization of forms in a given space, so that the overall effect is pleasing to the eye. If you have a sense for neatness, and a feeling for rhythm, that is already half the battle. Do not crowd too much into your picture. Yours lens should present a dramatic sector rather than the whole ... In pictorial composition, *less is more.*

In shooting a pin-up, make the human figure the center of attraction, using the studio or scenic background merely as a pictorial accent. Observe Nature closely, and you will find compositional elements in the lines of the shore, the formations of trees or mountains, the patterns of a landscape or a sand dune. Re-create those curves of Nature in your composition of the human figure, correlating the latter to the specific background. To accentuate the vitality of your model, use a diagonal arrangement of her figure in your rectangular compositional frame. Conversely, a horizontal or vertical placement of the figure will result in a static, or more restful atmosphere.

Lighting is not so much dependent on artistic intuition as composition, and can therefore be more easily discussed. Lighting is the technical complement to the expression of moods. Studio lights are to the photographer what brushes are to the painter; lights and shadows are to the one what colors are to the other. Spotlights were used for the studio pin-ups in this book because the author feels they afford better control and separation of the figure from the background. Back-side lighting with just enough front fill-in adds depth to the picture.

By using synchro-sunlight flash shooting, the same lighting system can be applied to outdoor photography. Use the sun, high and to one side, as the main spotlight on your model, and fill in with a flash from the front. Do not put your flash too close to the subject, as this will destroy the balance of lighting so essential to the harmony of the picture. And, finally, skillful lighting is what creates the illusion of three-dimensional reality. Proper back-side lighting will make your pin-up cutie practically step right out of the picture ... in your direction ... you can dream, can't you?

Komposition und Lichtführung

Kürzlich erläuterte ein renommierter Fachmann für Komposition auf einer Fotografentagung anhand des Gemäldes eines Alten Meisters seine Theorien über die „Poesie der Komposition“. Auf die spinnwebartigen Diagramme deutend, die das Gemälde überzogen, erklärte er: „Es hat mich Jahre gekostet, die dynamische Symmetrie dieses Bildes zu entschlüsseln, aber jetzt weiß ich endlich genau, warum es ein Meisterwerk ist.“ Und während er sich über die Stirn fuhr, fügte er freimütig hinzu: „Natürlich ist das alles reine Hypothese.“ Anders gesagt, er könnte auch total auf dem Holzweg sein. Selbst wenn er recht gehabt hätte, seine Theorien wären dem Maler, der sich vor hunderten von Jahren ohne die Hohe Schule der Geometrie nur auf seine Kreativität verlassen mußte, höchstwahrscheinlich neu gewesen.

Das gilt bis zu einem gewissen Grad auch für die Fotografie. Dank der besonderen Natur dieses Mediums ist es mit der Kamera allerdings wesentlich einfacher, eine „dynamische Symmetrie“ zu erreichen. Komposition ist im wesentlichen die Anordnung von Formen in einem vorgegebenen Raum, so daß der Gesamteindruck das Auge anspricht. Wenn man Sinn für einen klaren Stil und ein Gespür für Harmonie hat, hat man schon halb gewonnen.

Packen Sie nicht zuviel in ein Bild. Ihre Linse sollte sich lieber auf einen dramatischen Ausschnitt als auf die Totalansicht konzentrieren ... Bei der Bildkomposition ist weniger mehr.

Wenn man ein Pin-Up ablichtet, sollte die menschliche Gestalt im Mittelpunkt stehen, und der Studiohintergrund oder die natürliche Kulisse sollten lediglich malerische Akzente setzen.

Um die Modelle lebendig wirken zu lassen, arrangieren Sie die Figur diagonal innerhalb Ihres rechtwinkligen Bildrahmens. Umgekehrt erzielt man mit einer horizontalen oder vertikalen Ausrichtung des Modells eine statische, ruhigere Atmosphäre.

Beleuchtung ist die technische Ergänzung zum Ausdruck der Stimmungen. Studiolicht ist für den Lichtbildner, was der Pinsel für den Maler ist; Licht und Schatten sind seine Farben.

Für die Atelier-Pin-Ups wurden in diesem Buch Spotlichter benutzt, weil sie nach Ansicht des Verfassers die Gestalt besser vom Hintergrund abheben. Streiflicht mit nur einer Idee Vorderlicht verleiht dem Bild Tiefe. Bei Freilichtaufnahmen mit synchronisiertem Blitzlichtgerät kann man dieselbe Beleuchtungstechnik anwenden. Benutzen Sie die Sonne als Hauptlicht für Ihr Modell und verstärken Sie es durch einen Blitz von vorne. Gehen Sie mit dem Blitz nicht zu nahe an das Modell heran, denn das würde die für die Harmonie des Bildes so grundlegende Ausgewogenheit der Ausleuchtung zerstören.

Letztlich ist es die fachmännische Lichtführung, die eine Illusion lebendiger Dreidimensionalität erzeugt. Eine richtige Ausleuchtung wird Ihre Pin-Up-Schönheit praktisch aus dem Bild hervortreten lassen ... auf Sie zu ... träumen darf man ja schließlich, oder?

Composition et éclairage

Récemment, lors d'un congrès de photographes, un éminent conférencier spécialiste en composition a utilisé le tableau d'un grand maître pour illustrer ses théories sur « la poésie de la composition ». Indiquant d'innombrables diagrammes complexes qui recouvraient la toile, il a déclaré : « Il m'a fallut des années pour comprendre la symétrie dynamique de cette œuvre mais, à présent, je sais avec certitude pourquoi c'est un chef-d'œuvre ». Essuyant son front moite, il a ajouté avec candeur : « Naturellement, ce n'est qu'une hypothèse. » En d'autres termes, rien n'était moins sûr.

Même s'il avait raison, ses théories surprendraient certainement le peintre en question, qui, il y a plusieurs siècles, se basait uniquement sur son génie créatif sans le bénéfice de la géométrie.

A certains égards, il en va de même avec la photographie. Toutefois, du fait de la nature même de notre art, il est beaucoup plus aisé d'obtenir une « symétrie dynamique » avec un appareil photo.

Fondamentalement, la composition est l'organisation des formes dans un espace donné de sorte que l'effet général soit plaisant à regarder. Si vous avez le sens de la netteté et du rythme, vous avez déjà parcouru la moitié du chemin.

Ne surchargez pas vos images. Votre objectif devrait pointer vers une partie dramatique de la scène plutôt que vers l'ensemble … En matière de composition : « Inutile d'en rajouter ».

Lorsque vous réalisez une image de pin-up, faites en sorte que votre personnage soit le centre d'attention en utilisant votre toile de fond ou le décor naturel comme un simple détail pictural.

Si vous voulez accentuer la vitalité de votre modèle, cadrez sa silhouette en diagonale dans le rectangle de votre viseur. Inversement, une disposition verticale ou horizontale du corps créera une atmosphère plus statique et sereine.

L'éclairage est le complément technique de l'ambiance. Les lumières de studio sont au photographe ce que les pinceaux sont au peintre. Les ombres et les lumières sont au premier ce que les couleurs sont au second.

Les pin-up de studio présentées dans ce livre ont été réalisées avec des spots car, à mon sens, ils permettent de mieux contrôler la lumière et de faire ressortir le personnage de l'arrière-plan. L'éclairage par derrière avec quelques sources de lumière secondaires par devant ajoute de la profondeur au champ. En associant des flashs à la lumière solaire, on peut obtenir le même effet en extérieur. Utilisez le soleil, haut et de côté, comme source principale sur votre modèle et ajoutez un flash par devant comme source secondaire. Ne placez pas votre flash trop près du sujet, cela détruirait l'équilibre de la lumière essentiel à l'harmonie générale.

Enfin, un éclairage bien étudié peut créer l'illusion d'une image en trois dimensions. En éclairant judicieusement votre pin-up par derrière, vous la ferez littéralement jaillir hors de l'image … comme si elle se jetait dans vos bras. On peut toujours rêver, non ?

To create a provocative mood picture of supercharged magnetism, a coppery costume was draped around the figure, sarong fashion. The feeling of impending shock is brought out by use of a yellow filter to darken an otherwise blue sky adding somber contrast to the blonde hair. Shot in bright sunlight with a flash fill-in. 1/100 second at f/18, K-2 filter.

Um ein provokantes, atmosphärisch dichtes Bild von außerordentlicher Anziehungskraft zu schaffen, wurde das Modell in ein sarongähnliches Lurexkostüm gehüllt. Der Eindruck eines aufziehenden Gewitters wird durch einen Gelbfilter erzeugt, der den blauen Himmel toniger macht und einen dunklen Kontrast zum blonden Haar hervorruft. Bei hellem Sonnenschein mit einem Aufhellblitz fotografiert. 1/100 Sekunde bei f/18, K-2-Filter.

Pour cette image provoquante au magnétisme survolté, le modèle s'est drapé dans un costume cuivré façon sarong. L'impression d'explosion imminente est due à un filtre jaune qui obscurcit le ciel bleu et ajoute un contraste sombre aux cheveux blonds. Prise à la lumière du jour avec des flashs. 1/100ème de seconde à f/18, filtre K-2.

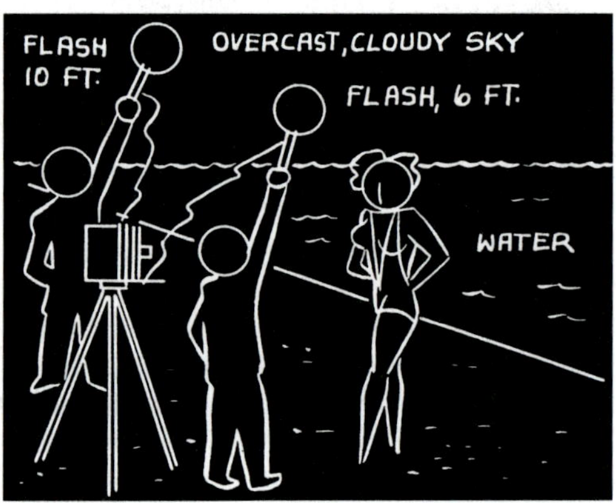

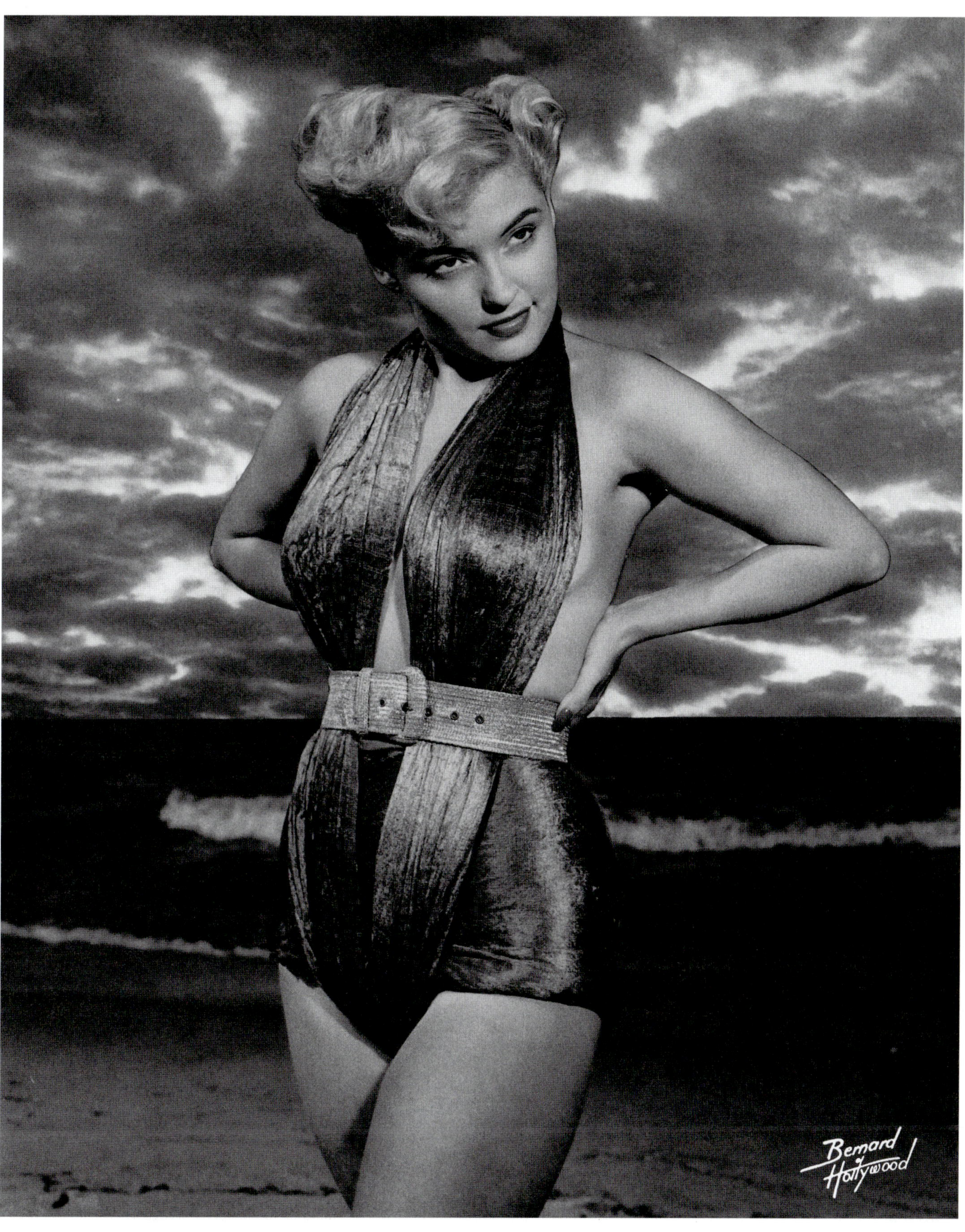

High Voltage

HOCHSPANNUNG · HAUTE TENSION

The most perfect composition is often suggested by the curves of Nature. Here a weather eaten piling has been used as a norm for the body swing. The rope serves as counterbalance and emphasis of movement already expressed through the diagonal composition. Red filter is used to darken sky and to make the face, sailor hat and thighs stand out.

Linien und Formen von Objekten der Natur animieren häufig zu den besten Kompositionen. Hier lieferte ein verwitterter Pfahl das Vorbild für die Körperhaltung. Das Tau dient als Gegengewicht und betont das dynamische Element, das schon in der diagonalen Komposition angelegt ist. Ein Rotfilter läßt den Himmel dunkler erscheinen und hebt das Gesicht, die Seemannsmütze und die Oberschenkel deutlicher hervor.

C'est dans les lignes de la nature qu'on trouve souvent l'inspiration pour la composition la plus parfaite. Ici, un pilier rongé par le temps a été utilisé pour accentuer l'inclinaison du corps. La corde permet de contrebalancer et de souligner le mouvement, déjà exprimé par la composition en diagonale. Un filtre rouge a été utilisé pour assombrir le ciel et faire ressortir le visage, le bonnet de marin et les cuisses.

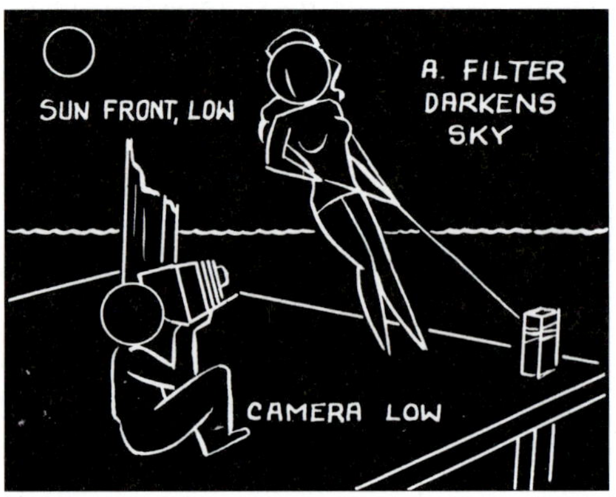

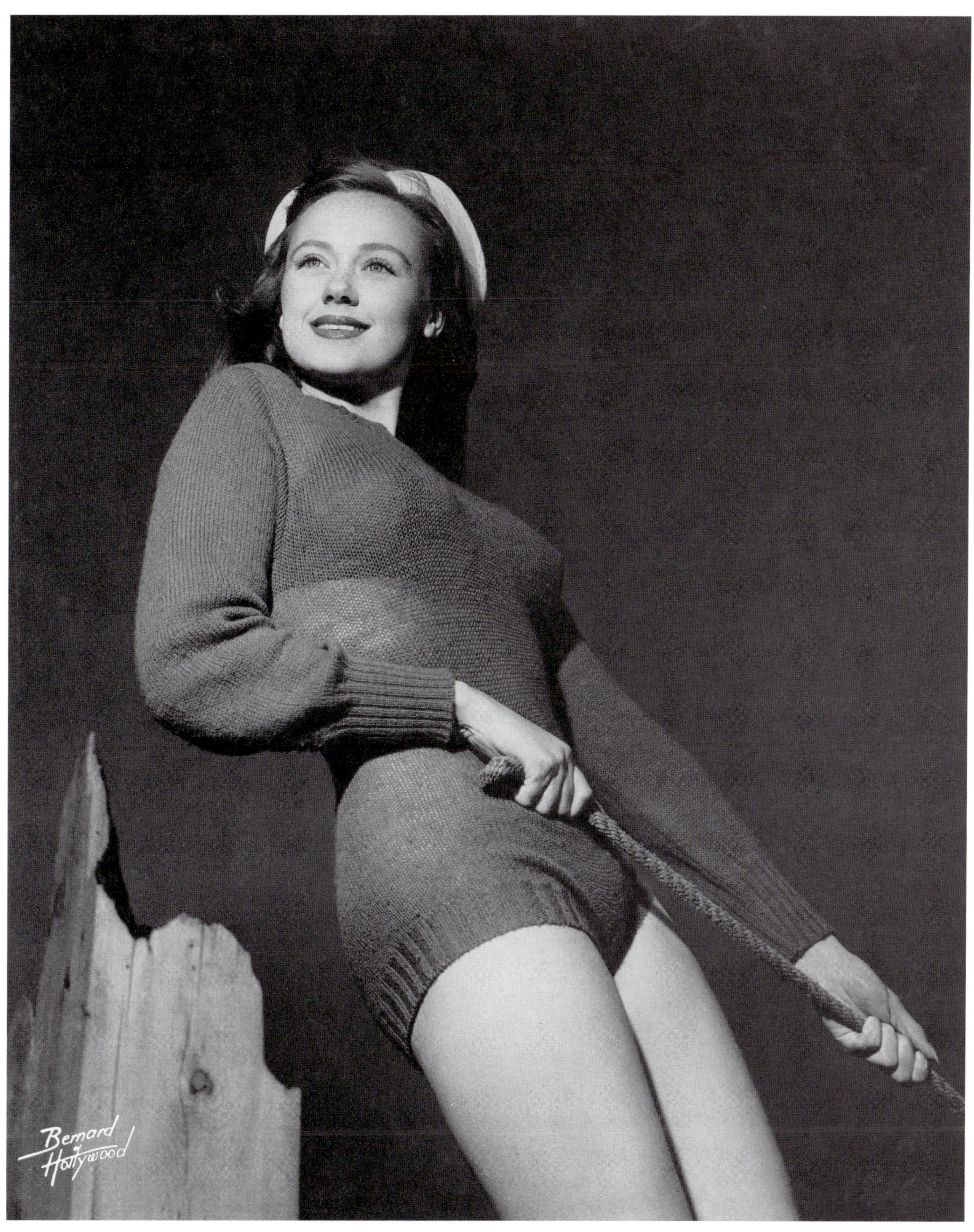

Ship Shape

LEINEN LOS! · ET VOGUE LE NAVIRE !

An extremely low camera angle is used to dramatize the long-limbed beauty of the subject. Early afternoon sunlight from the right records the plasticity of the figure and the pilings creating an almost stereoscopic effect. The polaroid filter puts subtle shades into an otherwise monotone sky. 4x5 Speed Graphic, 1/100 second at f/18, Panchro Press-B.

Um die langen Beine dieser Schönen zu betonen, wurde eine sehr tiefe Kameraposition gewählt. Das Sonnenlicht eines frühen Nachmittags hebt die Plastizität der Gestalt und der Pfähle hervor und schafft einen fast stereoskopischen Effekt. Der Polarisationsfilter bringt größere Kontraste in den ansonsten eintönigen Himmel. 4x5 Speed Graphic, 1/100 Sekunde bei f/18, Panchro Press-B-Film.

L'angle de vue à ras de terre accentue la longueur des jambes superbes de ce modèle. Le soleil de début d'après-midi souligne la plasticité de sa silhouette et des piliers, créant un effet presque stéréoscopique. Un filtre Polaroïd donne des nuances subtiles à un ciel autrement monotone. 4x5 Speed Graphic, 1/100ème de seconde à f/18, pellicule Panchro Press-B.

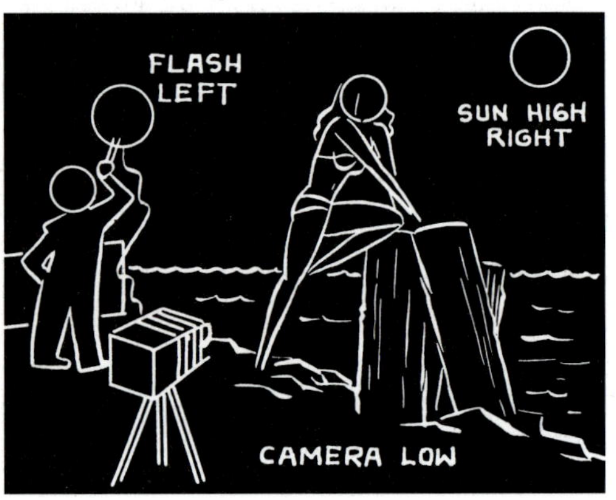

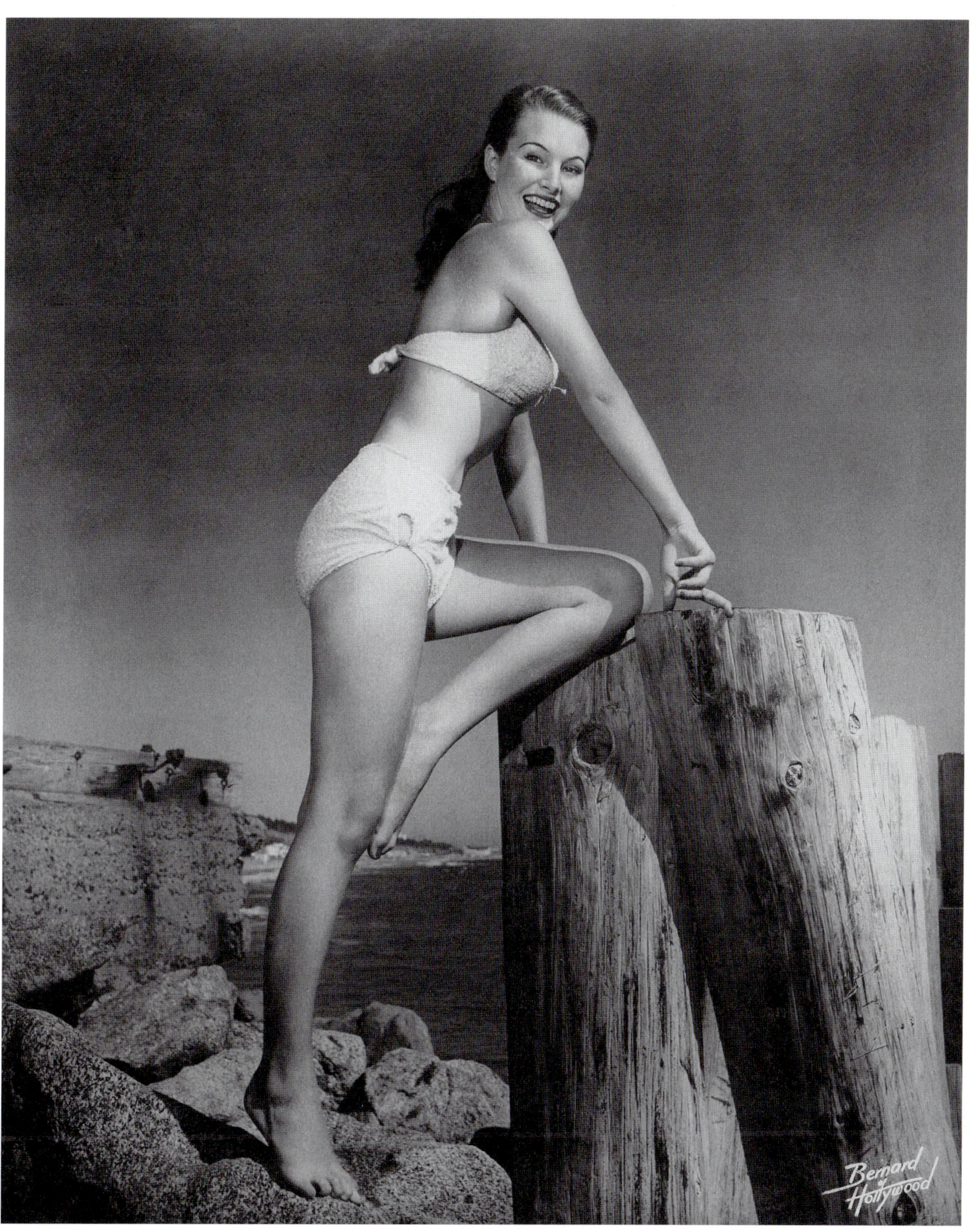

Rock Bottom

KÜSTENWACHE · PAR LE FOND

An interesting pattern of curves and lines is created by contrasting the vertical lines of the human body with the sweeping curves of tall desert reeds. The upward projection of the figure results from a low camera angle and a short foreground in contrast to the larger space over the head, leading the eye in an upright direction.

Der Kontrast zwischen den vertikalen Linien des menschlichen Körpers und den schwungvollen Kurven des hohen Riedgrases schafft ein spannungsreiches Muster. Die aufstrebende Perspektive wird durch die tiefe Kameraposition erzeugt und den verkürzten Vordergrund im Vergleich zum weiteren Raum über dem Kopf. So wird der Blick nach oben geführt.

En faisant contraster la verticalité du corps et la sinuosité des roseaux du désert, on obtient un intéressant motif de lignes et de courbes. L'objectif a été placé bas et le premier plan a été réduit au maximum pour faire ressortir la partie supérieure de l'image et attirer le regard vers le haut.

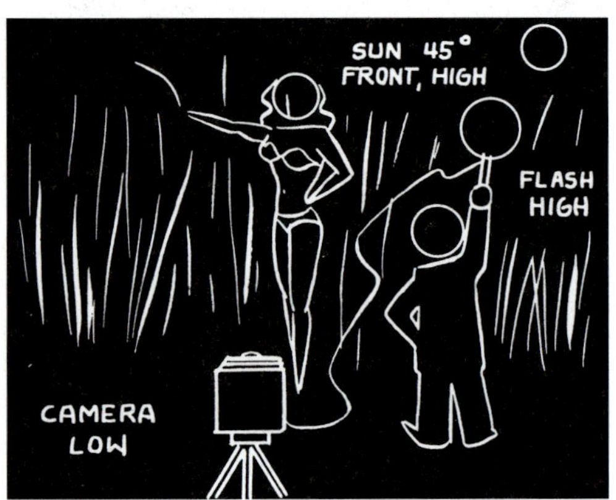

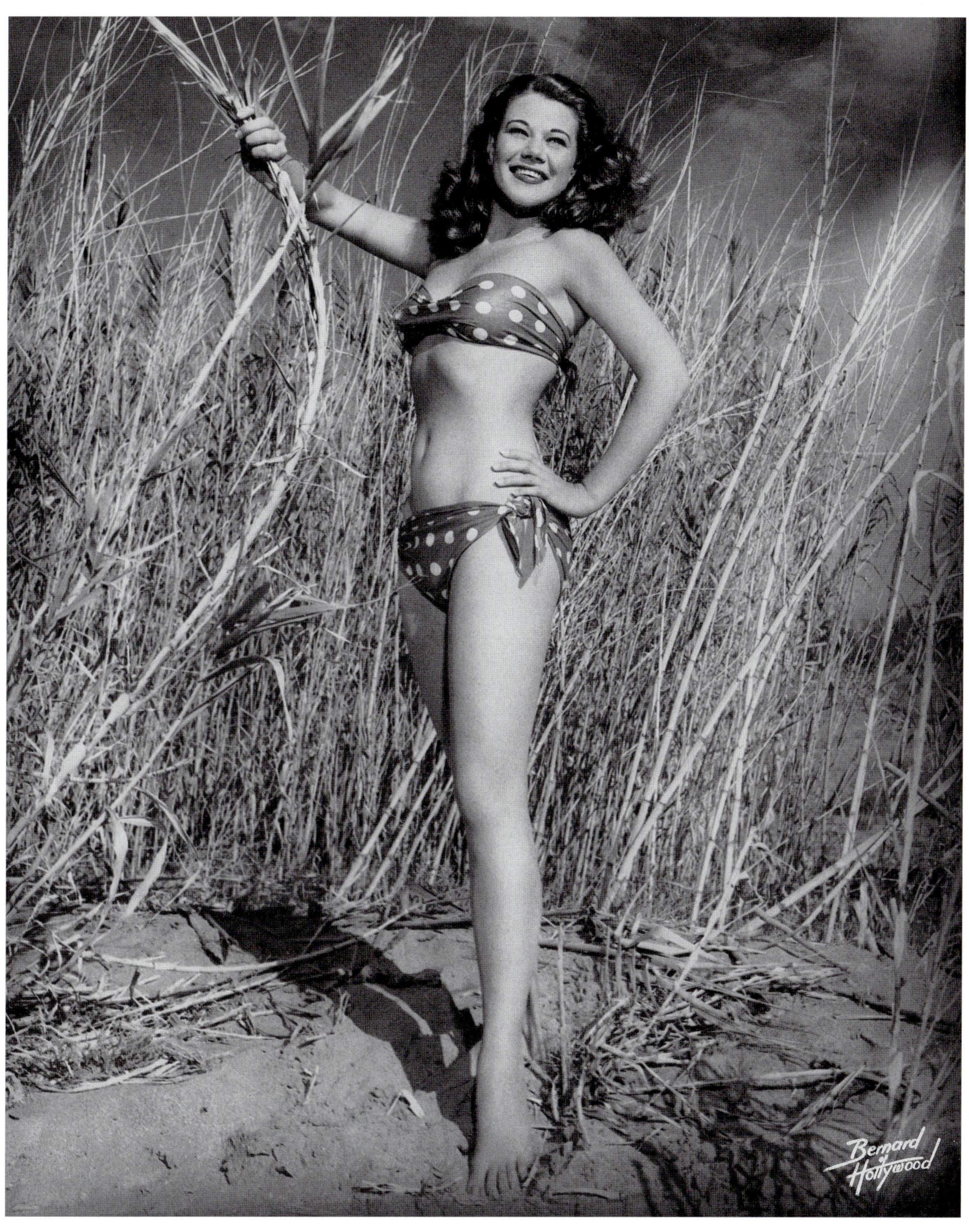

Recommended Reeding

GRASHÜPFER · ELLE PLIE MAIS NE ROMPT PAS

A very modern girl in a glamorized version of Grandma's corset suffers none of the straight-laced agony her old sisters had to go through, if this saucy twinkle means anything. The innocent playfulness of the situation is brought out by the extremely carefree pose. 1/10 second at f/11.

Ein Mädchen von heute in einer todschicken Version von Großmutters Korsett. Der schelmische Blick sagt alles – von Qualen in steifem Fischbein, wie sie ihre älteren Schwestern litten, kann hier keine Rede sein. Die unschuldige Verspieltheit der Situation wird durch die ausgesprochen zwanglose Pose betont. 1/10 Sekunde bei f/11.

Cette jeune femme moderne qui pose dans une version glamour du corset de nos grands-mères ne semble pas souffrir des contraintes de ses aînées, comme en témoigne son air malicieux. Le côté ludique et innocent de la situation est accentué par le naturel de la pose. 1/10ème de seconde à f/11.

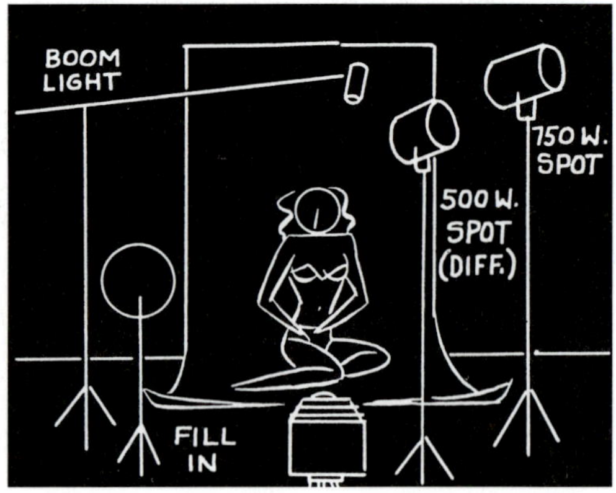

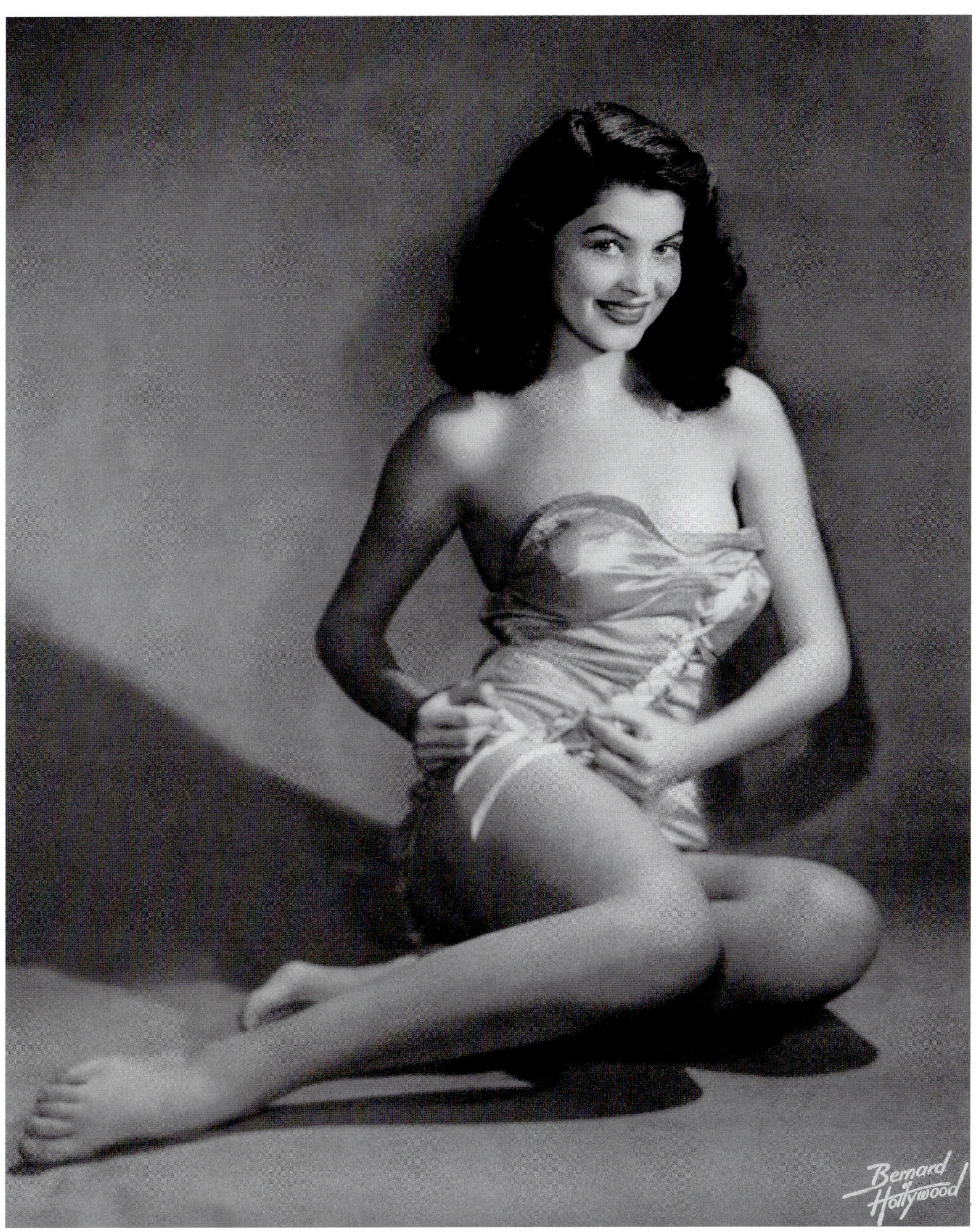

Strings for Holiday

HÜBSCH VERPACKT · CORSÉ !

The crouching position and costume camouflage serve to create the impression of a black panther about to pounce upon its prey. The use of bamboo backdrop suggests the tropical setting, while the almost translucent effect is achieved by placing a spotlight behind the bamboo screen simultaneously playing upon the model's black hair. 1/5 second at f/18.

Die geduckte Haltung und das Fellkostüm lassen an einen Panther denken, der im Begriff ist, sich auf seine Beute zu stürzen. Die Bambusmatte im Hintergrund unterstreicht das exotische Flair. Ein hinter den Bambusvorhang plaziertes Gegenlicht läßt diesen fast transparent erscheinen und betont gleichzeitig das schwarze Haar des Modells. 1/5 Sekunde bei f/18.

La position semi-allongée et le maillot de bain qui se fond dans le dessus de lit en léopard créent l'impression d'une panthère prête à bondi sur sa proie. L'arrière-plan en bambous suggère un décor tropical. L'effet presque translucide est obtenu en plaçant derrière l'écran de bambous un spot qui éclaire la chevelure noire du modèle. 1/5ème de seconde à f/18.

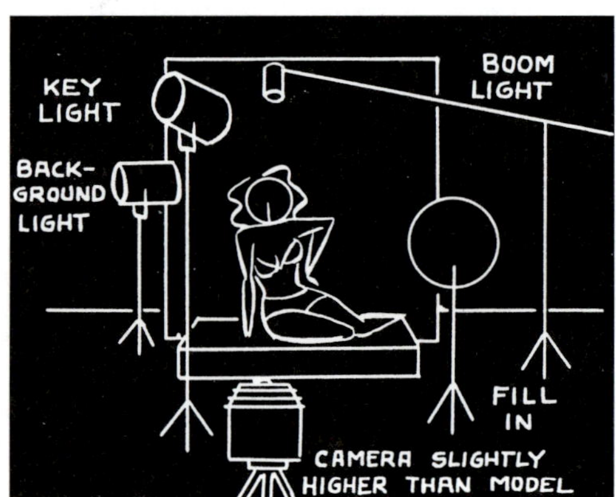

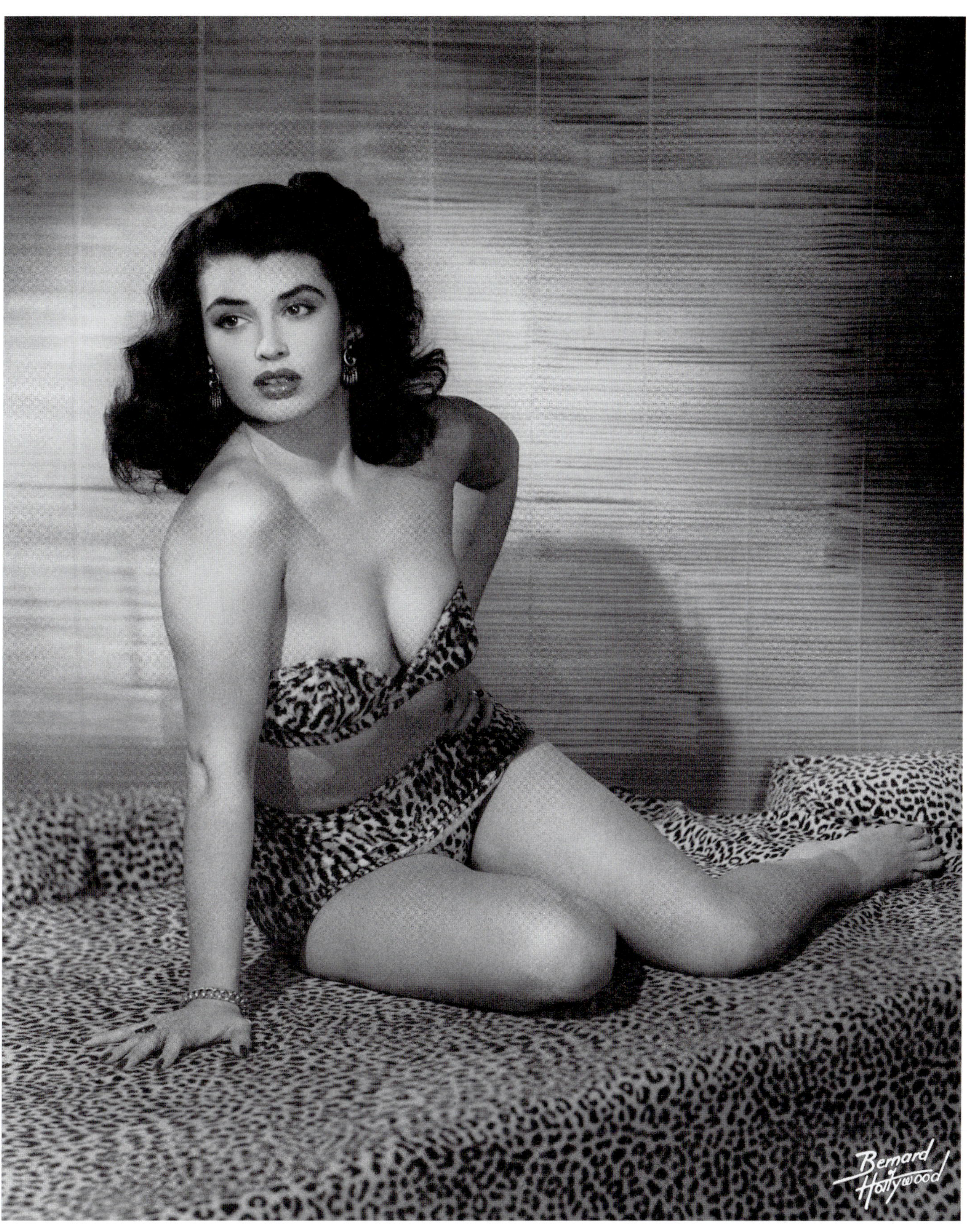

Tropicale

SPRUNGBEREIT · TROPICALE

Youth, playfulness and spontaneity exude from this natural action pose. The elongation of the legs is accentuated by the low camera angle and brevity of the costume improvised from two pieces of fluorescent satin.

Diese lebhafte Pose strahlt Jugendlichkeit, Verspieltheit und Spontaneität aus. Die tiefe Kameraposition und das knappe Kleidungsstück, das aus zwei Teilen schimmernden Satins improvisiert wurde, betonen die langen Beine.

Cette pose naturelle et dynamique respire la jeunesse, la gaieté et la spontanéité. La longueur des jambes est accentuée par la position basse de l'objectif et par le petit maillot improvisé avec deux bandes de satin fluorescent.

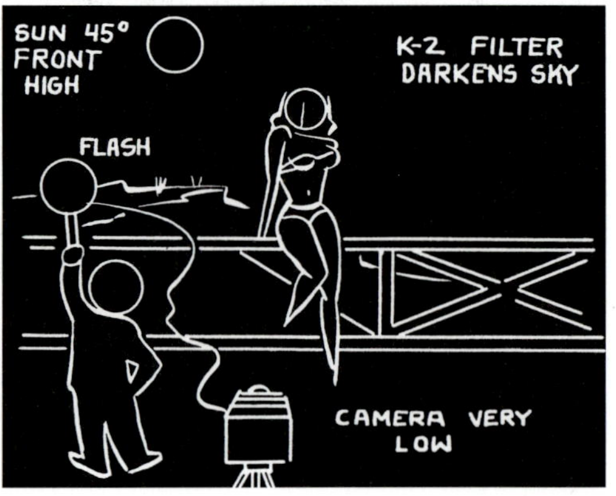

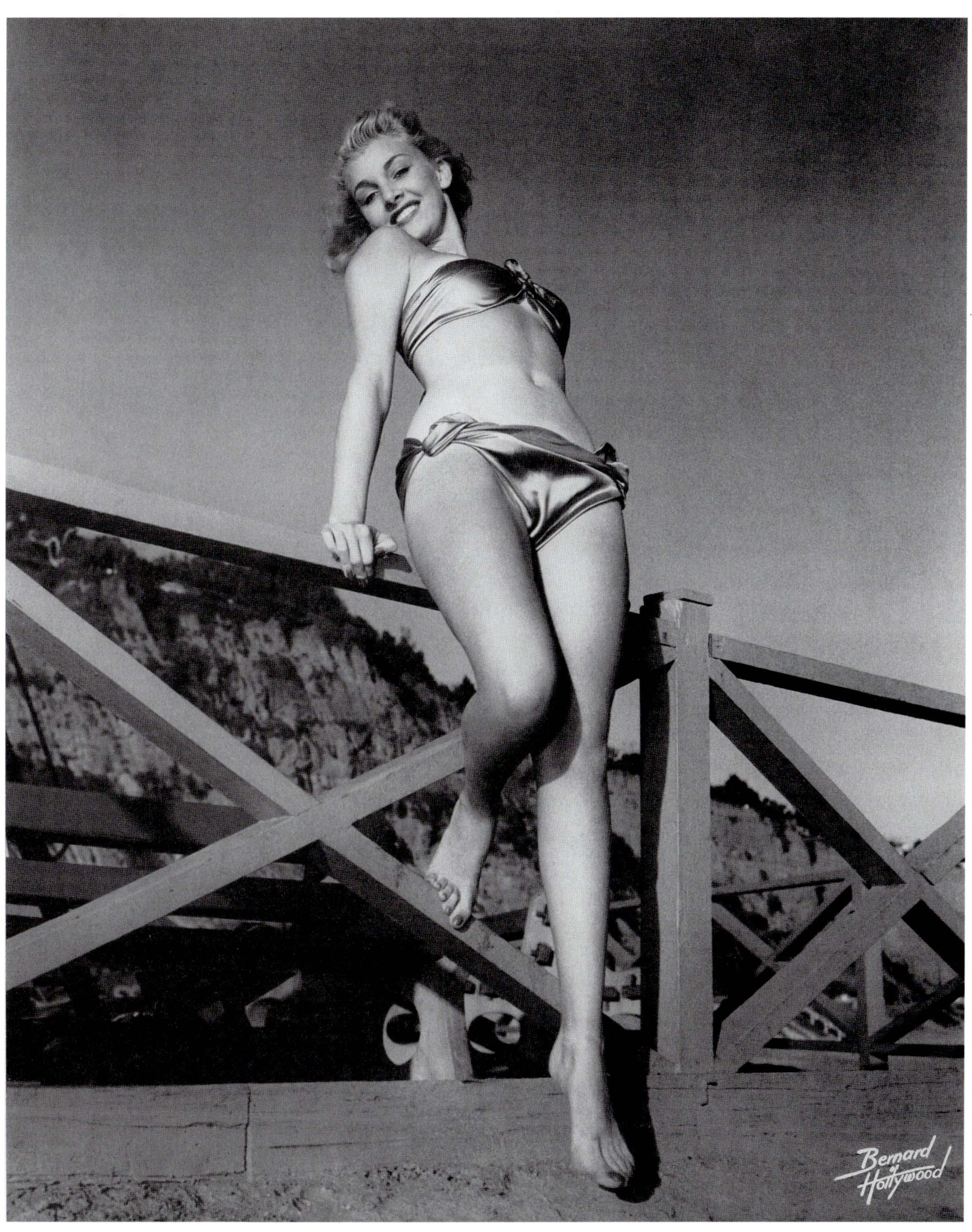

Last Hurdle

DIE LETZTE HÜRDE · LA DERNIÈRE HAIE

An unusually bold compositional study, easy on the eye, but hard to achieve for both subject and photographer. Visualization of the end result and careful rehearsing is necessary to catch the one climactic instant without exhausting the model. 4x5 Speed Graphic, 1/100 second at f/22, K-2 filter.

Eine ungewöhnlich ausdrucksstarke Komposition, hübsch anzuschauen, aber eine schwierige Aufgabe sowohl für das Modell als auch den Fotografen. Eine genaue Vorstellung vom angestrebten Endresultat und eine gründliche Vorbereitung sind notwendig, um diesen einen entscheidenden Augenblick einzufangen, ohne das Modell zu überanstrengen. 4x5 Speed Graphic, 1/100 Sekunde bei f/22, K-2 Filter.

Une composition particulièrement audacieuse, simple à regarder mais difficile à réaliser, tant pour le modèle que pour le photographe. Pour saisir l'instant idéal sans épuiser le modèle, il faut bien visualiser l'image que l'on souhaite obtenir et la répéter à l'avance. 4x5 Speed Graphic, 1/100ème de seconde à f/22, filtre K-2.

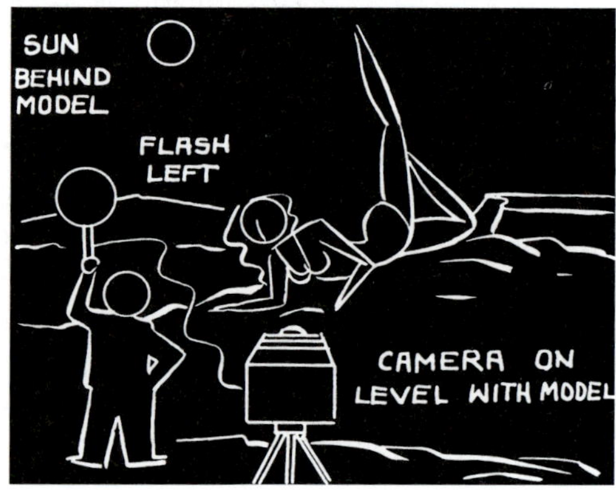

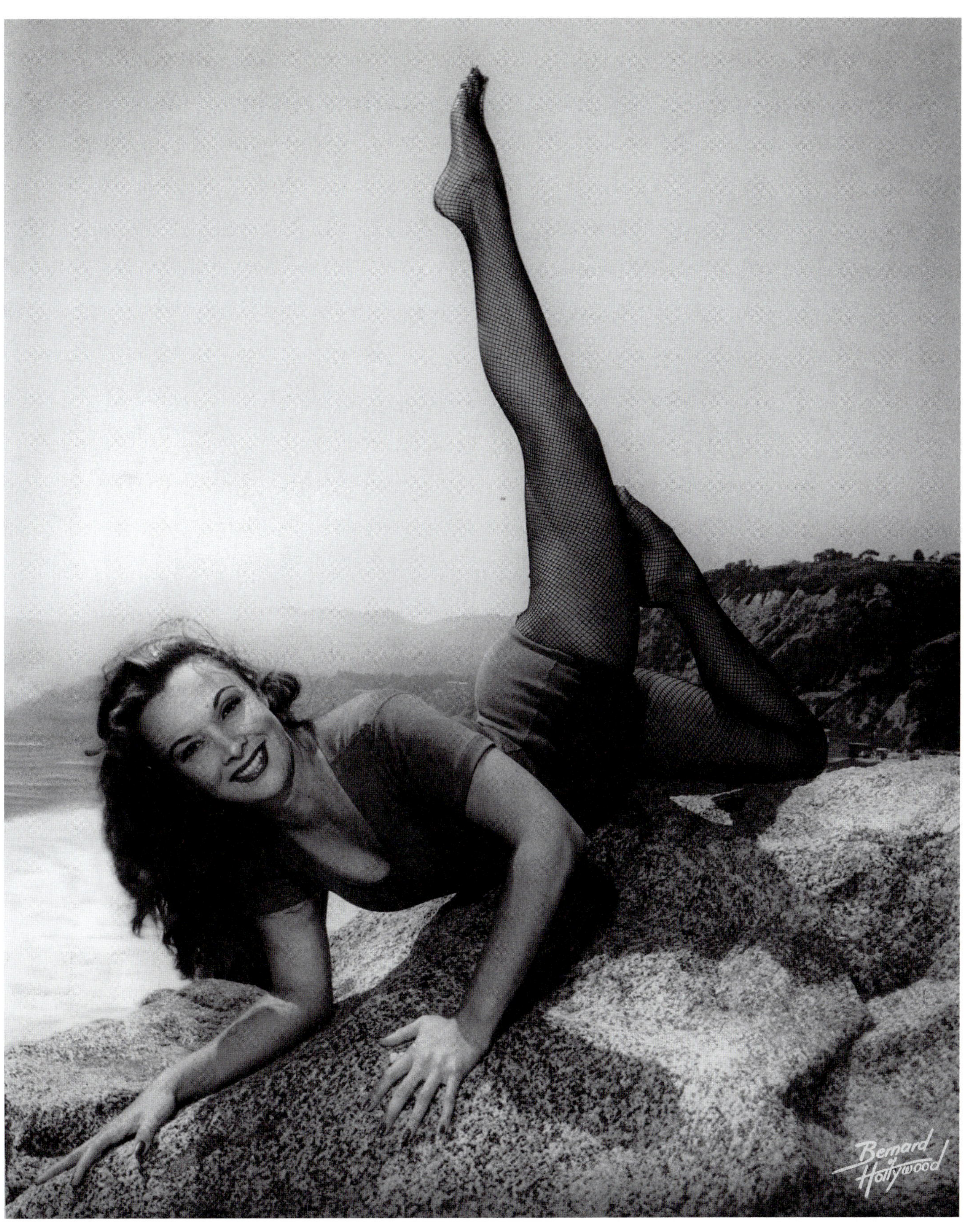

Skyscraper

GIPFELSTÜRMERIN · GRATTE-CIEL

Even a broken-down fence on any country road can serve as an effective setting. The danger of stationary posing is avoided here by tilting the camera to such a degree that the converging rail and mountain crest give depth and movement to the picture. The absolute diagonal posture of the model completes the dynamic pattern. Back-side lighting of the sun produces exceptional modeling of the legs which is maintained by keeping the flash fill-in at ten feet distance. 1/100 second at f/22, K-2 filter.

Selbst ein morscher Zaun an einer Landstraße kann eine wirkungsvolle Kulisse sein. Um eine zu statische Pose zu vermeiden, wird die Kamera so weit verschwenkt, daß die aufeinander zulaufenden Linien von Geländer und Bergkamm dem Bild Tiefe und Dynamik verleihen. Die konsequent diagonale Ausrichtung des Modells vervollständigt die dynamische Struktur. Das Streiflicht der Sonne bewirkt eine außergewöhnliche Modellierung der Beine. Um sie zu bewahren, kommt der Aufhellblitz aus drei Meter Entfernung. 1/100 Sekunde bei f/22, K-2-Filter.

Même une vieille clôture brisée sur une petite route de campagne peut servir d'accessoire efficace. Ici, on a évité le danger d'une pose trop statique en inclinant l'objectif de sorte que la rambarde et la silhouette de la montagne convergent, donnant ainsi de la profondeur et du mouvement à l'image. La posture diagonale du modèle complète le mouvement dynamique. Le soleil venant de derrière les jambes du sujet, ce qui est encore accentué par un flash placé à trois mètres de distance. 1/100ème de seconde à f/22, filtre K-2.

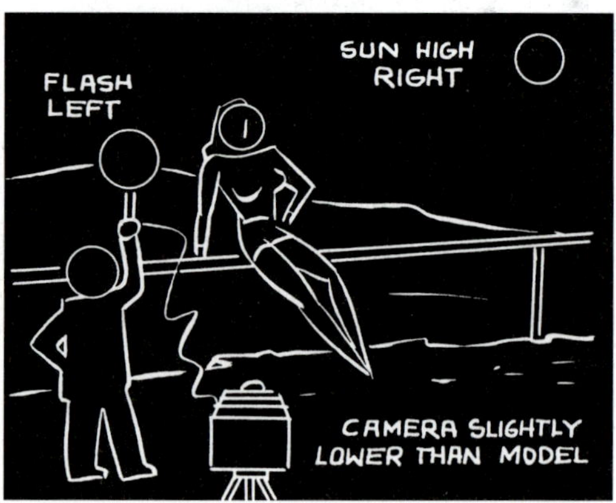

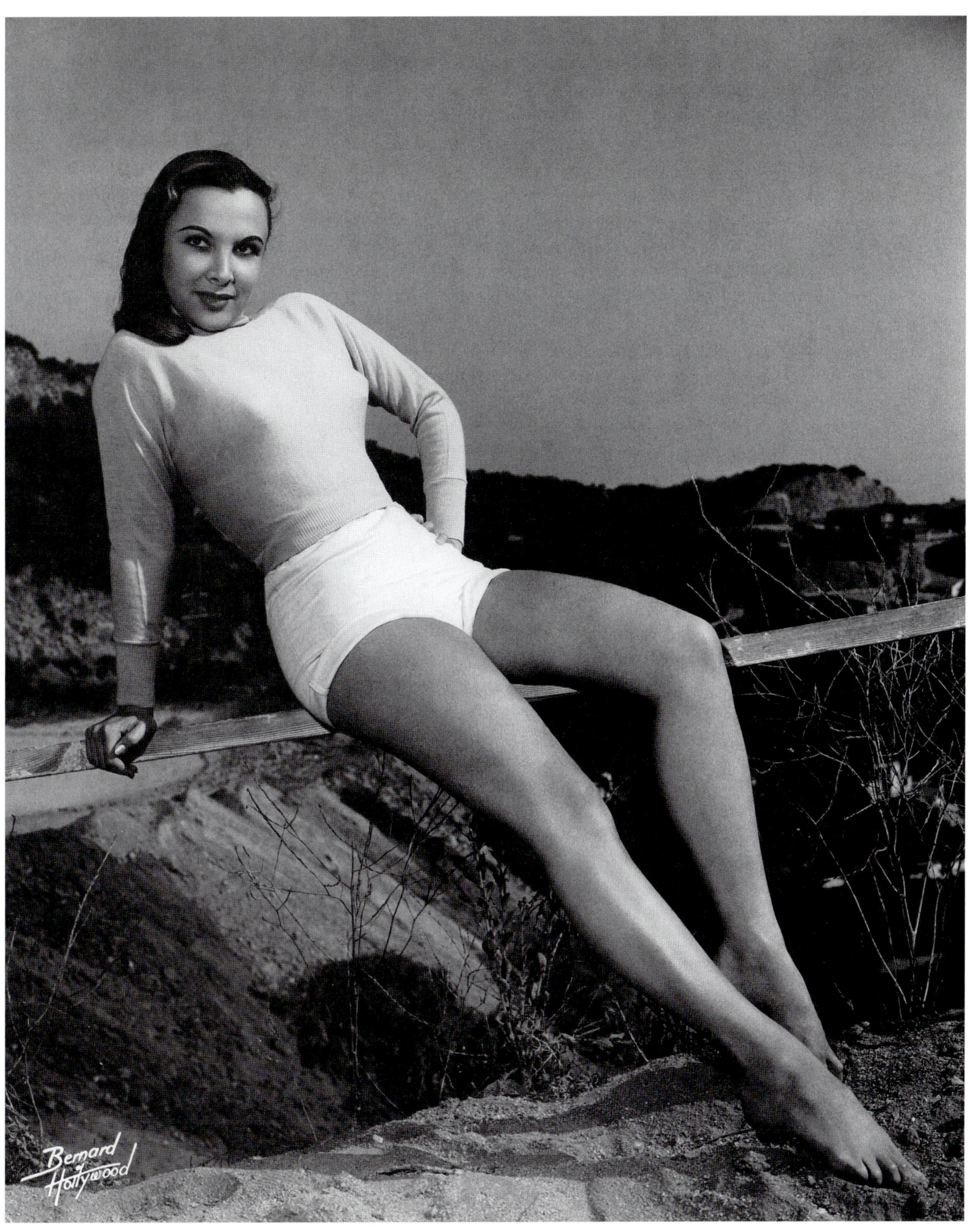

On the Beam

ZAUNGAST · EXERCICE À LA BARRE

Editorial demand for magazine covers often necessitates a pose which confines the entire figure to a small, rectangular area. This offers the advantage of giving the face close-up treatment while getting the whole body into the composition. 4x5 Ansco view camera, 1/100 second at f/10.

Für Zeitschriftencover ist oft eine Pose gefragt, die die Gestalt in ein layoutgerecht schmales, rechteckiges Format zwängt. Das bietet allerdings den Vorteil, daß man das Gesicht in Nahaufnahme zeigen und gleichzeitig den ganzen Körper ins Bild bringen kann. 4x5 Ansco view camera, 1/100 Sekunde bei f/10.

Lorsqu'on réalise une couverture de magazine, il faut souvent choisir une pose qui enferme le sujet dans un petit espace rectangulaire. Cela présente l'avantage de traiter le visage comme un gros plan, tout en intégrant l'ensemble du corps dans la composition. 4x5 Ansco view camera, 1/100ème de seconde à f/10.

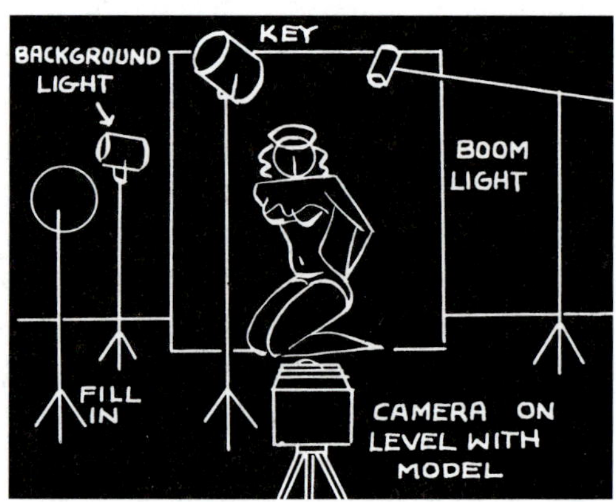

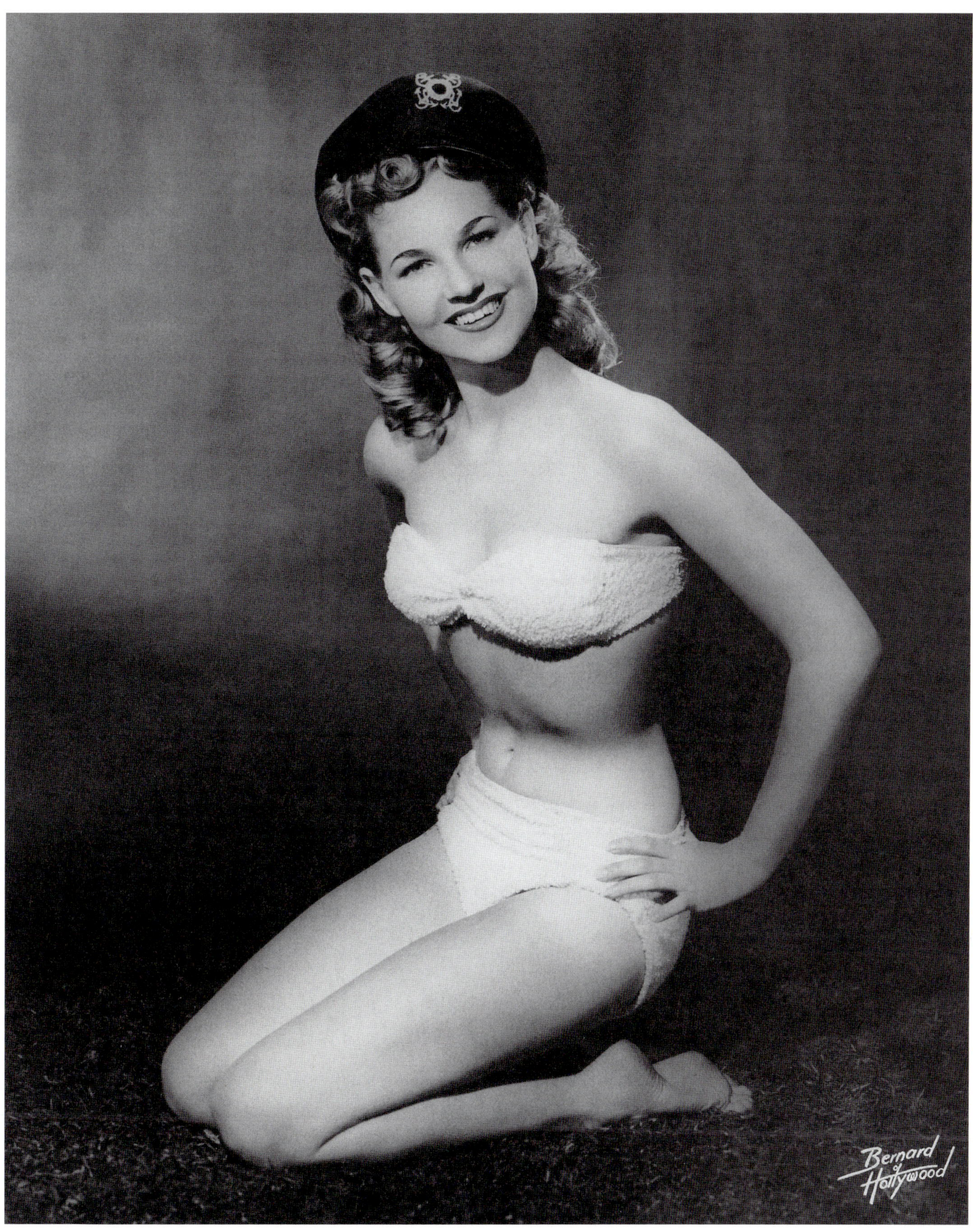

Sailor Maid

LOTSE AN BORD · LA MOUSSAILLONNE

A real tomboy far away from civilization … sweet and serene like the girl next door! This picture shows that effective photographs on the beach are not dependent on bright sunlight. Taken in the Indiana sand dunes at dusk on a very cloudy day, front side light was supplied by two flashes, the one on the face being diffused. 1/100 second at f/20.

Ein echter Wildfang fern der Zivilisation … nett und gutgelaunt wie das Mädchen von nebenan! Dieses Bild beweist, daß gelungene Aufnahmen am Strand nicht auf strahlenden Sonnenschein angewiesen sind. Es wurde in den Dünen Indianas an einem sehr wolkigen Tag in der Abenddämmerung aufgenommen. Das Vorderlicht kam von zwei Blitzlichtern, das auf das Gesicht gerichtete trug einen Diffusorvorsatz. 1/100 Sekunde bei f/20.

Un garçon manqué loin de toute civilisation … douce et sereine comme une fille bien de chez nous ! Cette image prouve que le soleil n'est pas indispensable pour réussir une bonne photo sur la plage : elle a été prise dans les dunes de sable de l'Indiana au crépuscule sous un ciel couvert. Deux flashs fournissent la lumière latérale, celui orienté sur le visage étant diffus. 1/100ème de seconde à f/20.

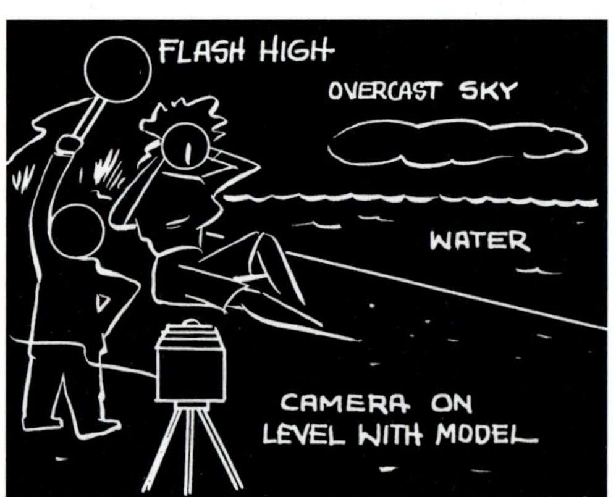

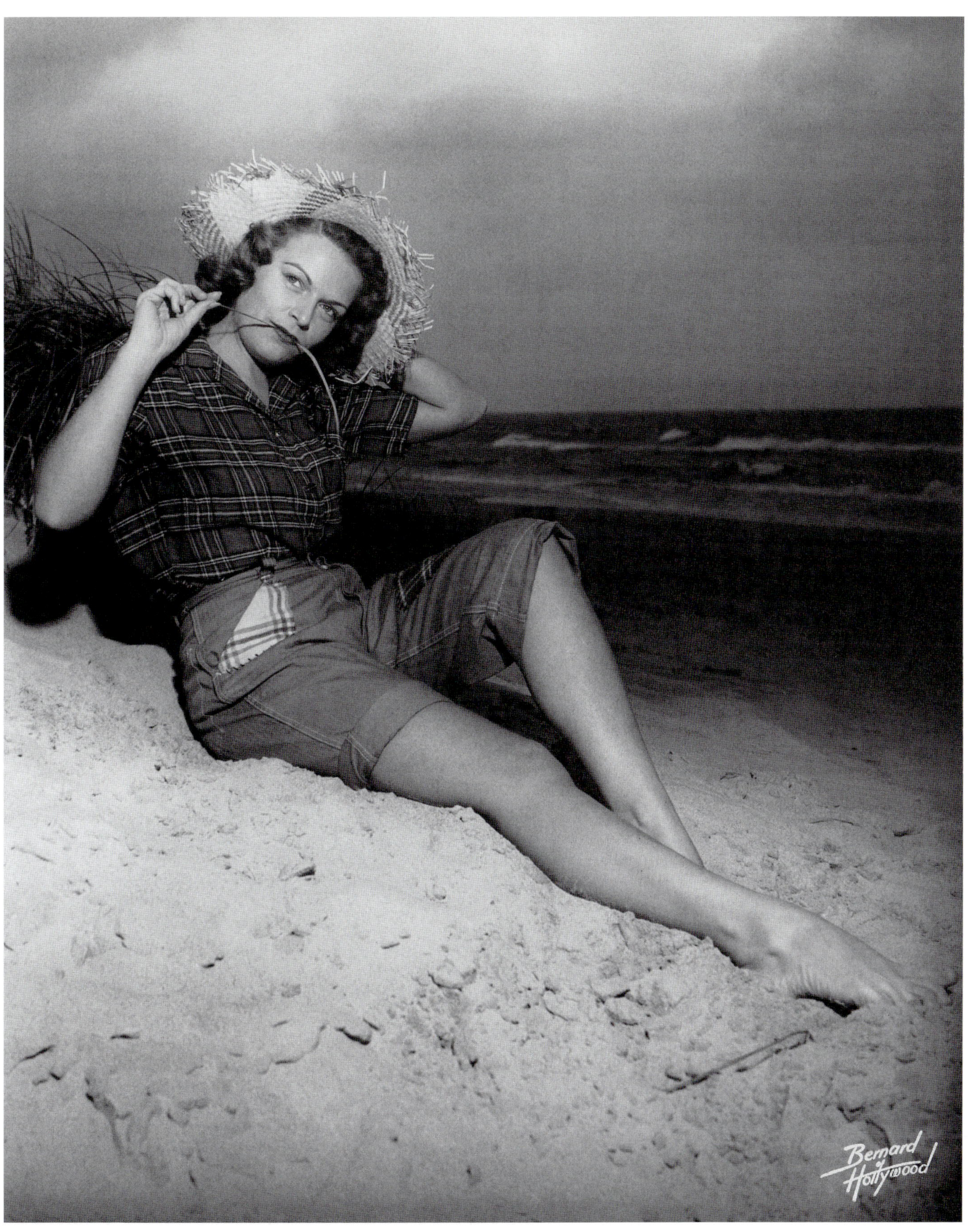

Peach Comber

STRANDPIRATIN · LA GARÇONNE

The model's graceful curves blend harmoniously with the shape of Nature, represented by this sweeping tree formation. Although the picture was shot in the shade, sufficient highlights are provided by flash fill-in and sun-tan lotion on the body. 1/100 second at f/18.

Die anmutigen Kurven des Modells fügen sich harmonisch in die natürliche Kulisse ein, hier die geschwungene Linie eines Baumstamms. Obwohl die Aufnahme im Schatten gemacht wurde, sorgen ein Aufhellblitz und das Sonnenöl auf der Haut des Modells für genügend Spitzlichter. 1/100 Sekunde bei f/18.

Les courbes gracieuses du modèle se fondent harmonieusement avec les formes de la nature, ici une branche sinueuse. Comme le sujet était dans l'ombre, on l'a éclairé au flash après avoir enduit son corps d'huile solaire. 1/100ème de seconde à f/18.

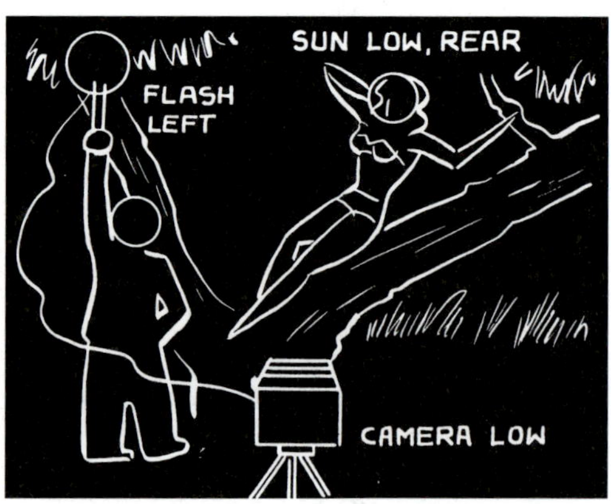

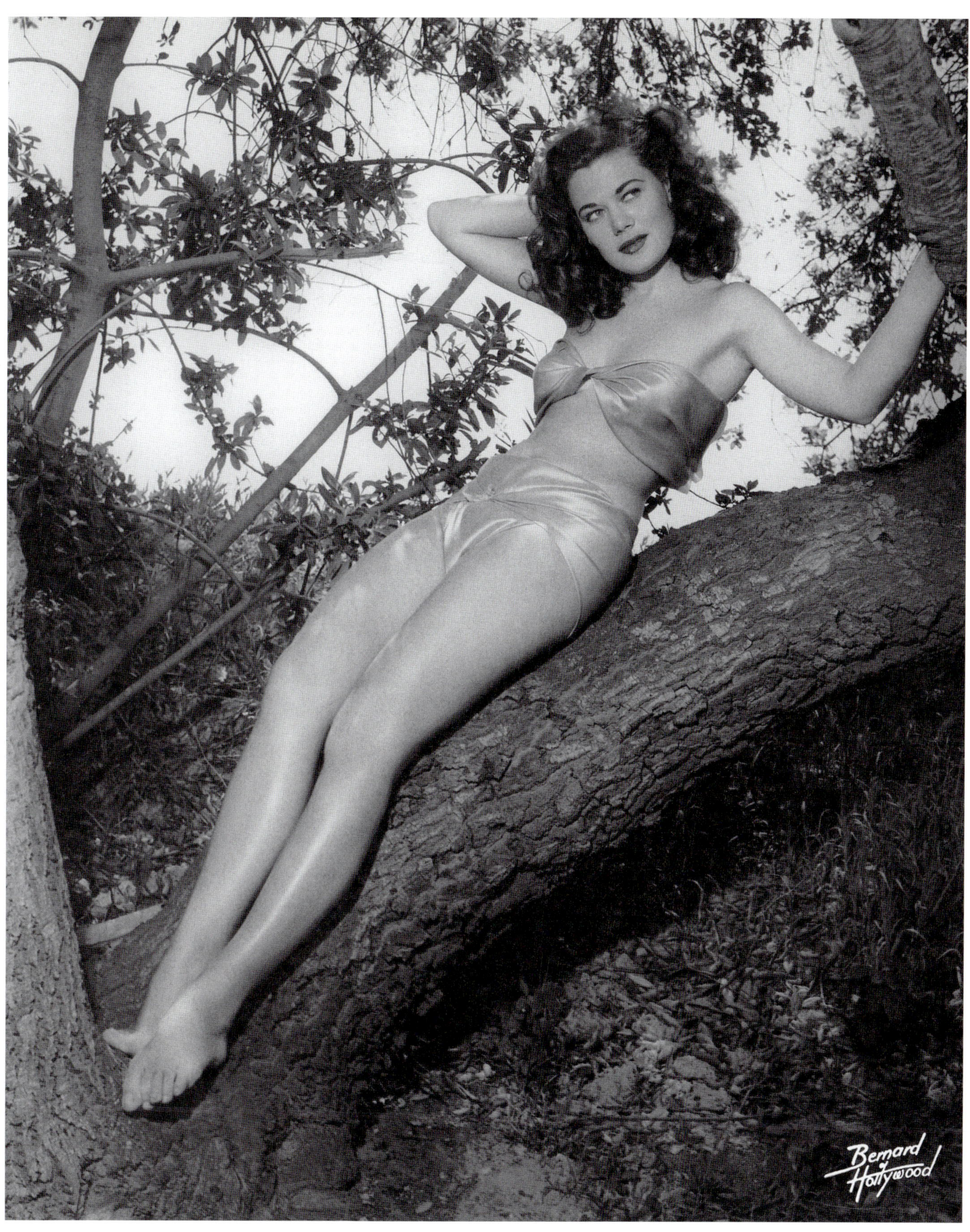

Branching Out

KLETTERPARTIE · COMME UN OISEAU SUR LA BRANCHE

This utopian island setting was created with the aid of a few simple studio props and the imagination of the model who draped her makeshift sarong out of burlap and fish netting. Simplicity of lighting lends heightened interest to the focal point of the picture: the alluring facial expression which speaks without words in any language. 1/5 second at f/16.

Diese Inselphantasie wurde mit Hilfe einiger einfacher Requisiten und dank des Einfallsreichtums des Modells realisiert. Den provisorischen Sarong hat sie sich aus einem Jutesack und einem Fischernetz selbst genäht. Die unkomplizierte Lichtführung betont den eigentlichen Blickfang des Bildes: das verführerische Gesicht, das eine Sprache spricht, die man auf der ganzen Welt versteht. 1/5 Sekunde bei f/16.

Ce décor imaginaire d'île tropicale a été créé grâce à quelques accessoires simples et l'imagination du modèle qui s'est improvisé un sarong dans une toile de jute et un filet de pêche. La simplicité de l'éclairage permet d'attirer le regard vers le point central de l'image : l'expression du modèle qui se passe de commentaire. 1/5ème de seconde à f/16.

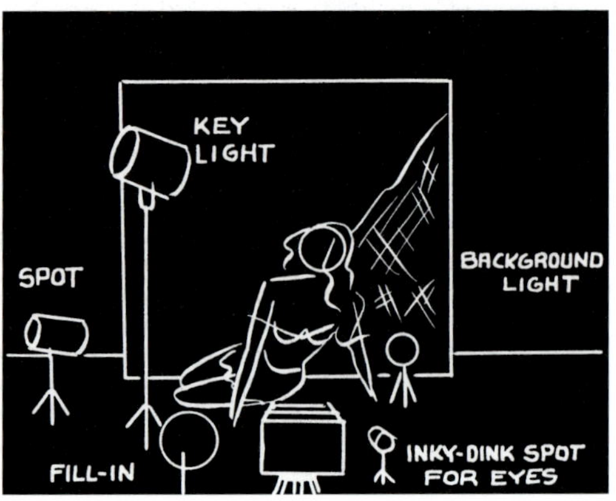

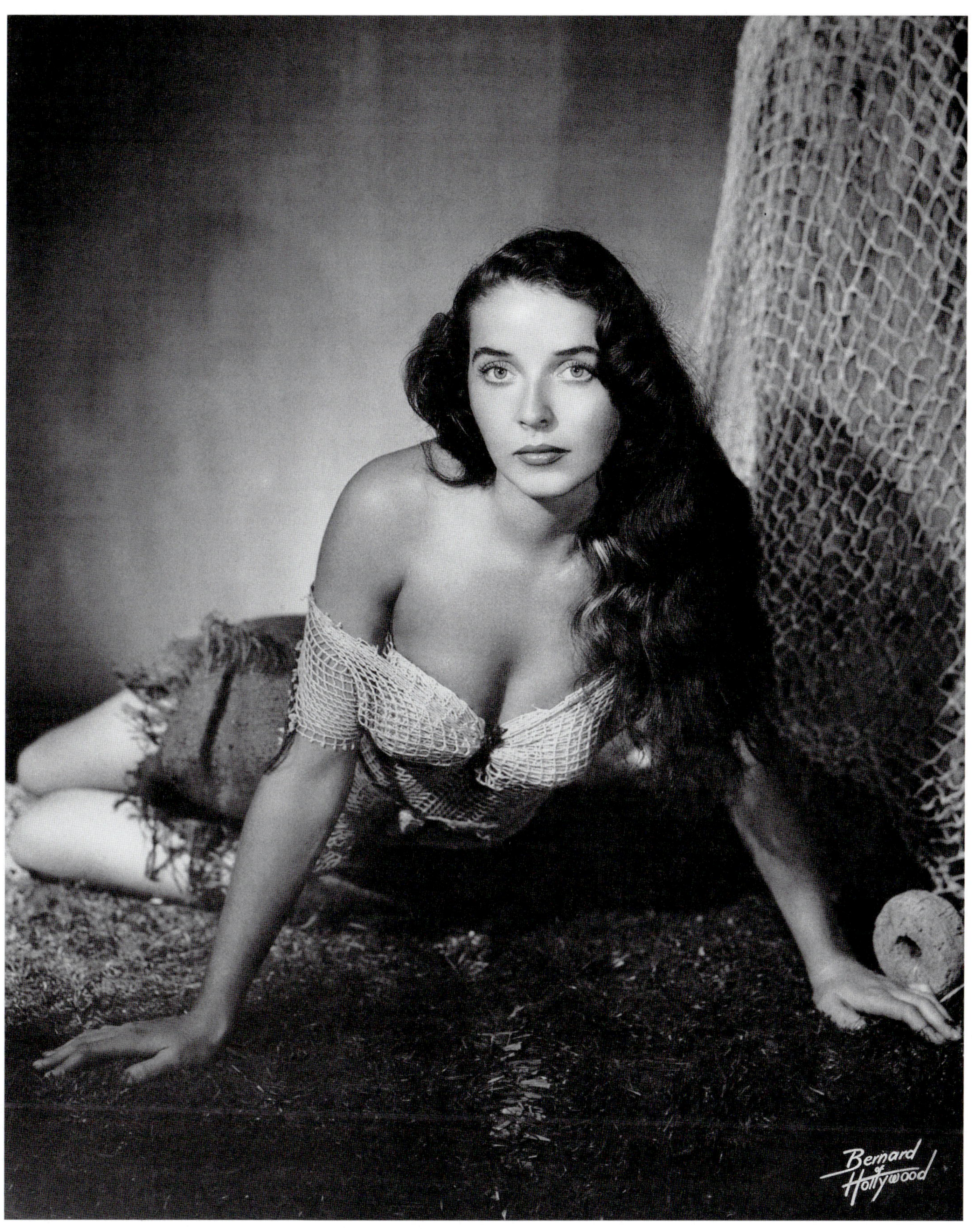

Bali Ha'i

AUF DER SCHATZINSEL · BALI HA'I

That an entirely conventional bathing suit can still be the proper costume for a vivacious pin-up is demonstrated in this refreshing study of a pert ingenue. A Bikini suit would have been out of character with the sweetness and naivete of the model.
1/10 second at f/11.

Diese erfrischende Studie eines kecken Mädchens demonstriert, daß auch ein ganz gewöhnlicher Badeanzug ein geeignetes Requisit für ein pfiffiges Pin-Up sein kann. Ein Bikini hätte kaum zu diesem anmutigen und unverdorbenen Modell gepaßt.
1/10 Sekunde bei f/11.

Parfois un maillot de bain d'une pièce est plus efficace pour créer une pin-up, comme en témoigne cette étude d'une malicieuse ingénue. Un bikini aurait été déplacé compte tenu de la douceur et de l'expression naïve du modèle. 1/10ème de seconde à f/11.

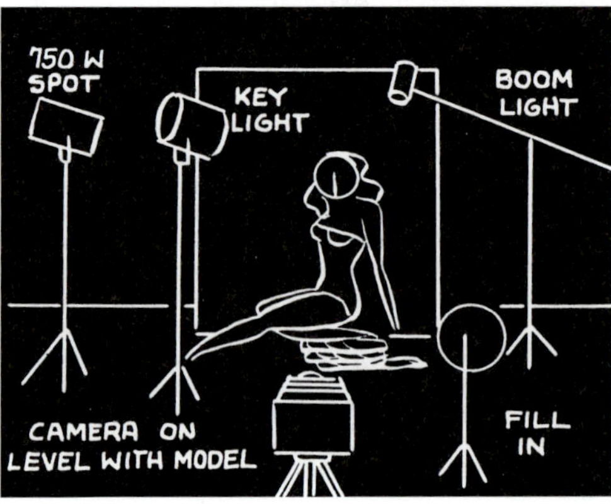

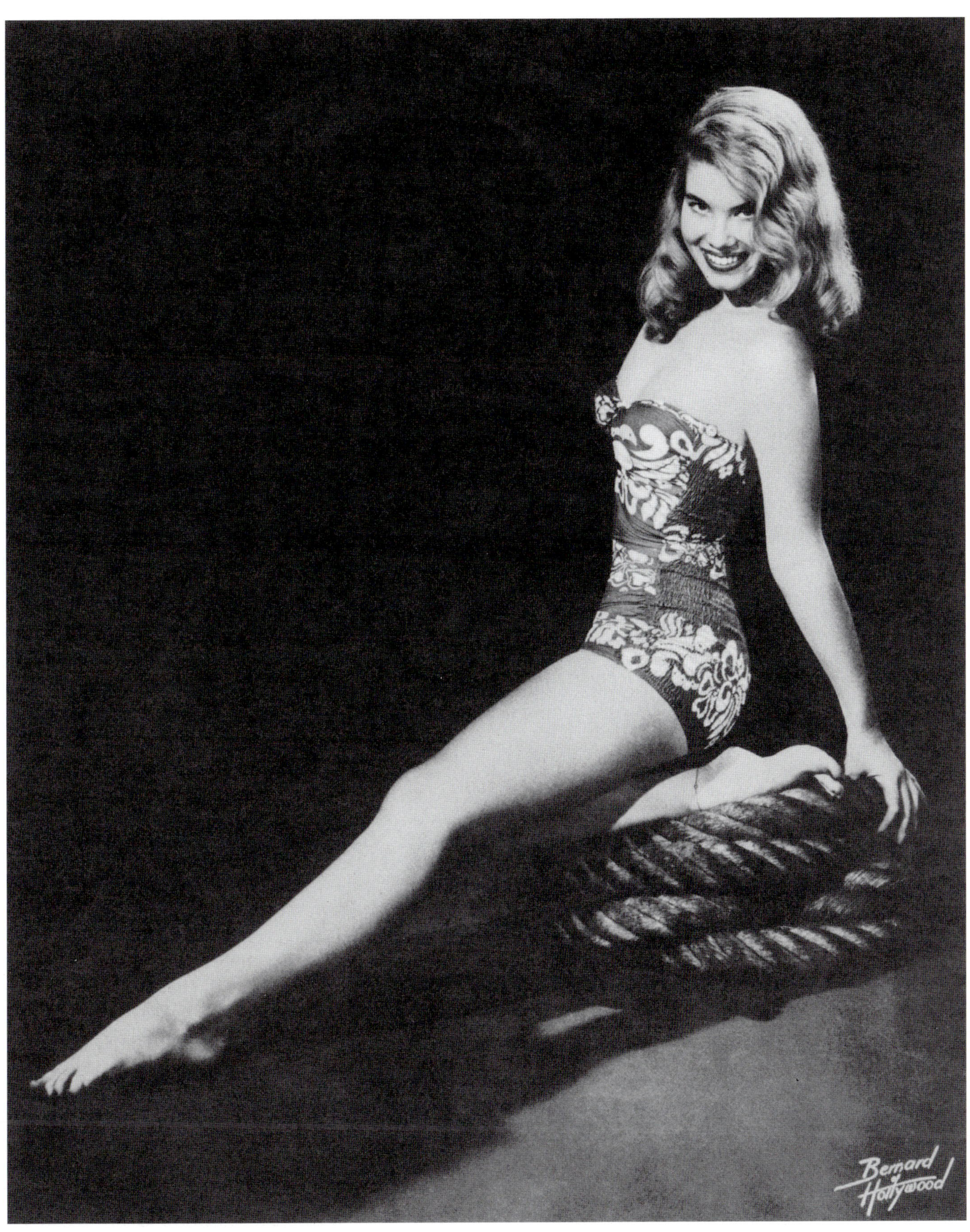

Cute Rope Trick

TAUFRISCH · TOUR DE CORDE

Uncluttered background and simplicity of lighting bring out the perfect figure and impish personality of the model to best advantage. Soft modeling light was achieved by using floodlights only, adding a single boomlight on the hair. 5x7 Ansco view camera, 1/10 second at f/11.

Ein neutraler Hintergrund und die unkomplizierte Lichtführung bringen die tadellose Figur und den schelmischen Charakter des Modells vorteilhaft zur Geltung. Das weich modellierende Licht wurde durch Flutlicht mit nur einem zusätzlichen Spot auf das Haar erzielt. 5x7 Ansco view camera, 1/10 Sekunde bei f/11.

Le fond dépouillé et l'éclairage simple font ressortir la silhouette parfaite et la personnalité mutine du modèle. La lumière douce a été obtenue avec deux projecteurs plus un spot de perche sur les cheveux. 5x7 Ansco view camera, 1/10ème de seconde à f/11.

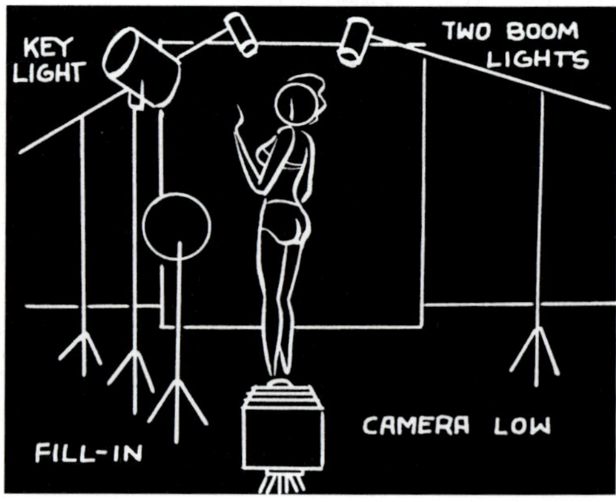

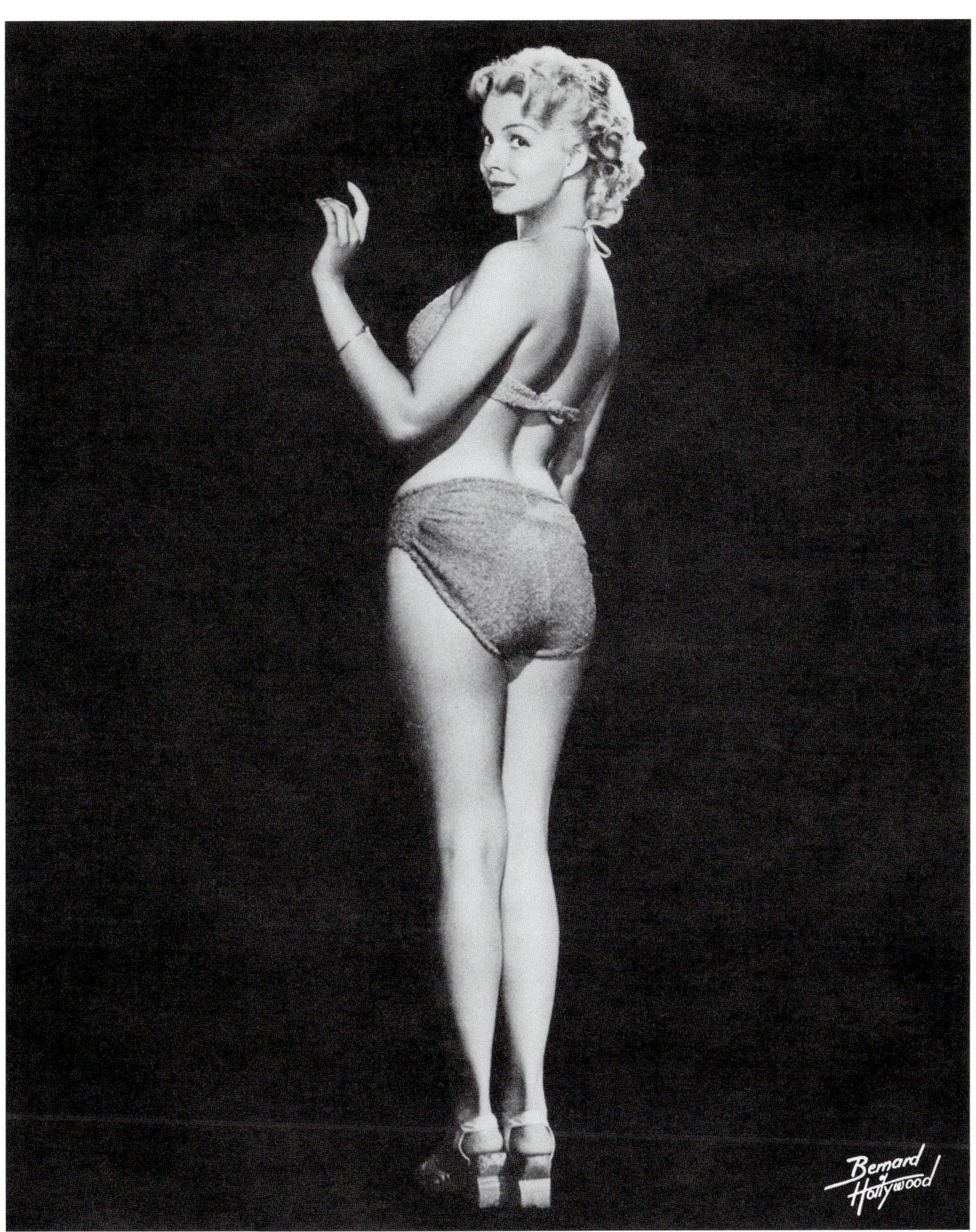

Be Seeing You

BIS SPÄTER! · À BIENTÔT!

Spark and Spontaneity in Posed Candids

The most beautiful lighting and composition will leave the spectator cold unless you pack spark into your pictures. The candid technique of the newspaper or magazine photographer needs some modification before it can be applied to the photography of pin-ups.

The trigger-happy fraternity is primarily interested in the "off-guard" picture – the uglier, the more grotesque it looks, the better. That is why we see so many atrocious photographs of politicians, divorcees or thugs in our daily columns. The extreme distortions of heads, hands and feet, the silly grins or furious grimaces bear as much resemblance to reality as an out-of-context quotation has to the meaningful coherence of the entire speech. This type of "candid" photographer does not portray honestly – he caricatures. The pin-up photographer, on the other hand, tends to glamorize his models. His "white lies" of perspective, lighting and timing will always be in favor of the subject. However, in spite of this partiality, he will come much closer to reality by freezing the action in its most characteristic and appealing moment. To find the right split-second when a single static picture will create the illusion of dynamic continuity and unbroken rhythm is the difficult task of the "posed candid" technique, which the author advocates.

The expression "posed candid" sounds like a contradiction in itself; however, after some reflection it makes sense. In taking the picture of a dancer, for instance, you let her go through her entire routine, and mentally shoot those poses which strike you as characteristic and appealing. After this visual, pre-shooting editing, concentrate on those highlighting movements. After proper rehearsal, you will be able to make any number of fast exposures, which will have an absolutely candid flavor. Take the concluding pictures in this book, for example: The model was carefully briefed and actual bits of dialogue given her, in order to make these carefully rehearsed pictures appear spontaneous.

This visualization of the final result is the professional technique in contrast to the hit-and-miss approach of the amateur.

It will save you not only a lot of film, but it will get you a haul of pin-up pictures whose spark and spontaneity will have the desired explosive effect on the spectator.

Above all, have fun shooting your pin-ups! The carefully rehearsed, yet seemingly effortless technique of circus acrobats performing their back-breaking stunts reveals the ultimate secret of every true artistry: conquer technique until it becomes second nature and then – forget it!

Schwung und Spontaneität im inszenierten Schnappschuß

Die beste Ausleuchtung und Komposition läßt den Betrachter kalt, wenn es nicht gelingt, den Bildern Leben einzuhauchen. Die Schnappschußtechnik der Zeitungsfotografen bedarf allerdings einiger Modifikationen, bevor sie für die Pin-Up-Fotografie einsetzbar wird.

Die Jungs mit der schnellen Hand am Auslöser interessieren sich in erster Linie für den Moment der Überrumpelung: je häßlicher und grotesker das Bild, desto besser. Daher bekommen wir so viele grauenhafte Fotos von Politikern, geschiedenen Ehepartnern und Gewalttätern in der Tagespresse zu sehen. Die extremen Verzerrungen von Köpfen, Händen und Füßen, das dumme Grinsen oder die wilden Grimassen haben soviel mit der Realität gemein wie ein aus dem Zusammenhang gerissenes Zitat mit einer kompletten Rede. Diese Sorte von „Schnappschuß"-Fotografen porträtiert nicht ernsthaft, sie karikiert. Der Pin-Up-Fotograf dagegen neigt dazu, sein Modell zu überhöhen. Seine kleinen Mogeleien bei Perspektive, Beleuchtung und Timing kommen immer dem Modell zugute. Und doch wird er, trotz seiner Parteinahme, wesentlich näher an die Realität herankommen, weil er einen besonders charakteristischen Moment einfängt. Den richtigen Sekundenbruchteil zu finden, in dem ein einzelnes statisches Bild die Illusion einer bewegten Szene vermittelt, ist die schwierige Aufgabe der „inszenierten Schnappschuß"-Technik.

Der Ausdruck „inszenierter Schnappschuß" klingt wie ein Widerspruch in sich selbst; doch nach einiger Überlegung macht er Sinn. Wenn man etwa eine Aufnahme von einer Tänzerin macht, läßt man sie ihre ganze Nummer tanzen und fotografiert im Geiste sämtliche Posen, die einem als besonders charakteristisch und ansprechend erscheinen. Im Anschluß an diese optische Vorauswahl konzentriert man sich dann auf die entscheidenden Abläufe. Nach gründlichen Proben wird man in der Lage sein, beliebig viele Aufnahmen mit kürzester Belichtungszeit zu machen, die auf perfekte Weise spontan wirken. Man betrachte etwa die Fotos in diesem Buch: das Modell wurde in jedes Detail eingewiesen und bekam sogar einige Dialogzeilen, um die sorgfältig einstudierten Aufnahmen spontan erscheinen zu lassen.

Sich ein Bild vom Endergebnis machen zu können, das ist der Unterschied zwischen einem professionellen Vorgehen und der „Zufallstreffer-Technik" des Amateurs. So spart man nicht nur jede Menge Film, sondern erhält auch eine gute Ausbeute an Pin-Up-Fotos, deren Lebendigkeit und Spontaneität den gewünschten Effekt auf den Betrachter nicht verfehlen werden.

Vor allen Dingen sollten Sie Spaß am Fotografieren Ihrer Pin-Ups haben! Die sorgfältig geprobten und dennoch so mühelos erscheinenden halsbrecherischen Stunts der Zirkusakrobaten verraten das eigentliche Geheimnis wahrer Kunstfertigkeit: Die technischen Feinheiten müssen einstudiert werden, bis man sie im Schlaf beherrscht. Und dann muß man sie wieder komplett vergessen!

De la spontanéité dans les instantanés posés

Le plus bel éclairage et la composition la plus sophistiquée laisseront le spectateur de glace si vous ne mettez pas un peu de piment dans vos images. Cependant, pour réaliser une bonne pin-up, on ne peut appliquer telle quelle la méthode du cliché pris sur le vif tant prisée des photographes de presse et des paparazzis.

Cette confrérie à la détente facile cherche principalement à « surprendre » ses sujets : plus la photo est laide, plus la pose est grotesque, plus ils sont contents. C'est pourquoi les pages de nos quotidiens sont inondés d'images hideuses de politiciens, de starlettes et de voyous. La distorsion extrême des visages, des mains et des pieds, les sourires niais ou les grimaces ridicules ont aussi peu à voir avec la réalité qu'une citation prise « hors contexte » en a avec la cohérence d'un discours élaboré. Ces photographes de presse ne présentent pas honnêtement leurs sujets, ils les caricaturent. De son côté, le photographe de pin-up tend à les sublimer. Ses « embellissements » de la perspective, de la lumière et de la pose sont toujours en faveur du modèle. Toutefois, en dépit de ce parti pris, il s'approchera beaucoup plus de la réalité en figeant l'action à son moment le plus caractéristique et parlant. Trouver l'exacte fraction de seconde où une simple image statique créera l'illusion d'une continuité dynamique et d'un rythme ininterrompu, c'est là la tâche ardue de « l'instantané posé », une technique chère à l'auteur.

Le terme « instantané posé » semble être une contradiction en soi. Cependant, quand on y réfléchit, il tient debout. Si vous voulez photographier une ballerine, par exemple, regardez-la exécuter l'ensemble de sa chorégraphie en photographiant mentalement les moments qui vous semblent les plus caractéristiques et attrayants. Visualisez soigneusement dans votre tête les images qui vous intéressent, puis demandez-lui d'isoler les mouvements correspondants. Après une bonne répétition, vous pourrez réaliser autant de clichés à exposition rapide que vous voudrez. Ils auront l'air parfaitement spontané. Prenez les dernières images de ce livre : les modèles ont été soigneusement briefées et ont même appris quelques bribes de dialogues afin que leurs poses soigneusement répétées à l'avance paraissent le plus naturelles possible.

C'est à la capacité de visualiser le résultat final qu'on reconnaît le professionnel, par opposition à l'amateur qui mitraille tout ce qui bouge.

Non seulement cela vous épargnera beaucoup de pellicule, mais cela vous permettra de réaliser beaucoup d'images de pin-up dont la vitalité et la fraîcheur feront mouche chez tous ceux qui les regarderont.

Par-dessus tout, amusez-vous ! Prenez exemple sur les acrobates de cirque : ce n'est qu'au prix d'un long entraînement qu'ils peuvent réaliser des cascades périlleuses sans le moindre effort apparent. C'est là le vrai secret de tout art : il faut maîtriser la technique afin de pouvoir l'oublier.

Credits

18 "A Couple of Good Reasons"
Ann Melton, dancer and model

21 "Hi There!"
Neva Gilbert, model and television actress

29 "Desert Storm"
Minka Diaz, model

31 "Sailor Beware"
June McCall, model and television actress

33 "Beauty and the Beach"
Barbara Nichols, model and television actress

35 "Jungle Juno"
Val Njord, "Miss International Beauty"

37 "Cold Outside"
Barbara Nichols, model and television actress

39 "Beauty Rest"
Lorraine Crawford, motion picture actress

41 "Flotsam"
Ramsay Ames, motion picture actress, bandleader

43 "Star and Stripes"
Vivian Mason, motion picture actress

45 "Gamin"
Ava Norring, cover girl and television actress

47 "Sea Siren"
Judy Landon, dancer and motion picture actress

49 "Across the Board"
Jane Greer, motion picture actress (RKO)

51 "Well Balanced"
Jeannette Donnell, illustrator's model

53 "Making the Grade"
Marilyn Monroe, motion picture actress (20th Century-Fox)

55 "Sultry Savage"
Val Njord, "Miss International Beauty"

63 "Nocturne"
Joy Lansing, motion picture and television actress

65 "Hollywood Calling"
June Dempsey, model

67 "Winter Joy"
Joyce Holden, motion picture actress (Universal-International)

69 "Summer Harvest"
Annabelle Harnad, model

71 "Island Dressing"
Joy Lansing, motion picture and television actress

73 "Good Connection"
Laurette Luez, motion picture actress

75 "Figurehead"
Winonah Smith, dancer, "Miss Brevity" (Florida)

77 "Sitting Pretty"
Barbara Blaine, dancer and model

79 "Body and Soil"
June McCall, model and television actress

81 "Lighter than Air"
Pat Hall, cover girl, actress, designer

83 "Design for Loving"
Gwenn Caldwell, model, motion picture and television actress

85 "Quick Adjustment"
Gwenn Caldwell, winner of "Most Beautiful Legs"

87 "Early American"
Lili St. Cyr, exotic dancer